AF575651

POSTER MAN

POSTER MAN

0 YEARS OF ICONIC GRAPHIC DESIGN

EYMOUR CHWAST

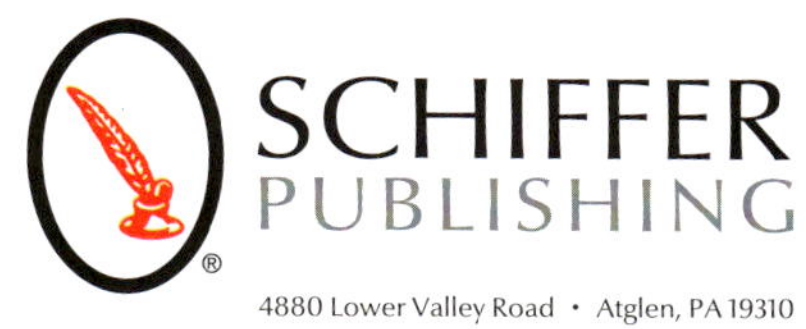

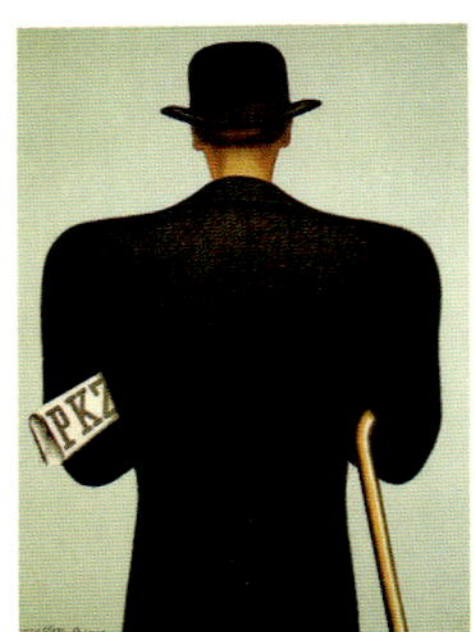

This book is dedicated to
Niklaus Stoecklin, creator
of my favorite poster.

Other Schiffer Books on Related Subjects:

Robbie Conal: Streetwise: 35 Years of Politically Charged Guerrilla Art, G. James Daichendt, ISBN 978-0-7643-5908-8

It Must Be Art: Big O Poster Artists of the 1960s and 70s, Michael Fishel & Nigel Suckling, ISBN 978-0-7643-5548-6

Eye See You: The Art of Oliver Hibert, Angelo Madrigale & Oliver Hibert, ISBN 978-0-7643-5443-4

Library of Congress Control Number: 2020943409

Designed by Seymour Chwast
Associate Designer: Camille Murphy
Type set in Trade Gothic Light & Bold and Champion Middleweight

ISBN: 978-0-7643-6122-7
Printed in China

On back cover: "End Bad Breath," 1968; "The End Place," 1967

Published by Schiffer Publishing, Ltd.
4880 Lower Valley Road
Atglen, PA 19310
Phone: (610) 593-1777; Fax: (610) 593-2002
E-mail: Info@schifferbooks.com
Web: www.schifferbooks.com

The Breadth of Style and Concept
By Shepard Fairey

Seymour Chwast is a lot more than a Poster Man, but for someone whose practice covers so many styles and mediums, he's made more than his share of memorable posters. I'm a huge believer in the power of the poster, so I'm glad that a stellar range of Chwast's works in that medium has been aggregated for all of us to study and enjoy. The breadth of style and concept showcased in the enclosed posters is impressive not just because it demonstrates Chwast's versatility, but also because the artworks are eclectic but never schizophrenic. These images take many approaches, blending whimsical illustrations with precise typography, graphic elements, and found images, but after a few encounters, you can almost certainly recognize a Chwast piece. A lot of artists or designers can execute strong composition, concept, typography, or illustration. Seymour Chwast is one of the few who can master all of those in one piece with sharp wit as a consistent bonus ingredient.

Seymour Chwast is one of the first graphic designers and illustrators I ever knew by name. I was familiar with a few pieces of Chwast's art and design before I connected them with his name, but once I got to art college, the name Seymour Chwast was practically ubiquitous. I arrived at the Rhode Island School of Design in 1988 with a love of drawing and stencil-making, but not much knowledge of art and design history or notable contemporary practitioners of either. As my freshman year at RISD came to a close, I had to choose a focus. I settled on illustration as my major because I liked to draw, but also because it was the department that allowed for the most electives, permitting me to take printmaking, photography, and graphic design classes on top of my illustration requirements. The different departments at RISD were notoriously snobby toward each other, but because I was taking illustration classes and a graphic design class, I was witness to one glaring example of consensus. Both departments admired the work of Push Pin Studios for the studio's integration of illustration and graphic

Bob Dylan, Joan Baez, and Chwast's "Booth Gin" poster, photographed by Daniel Kramer, 1964. Image courtesy of the SVA Picture Collection.

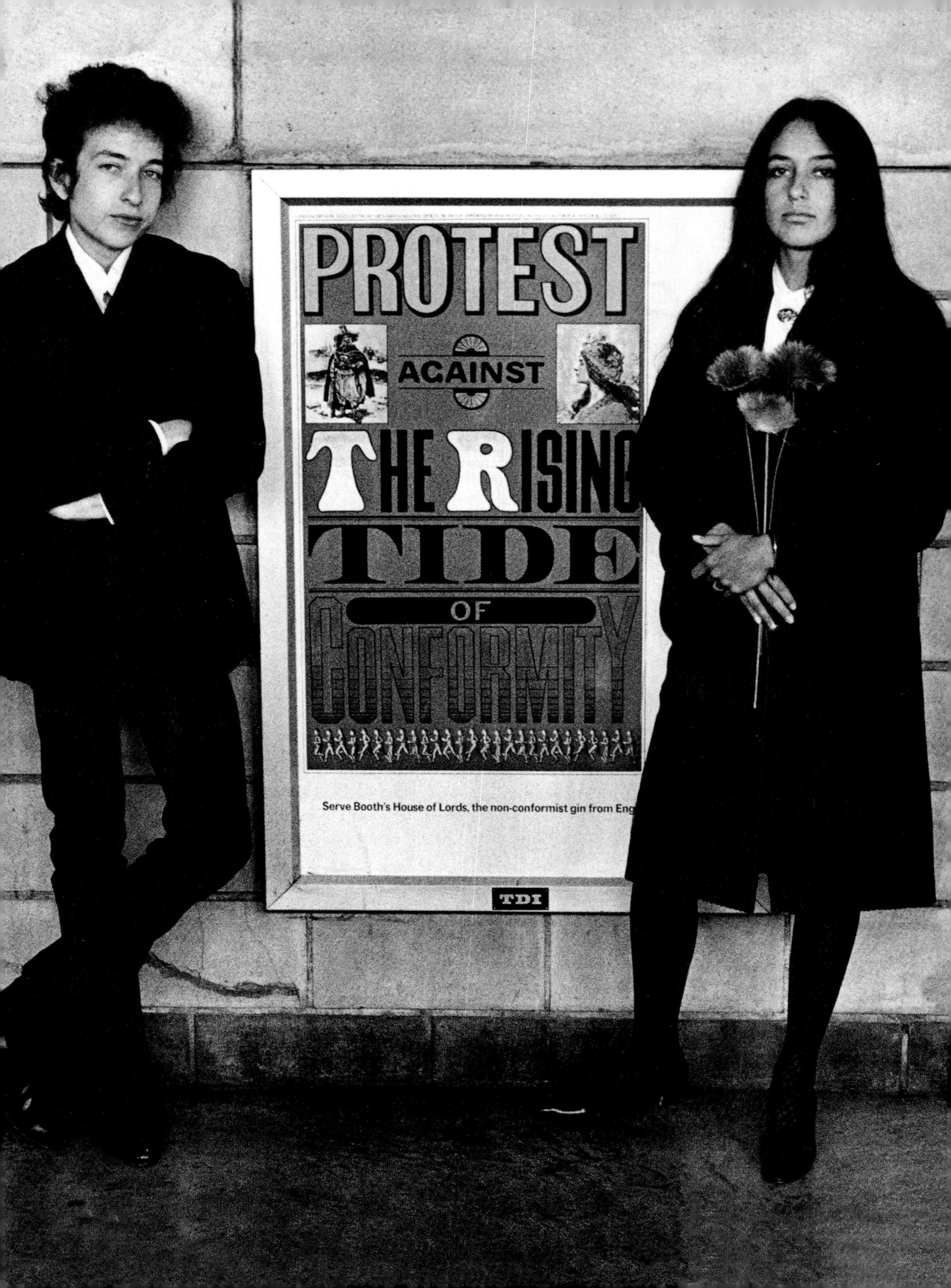

PROTEST
AGAINST
THE RISING
TIDE
OF
CONFORMITY
Serve Booth's House of Lords, the non-conformist gin from Eng
TDI

design, or graphic design and illustration, depending on departmental prejudice. I distinctly remember the works of Push Pin touted as the "gold standard" for the industry, and the names associated with that gold standard were Push Pin partners Seymour Chwast and Milton Glaser. I was told authoritatively that Push Pin was a major force in shaping the aesthetics of the '60s and '70s. As a young contrarian, I was immediately suspicious of anything celebrated or from an older generation, so I made no effort to research Push Pin Studios, Glaser, or Chwast. However, despite my obstinance, I was soon seduced, or maybe more punched in the gut, by one of Seymour Chwast's images when I was researching for an art theory class.

I had decided to write a paper about protest art, or what I termed Positive Propaganda, based on initial inspiration from artists/designers Barbara Kruger and Robbie Conal, who both used their work to comment on social and political issues. While looking for other protest art examples, I discovered Seymour Chwast's poster *End Bad Breath*, a critique of the Vietnam War, which shows Uncle Sam with a mouth full of bombers and burning houses. At that time, punk rock was the soundtrack to my life, and I loved punk's visuals, which skewered sacred symbols as a way of questioning and subverting the dominant power structure. Chwast's *End Bad Breath* was punk rock from another era! The rough block-print style of the illustration imbued it with bohemian but of-the-people irreverence. The satire of a mouthwash advertisement implied that "everything may be packaged as a product, but the Vietnam War is one we won't buy"! *End Bad Breath* featured prominently in my Positive Propaganda paper as an example of art that presented a counterargument to the agenda of those with the most power to dominate the narrative and dictate policy. That paper also helped me to refine some of my developing ideas about what the best art and design could achieve, and how I might ultimately like to use my voice through those mediums.

I was inspired by the *End Bad Breath* poster to search for more of Chwast's art and design, which I could do at the RISD library. On top of books, there was a vast clipping file at the library that cross-referenced names and topics like an analog Google search. I was combing through the folders of the clipping file when I stumbled upon Chwast's ad for Booth's Gin that read "Protest Against the Rising Tide of Conformity." With a small line of men in suits running like lemmings across the bottom. I loved the sentiment of that slogan, and the piece of design was barely recognizable as an ad because it featured only a small Booth's bottle in the lower right corner. The poster used a strong composition of wood-block-style display type and was reminiscent of a carnival poster. I liked the way the poster had a disarming nostalgic style for a provocative modern slogan. I also thought to myself, "Maybe commercial design doesn't have to be spineless, watered-down crap!" Years later, after my screen-printing business failed, I began to do commercial graphic design and illustration as my primary source of income. I screen-printed posters at night, but during my day job as a graphic artist, I considered Chwast's "Protest Against the Rising Tide of Conformity" as a model for how I might be able to inject my agenda into the images I created for clients. If the client's audience responded well to my design, I might get paid to do more work by pushing my ideas and aesthetics through the client's distribution mechanisms. I have a smart friend who explained to me that this hijacking strategy is called *détournement* and was used by the Situationist International to subvert the meanings of dominant culture aesthetics. I wouldn't call the majority of Seymour Chwast's works *détournement*, but his strong point of view in his personal work and much of his commercial work should give any designer hope that they can project a unique voice even while simultaneously fulfilling a client's needs or working within rigid parameters.

Chwast regularly demonstrates that even recurrent motifs feel fresh when executed with a new concept and stylistic approach or mutation. Potent and universal symbols like Uncle Sam, the Statue of Liberty, doves, guns, and pens appear in many of these posters, serving the image's communication without feeling repetitive or tired because the fashion of the creative approach is distinctive in each poster. There are many different looks and concerns in these posters, so what are the unifying threads? Fun might be too bland a word, but there is a pervasive and infectious sense of fun in these posters. Maybe a better way of putting it is that there is an irrepressible personality and sense of mischief embedded in almost every one of these works, whether the project is social or commercial in nature, and some are both. I see Seymour Chwast as an artist more than a designer because he seems to thrill in the modest coup of manifesting unique expression where others would settle for a bland, if competent and respectful, visual communication. We are all lucky Seymour Chwast likes some spice in his soup. Peruse these pages and drink up!

Seymour "Poster Man" Chwast
By Steven Heller

The collected posters by Seymour Chwast fit snuggly into a tradition of illustrative nineteenth- and early-twentieth-century French *artistes affiches publicitaires*, German *Werbeplakatkünstler*, and English advertising placard masters. Although the styles are his own "Chwastian" interpretations, his posters embody the spirits of such artists as Jules Cheret, A. M. Cassandre, Lucian Bernhard, Ludwig Hohlwein, and the Beggarstaff brothers, among the most famous. He has also contemporaneously applied Victorian, Art Nouveau, Jugendstil, Art Moderne, and other decorative approaches as graphic accents to enliven his colorful and playful drawings and letterforms.

Chwast's posters, like his editorial illustrations, book covers, packages and other graphic designs, are conceptually driven, sometimes decorative, occasionally abstract and frequently comical, whimsical, and expressive. Even dark subjects (like the brutality of war) are usually handled with surprising lightness and subversive wit.

My first introduction to a Chwast poster was not a Chwast poster, per se, but rather a (now famous) 1964 photograph by Daniel Kramer, which featured a Chwast poster on a airport waiting room wall. The black and white photo was of my sixties culture heroes, Bob Dylan and Joan Baez [page 7] standing on either side of Chwast's work. The photo was made into a poster and sold at Postermat, a once-popular New York chain that sold pop cultural merchandise, including some of Chwast's own work. The Chwast poster within the Dylan/Baez poster read "PROTEST THE RISING TIDE OF CONFORMITY," which was typeset with a mixed assortment of nineteenth-century decorative wood type styles, was actually an advertisement for Booth's Gin—not really protesting anything—simply promoting this famous London brand of liquor. Obviously, it was meant to appeal to an emerging nonconformist sensibility.

Nonetheless, the ironic juxtaposition of the commercial poster with two of the most famous protest folk singers of the decade imbued the one-sheet with a kind of social consciousness and validation. The fact that Chwast was, himself, a longtime progressive, civil rights and antiwar advocate further added another level of meaning to the image and took on a life of its own. This Dylan/Baez poster was among the most popular youth culture images of the age, and the Chwast "PROTEST" poster itself became ubiquitous.

It was also an inspiration for me when in 1967 I started designing hippie/underground newspapers and magazines using vintage wood type that I admit having copied from Chwast. When I was around seventeen, Chwast, whom I did not personally know at the time (and would not meet until almost a decade later), was my influence for the graphic look he helped to create during the midsixties, known as the "Push Pin Style," known for reviving old letterforms combined with witty illustrations into a counterculture aesthetic.

I was always attracted to Chwast's poster designs—of which there were many—hanging on walls and reproduced in annuals. What I enjoyed about them is that over the years, he liberally applied different drawing and design styles (and continues to do so five decades later), yet they always were Chwastian. Among my early favorites was a 1968 poster titled *War Is Good Business Invest Your Son*, which was a similar vintage aesthetic to the Booth's "Protest" poster, albeit with a more biting political slogan. Since it related to my own status as a draft-age teenager, it was one of many posters I had taped on the walls of my bedroom.

Chwast did not just specialize in political posters, but a sizeable percentage of his poster output indeed advocated for peace or protested against injustice, pollution, and gun violence. Arguably his most famous poster was a polemical response to the bombing of Hanoi during the Vietnam War. Also produced in 1968, it involved a woodcut rendering of the head of Uncle Sam, his mouth wide open with bombs being dropped by aircraft. Titled *End Bad Breath*, it was a not-so-subtle satire of the conventional advertising tropes, only refitted as an end the war protest

Of the 175 posters he has designed during his lifetime—and he has always made the time to design them when the opportunity presents itself—there are a large number of subway, train station, bus shelter and other advertisements for media (*Forbes* magazine), entertainment (Mobil and PBS), cultural events (Brooklyn Children's Museum), paper companies (Mohawk), food (Carta di Pasta), public service, and his own exhibitions and public speaking.

Many of these posters in this book have so captured the eyes of their beholders that they have been appreciatively collected, framed, and hung on walls because of their wit, playfulness, and joy. Although the poster medium is giving way to animated LEDs and signboards, Chwast remains a Poster Man—and will continue to design them for as long as he can.

COMMERCE

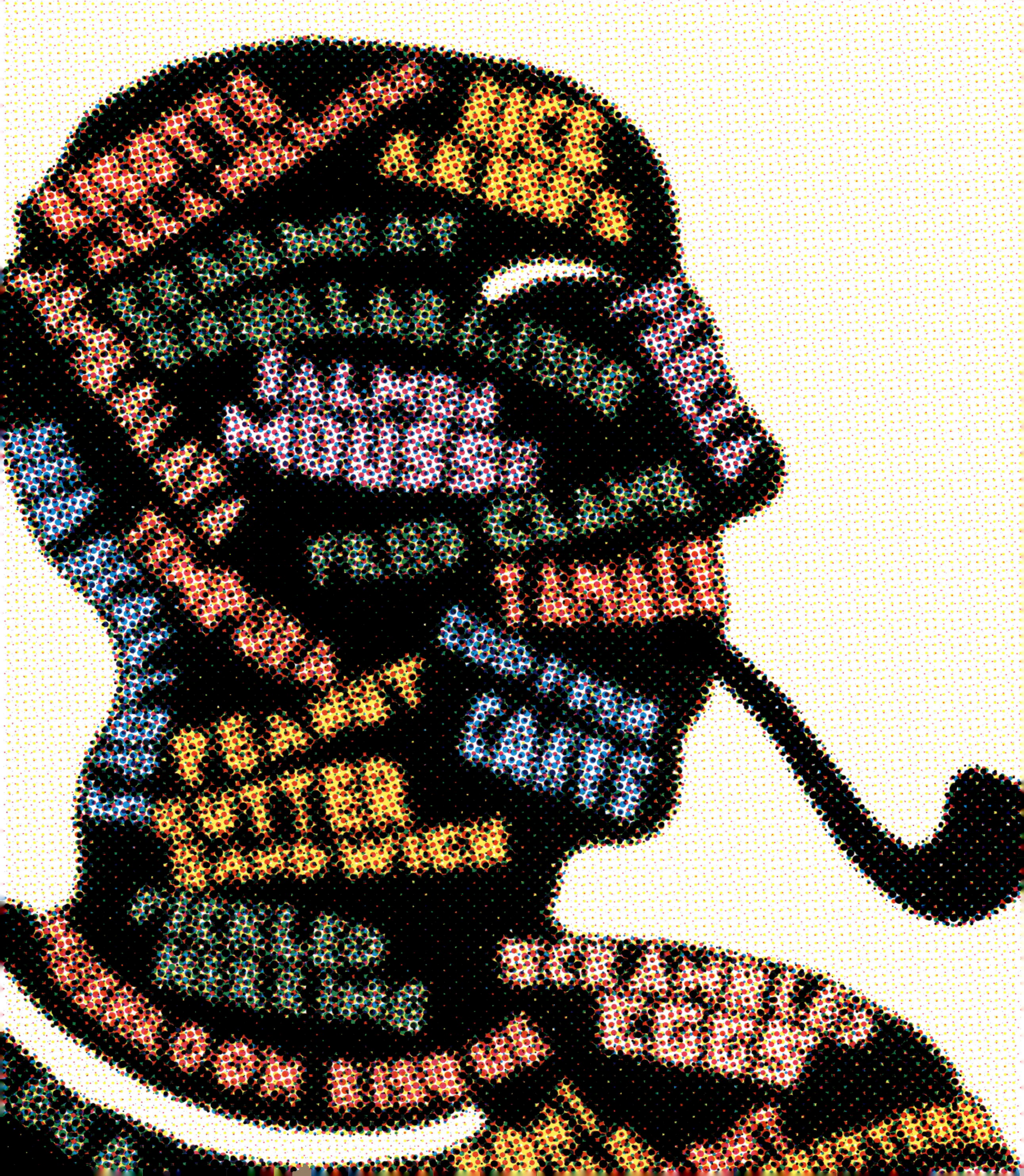

Below: **NEW FILMS.** My design represents one of New Line Cinema's Film Series for college students. Another poster in the series is on page 98.

Opposite: **SEVILLA.** The theme for the Universal Exposition of Seville (Expo '92) was "The Age of Discovery," celebrating the 500th anniversary of Christopher Columbus reaching the Americas after launching from Seville's port.

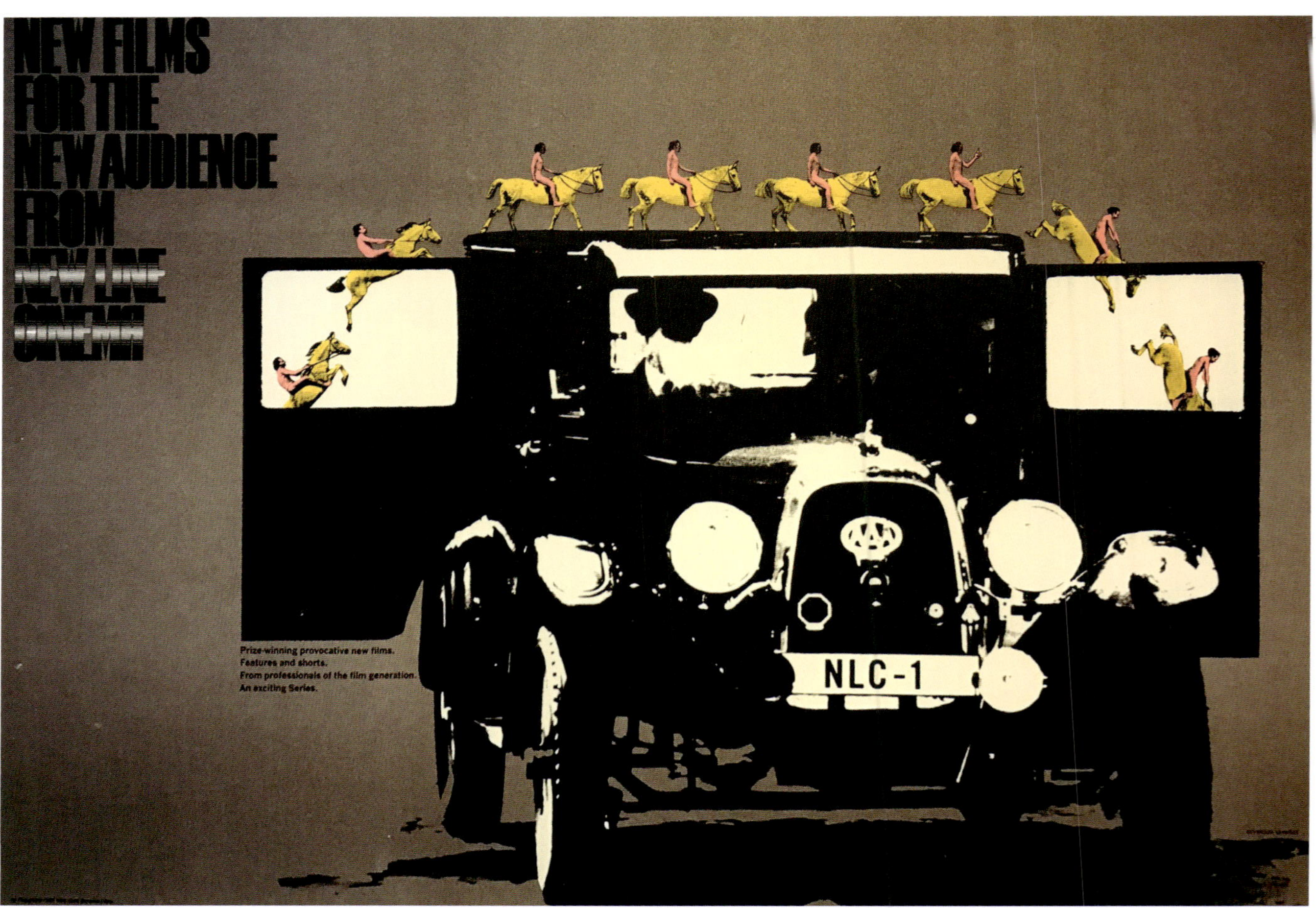

Pen and ink, pencil, color film, offset, 18" x 24", 1989

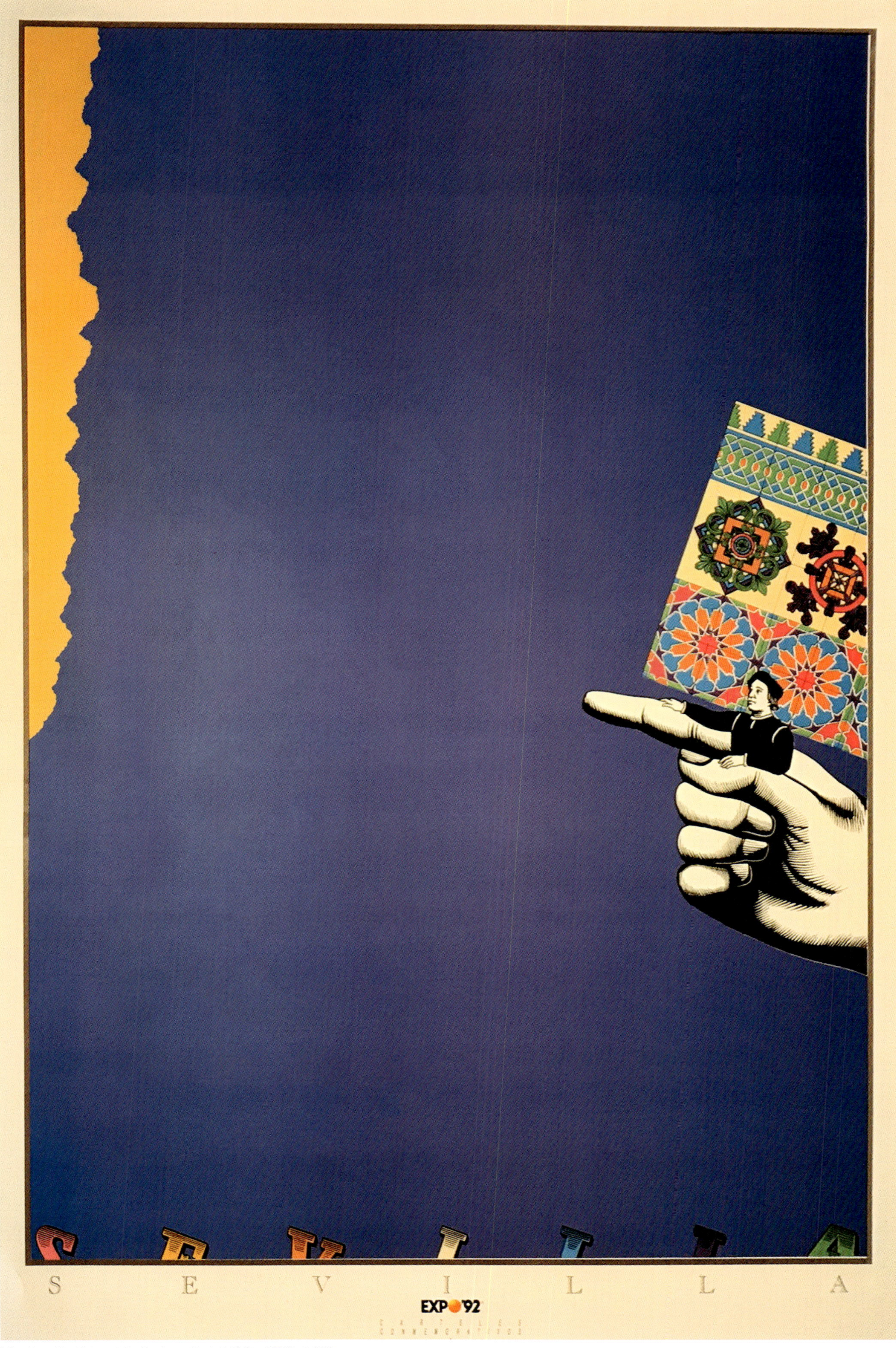

Mixed media, flat matched color, offset, 18½" x 27½", 1992

PEUGEOT

Peugeot demonstrated their bicycles with racing events.

PEUGEOT BALADE SAUVAGE
PEUGEOT INTERPLAGES

Puegeot is known for cycling and hosting the Tour de France bike race through parts of the country. A European art director asked me to parody old European posters, which was odd, since there was no shortage of designers on the Continent familiar with the history with design. For the poster opposite, I was inspired by Ludwig Hohlwein for the style and René Magritte for the surrealist concept.

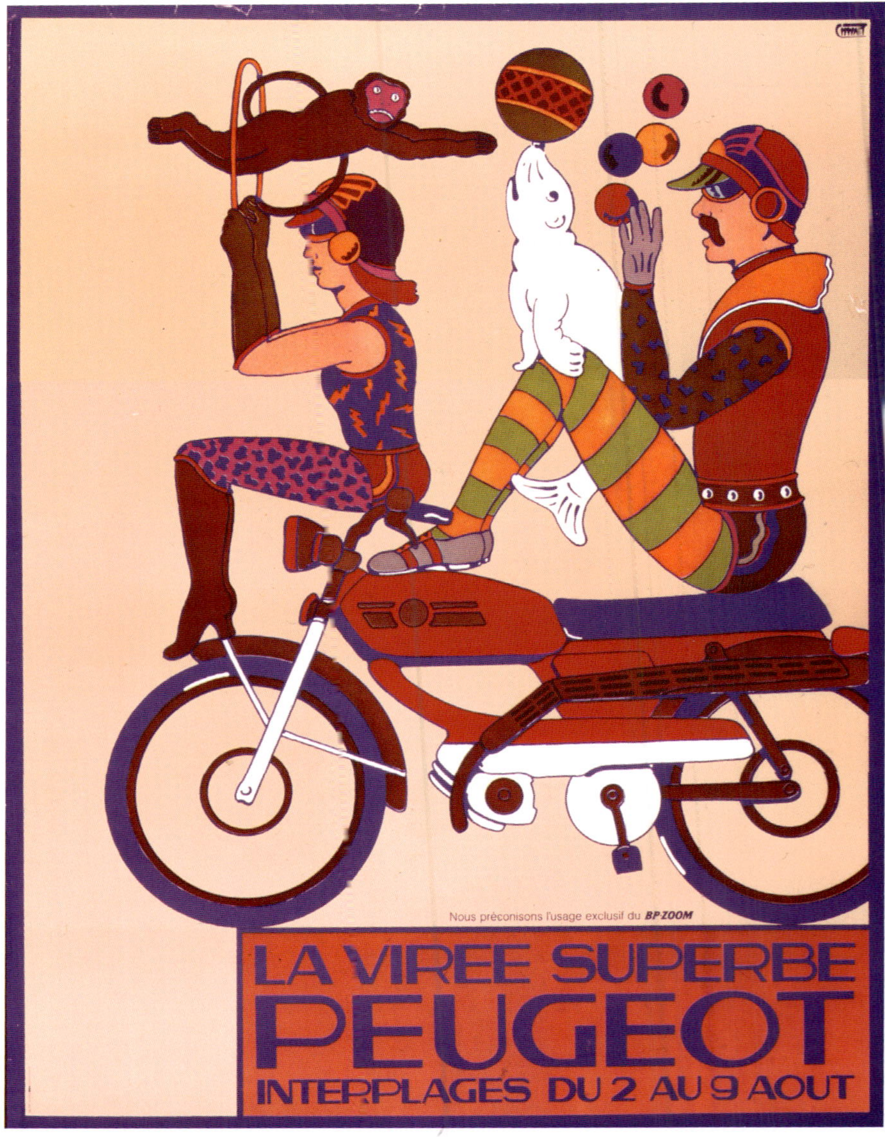

Pen and ink, color film, offset, 31½" x 23¾", 1978

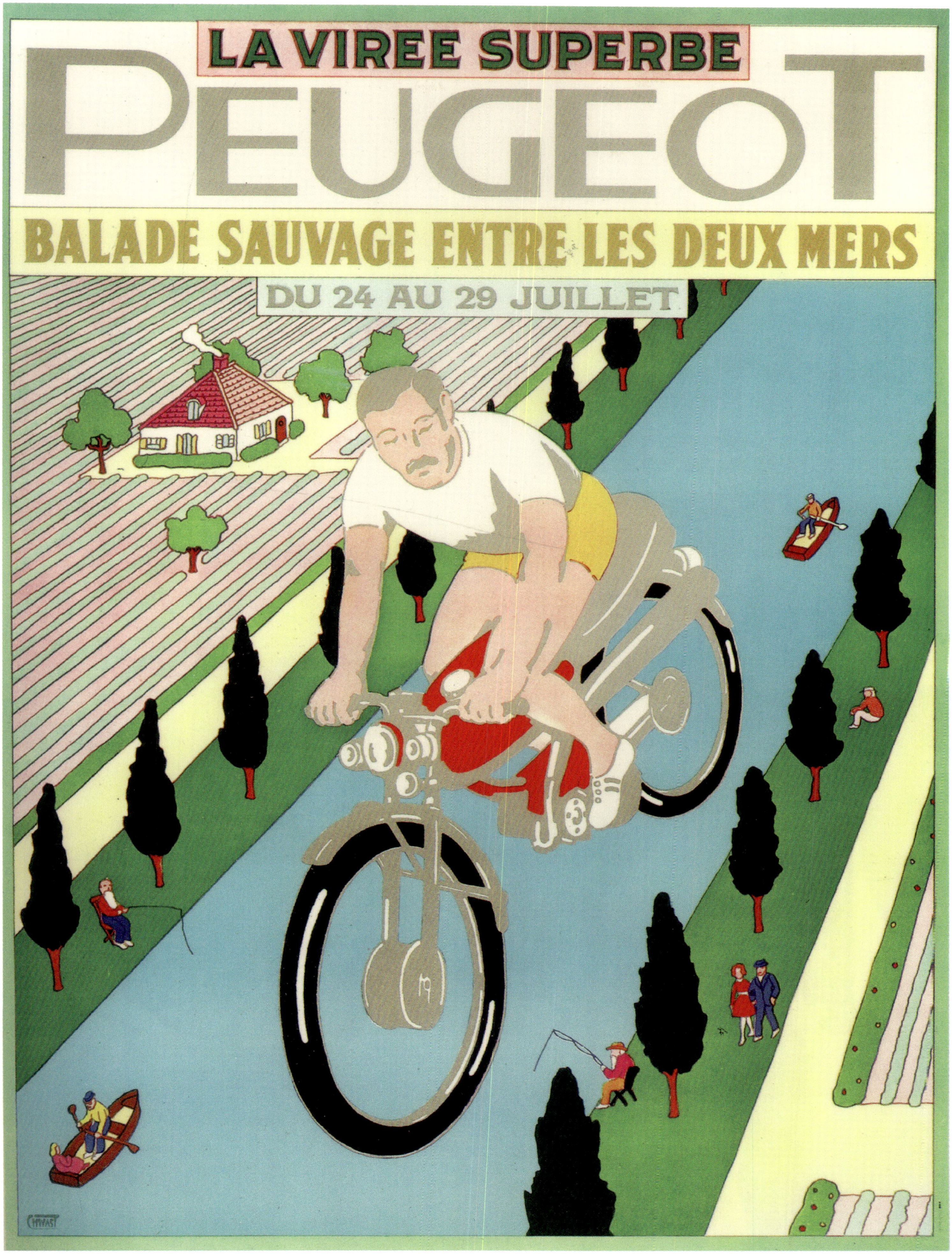

LA VIREE SUPERBE

PEUGEOT

BALADE SAUVAGE ENTRE LES DEUX MERS

DU 24 AU 29 JUILLET

CHWAST

Pen and ink, color film, offset, 31½" x 23¾", 1978

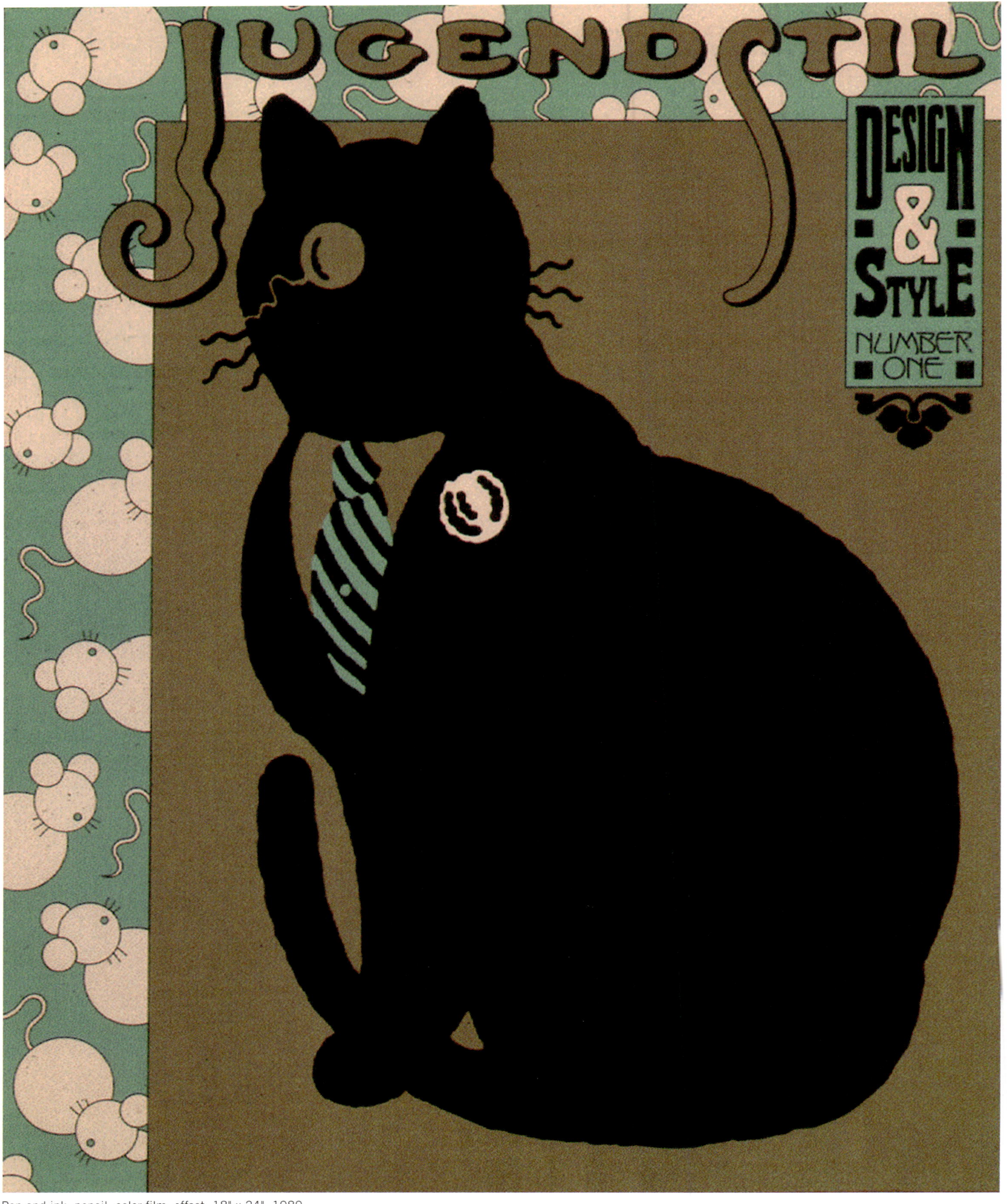

Pen and ink, pencil, color film, offset, 18" x 24", 1989

PAPER

Opposite: **JUGENDSTIL.** The cover of the first issue of *Design and Style*, which I designed with Steven Heller. The issues covered Jugendstil (Youth Style), Paris Deco, Surrealism, De Stijl, Streamline, Futurism, and Bauhaus. We showed examples of graphic design, architecture and typography in each style. The paper and production for these brochures were supplied by Mohawk Fine Papers.

Below: **THE WEDDING RING.** Neenah Paper sponsored a series of posters, each highlighting a punctuation mark. My poster featured a parenthesis.

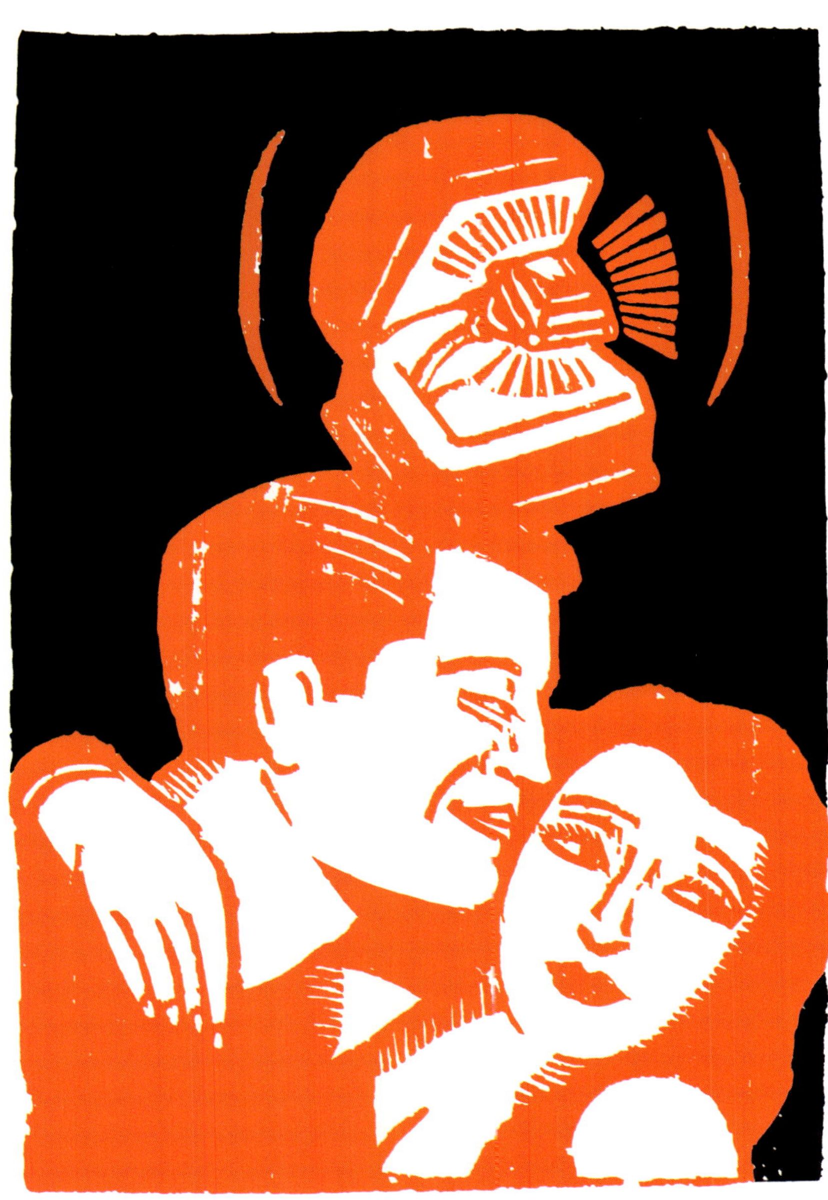

Woodcut on paper, flat matched color, offset, 24" x 36", 1968

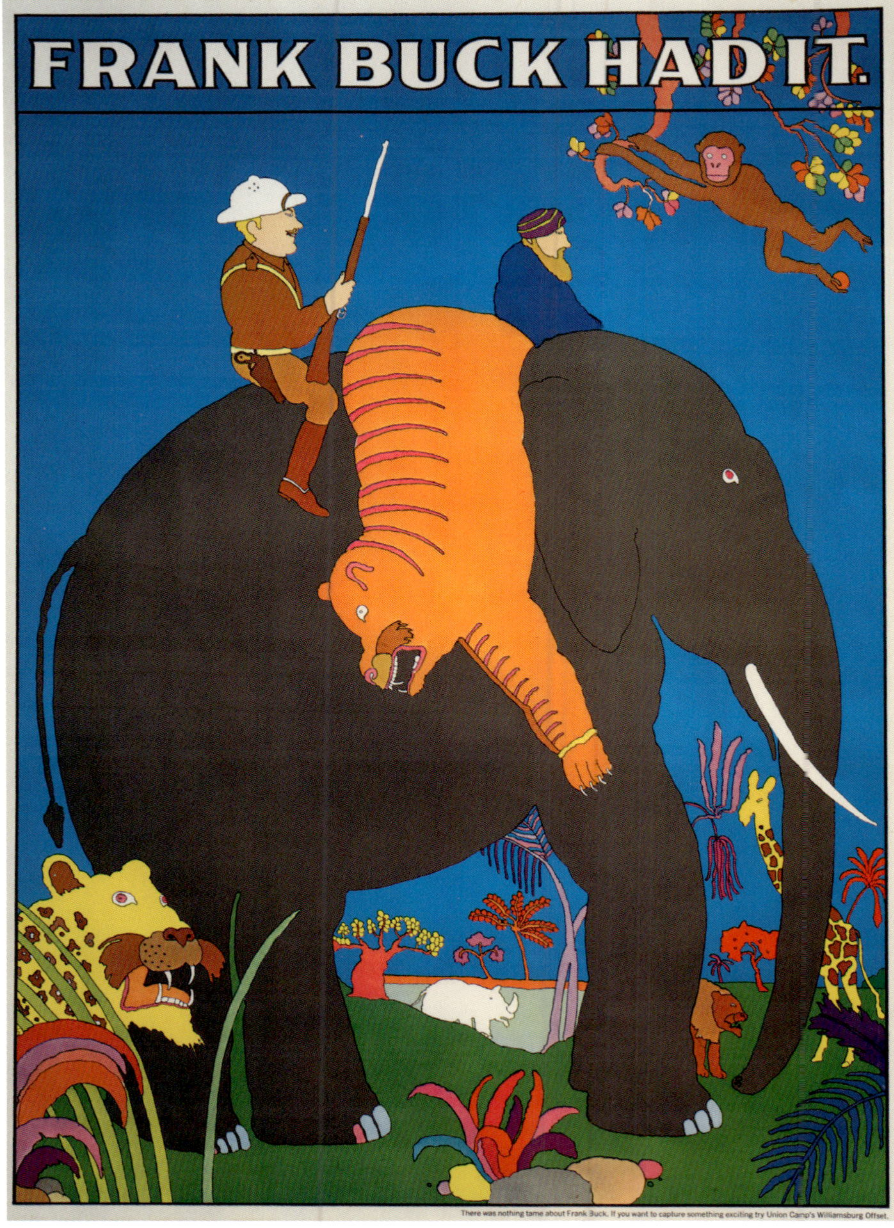

Pen and ink, color film, offset, 18" x 24", 1989

PAPER

FRANK BUCK
SIGMUND FREUD

Sigmund Freud and Frank Buck were just two of the people who were the subjects of posters promoting Union Camp Paper. I went along with the headline in spite of the fact that I didn't understand the connection with the paper. The little drawings in the Freud poster were meant to have sexual significance.

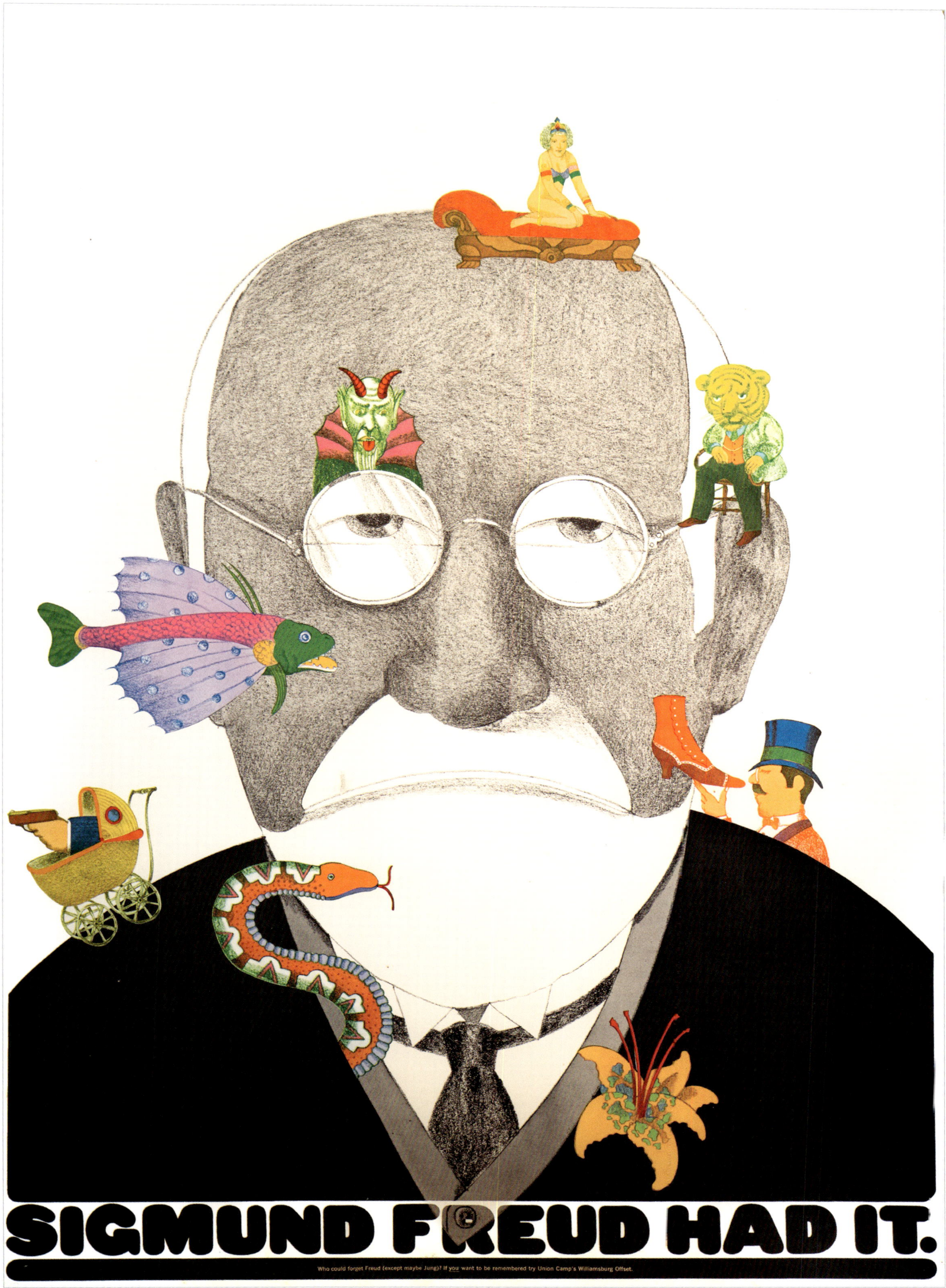

Pencil, flat matched color, offset, 25" x 35", 1968

"L" POSTER
"C" POSTER
Paula Scher art directed the alphabet for twenty-six posters for Champion Paper. Thirteen designers each had two letters to interpret.

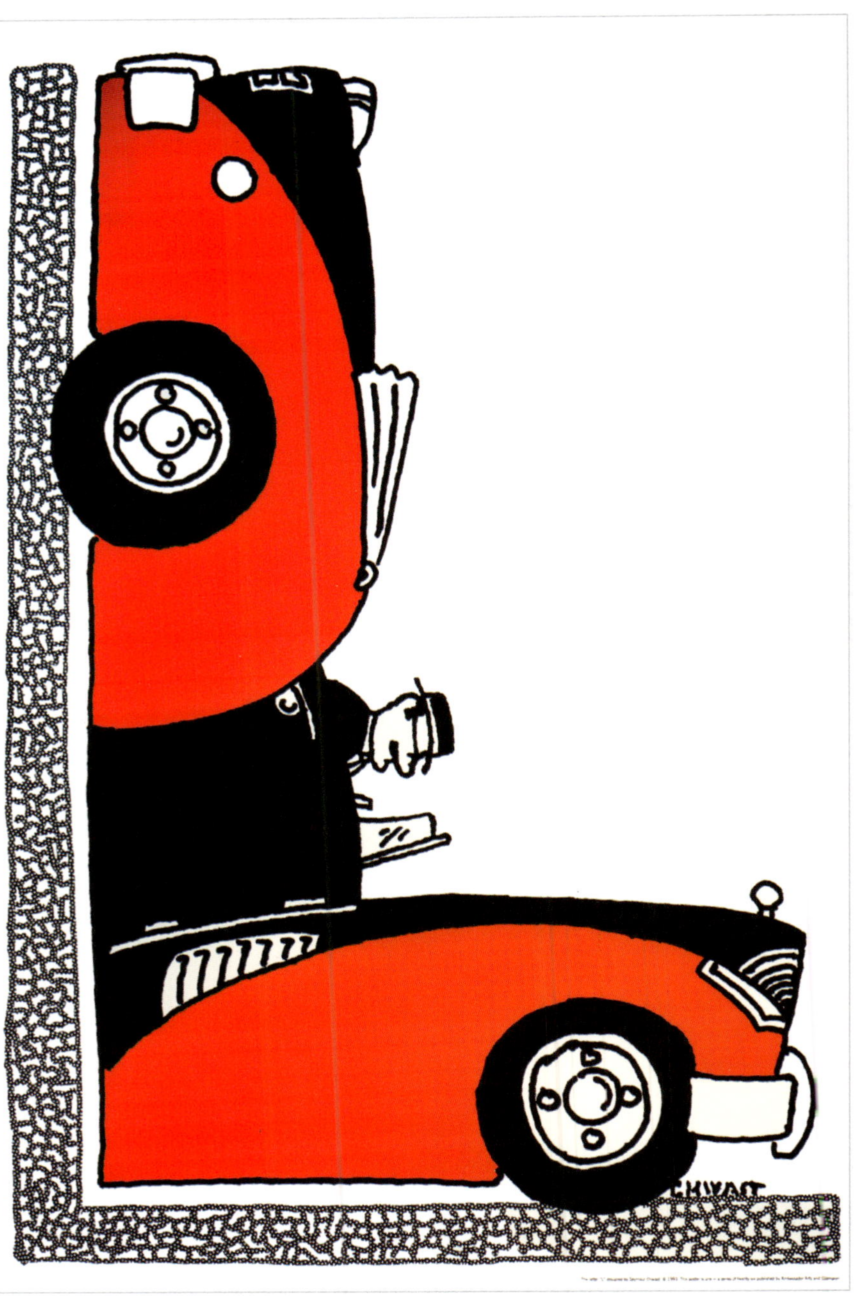

Pen and ink, color film, offset, 18" x 24", 1989

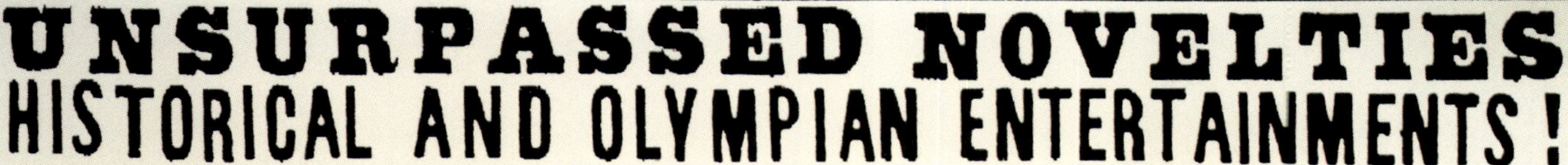

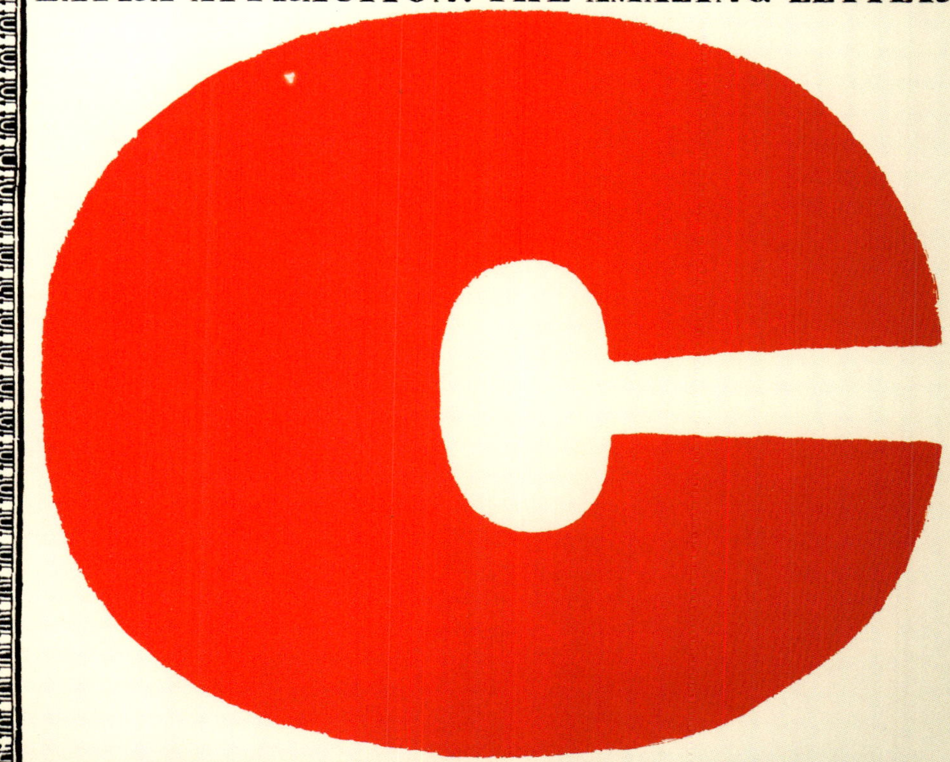

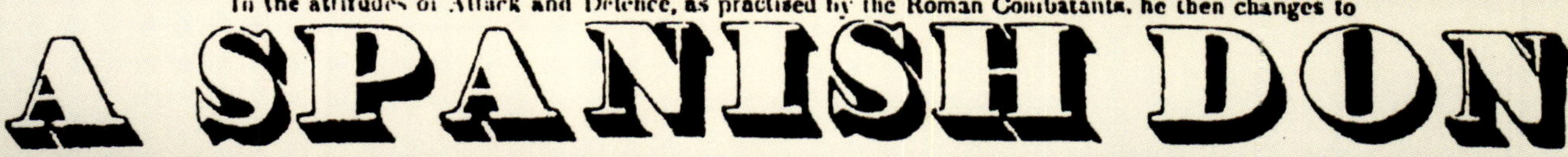

Found type, flat matched color, offset, 23" x 35", 1968

ADVERTISING ZANDERS, 4 POSTERS
These posters were done for Zanders Paper. Two different grades of paper are demonstrated on one poster. The copy is under the flap. Lift it and you find more than you ever wanted to know.

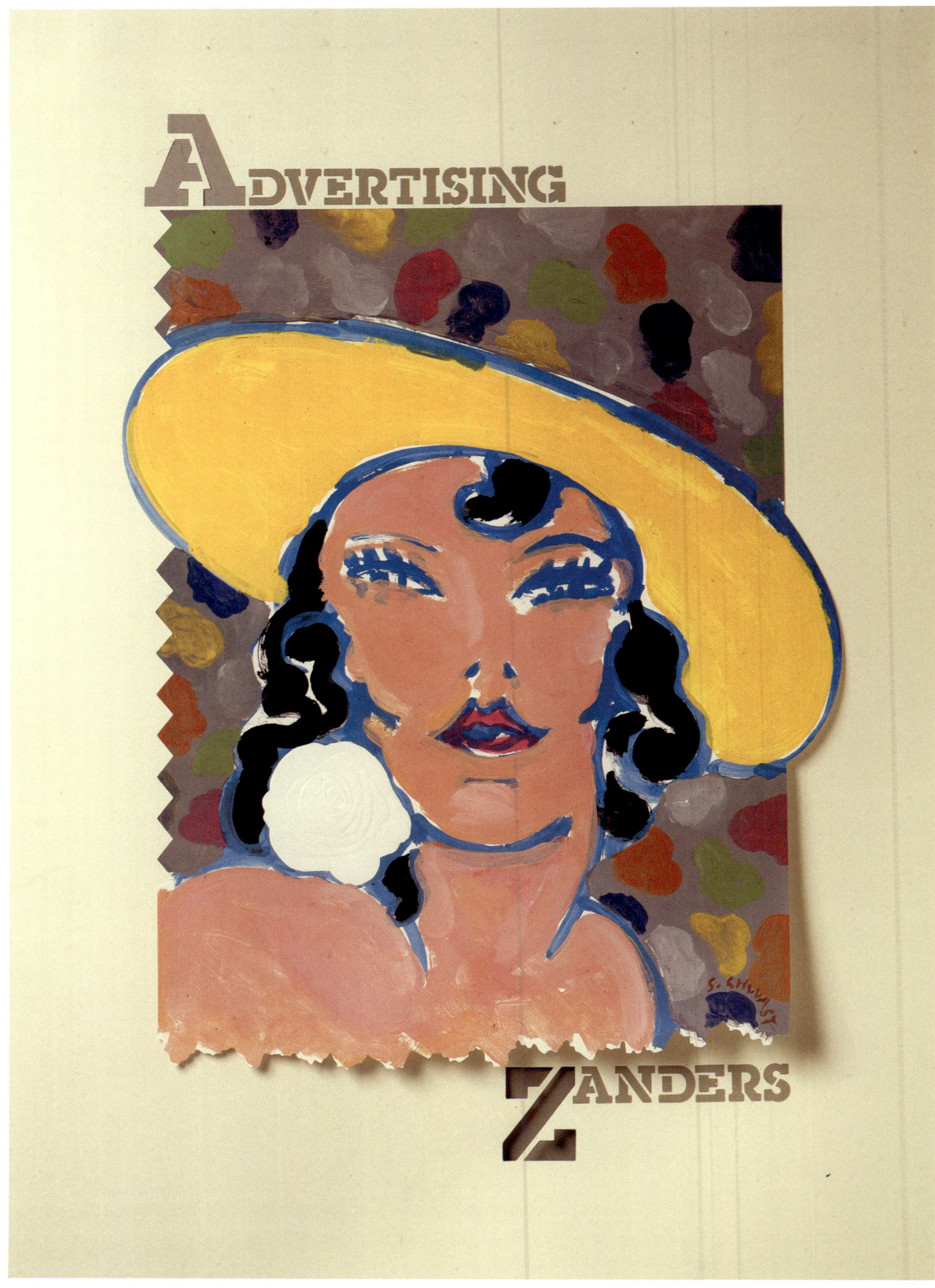

Acrylic on paper, offset, 23½" x 33", 1989

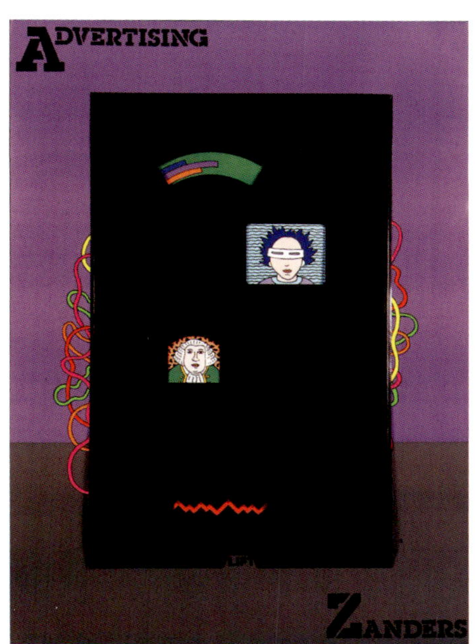

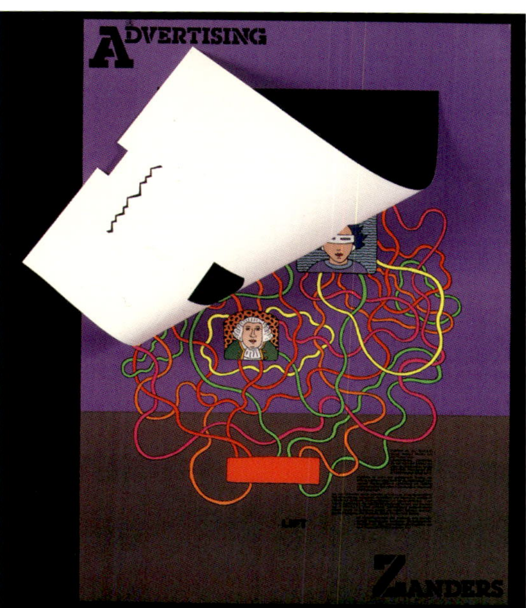

Mixed media, matched color, offset, 23½" x 33", 1989

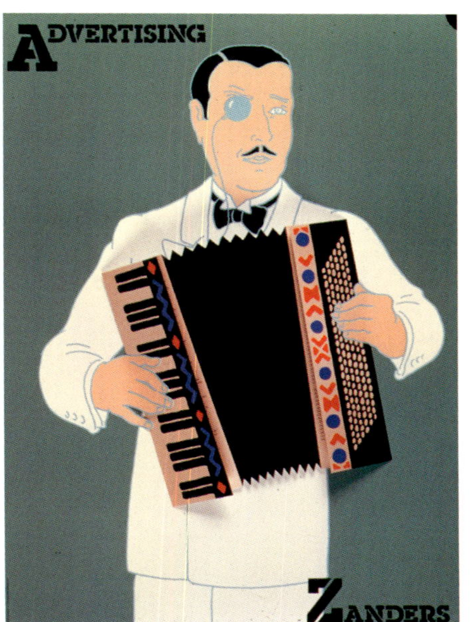

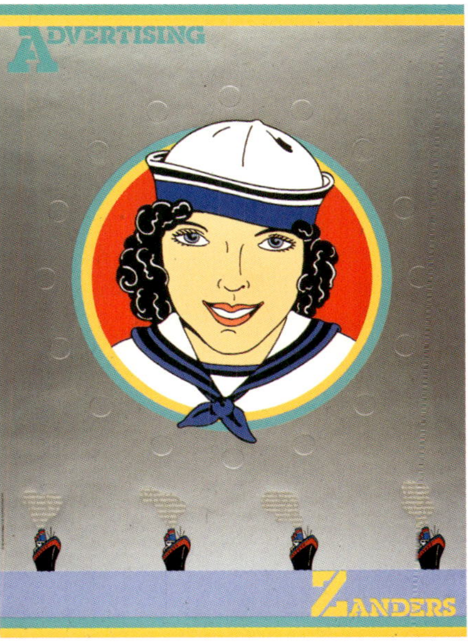

Left and right: Pen and ink, matched color, offset, 23½" x 33", 1989

FORBES

FORBES, 5 POSTERS
Posters for *Forbes* on this and the following spreads were for a campaign seen on the New York subways. Smaller versions became full-page ads in a magazine. I worked from sketches the advertising agency sent me. The ideas were theirs.

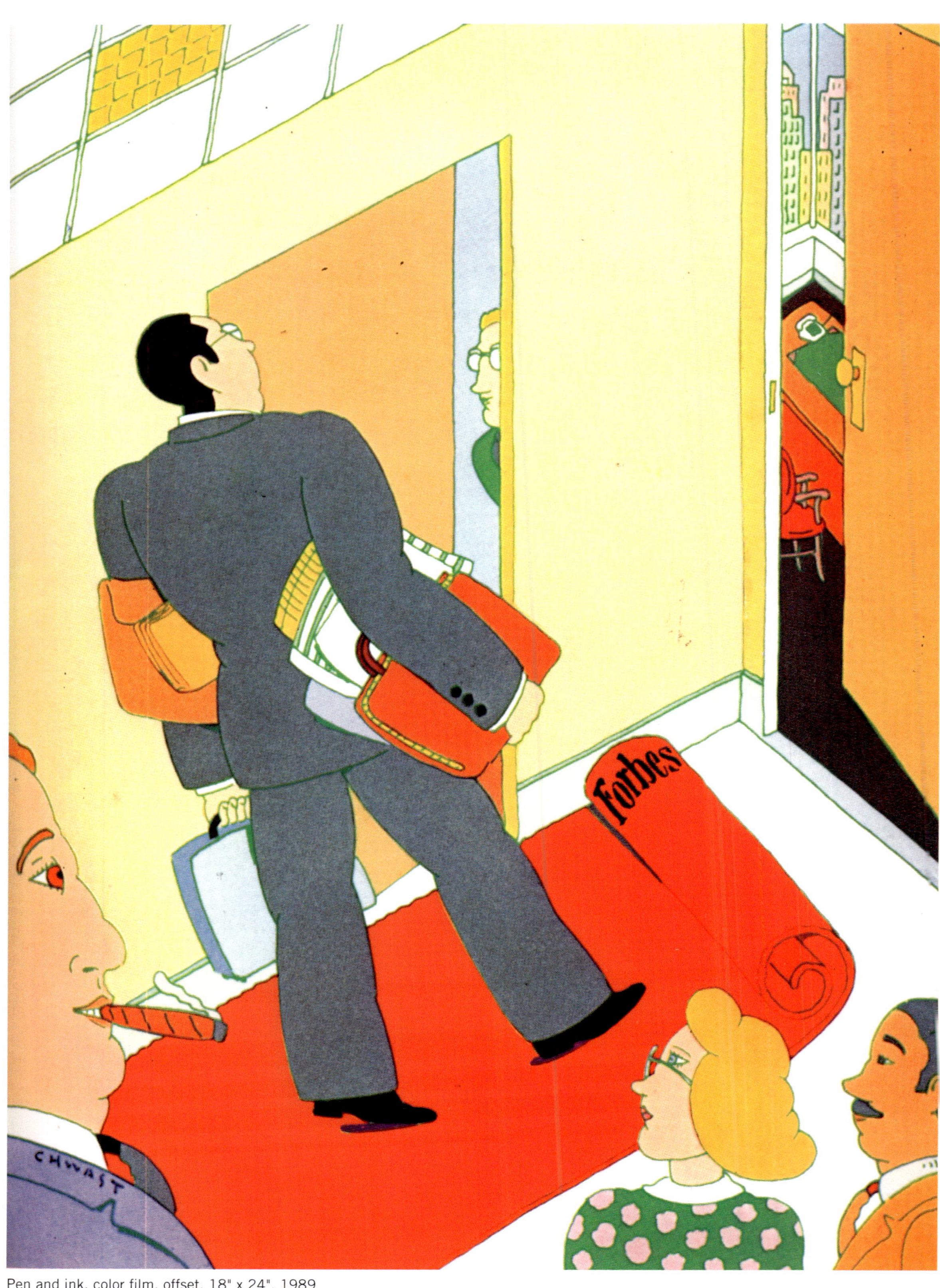

Pen and ink, color film, offset, 18" x 24", 1989

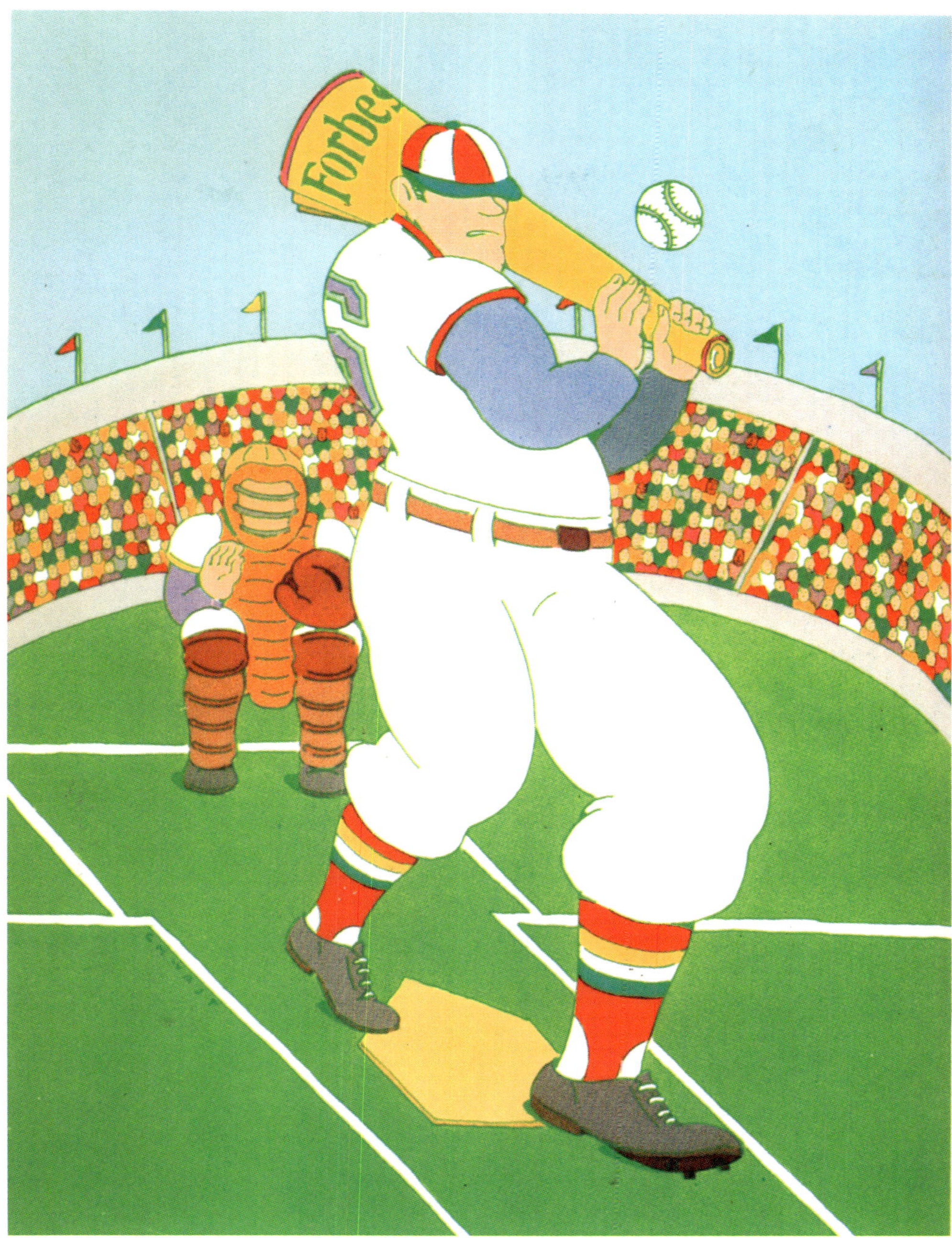

Pen and ink, color film, offset, 18" x 24", 1986

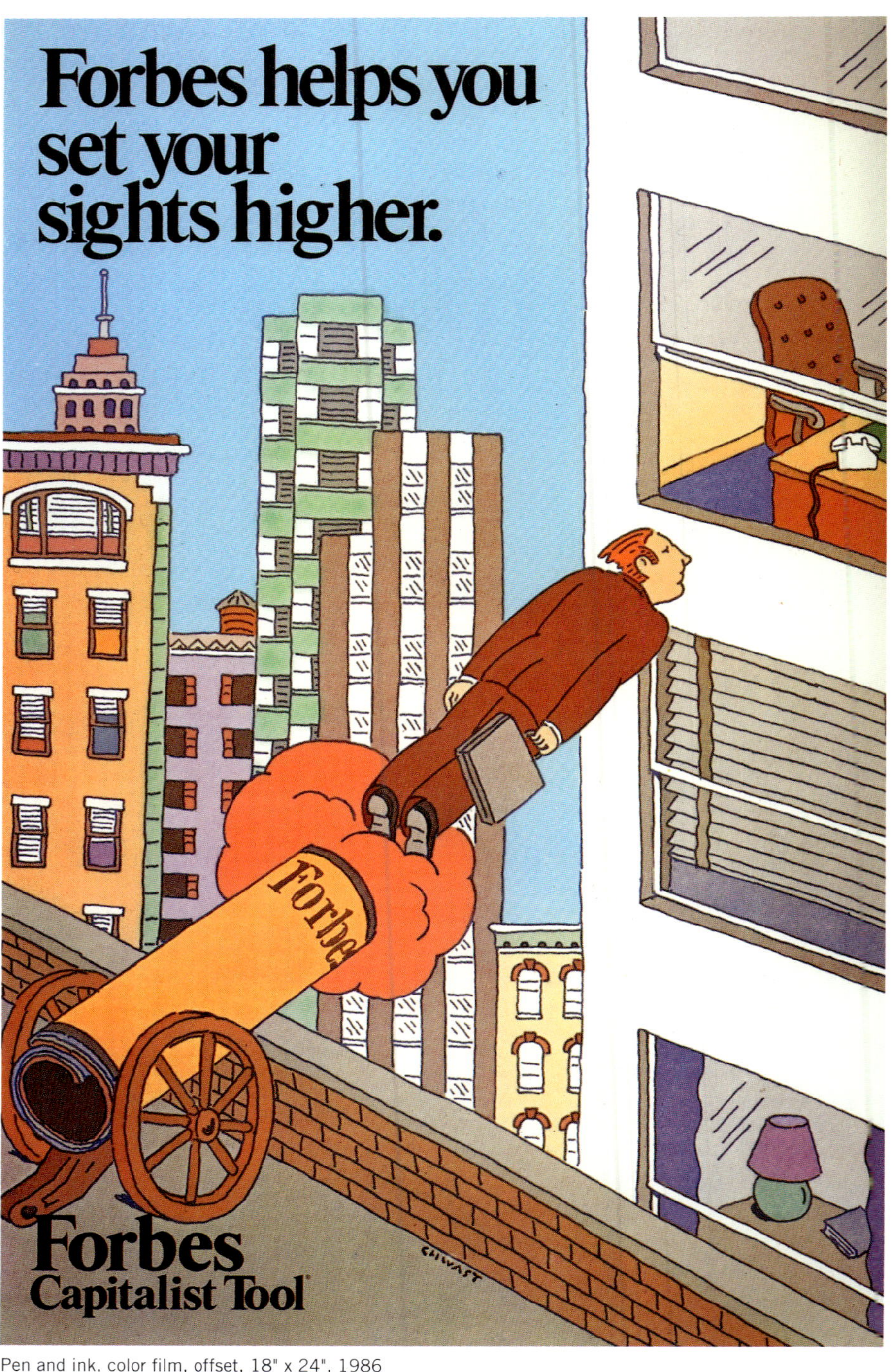

Pen and ink, color film, offset, 18" x 24", 1986

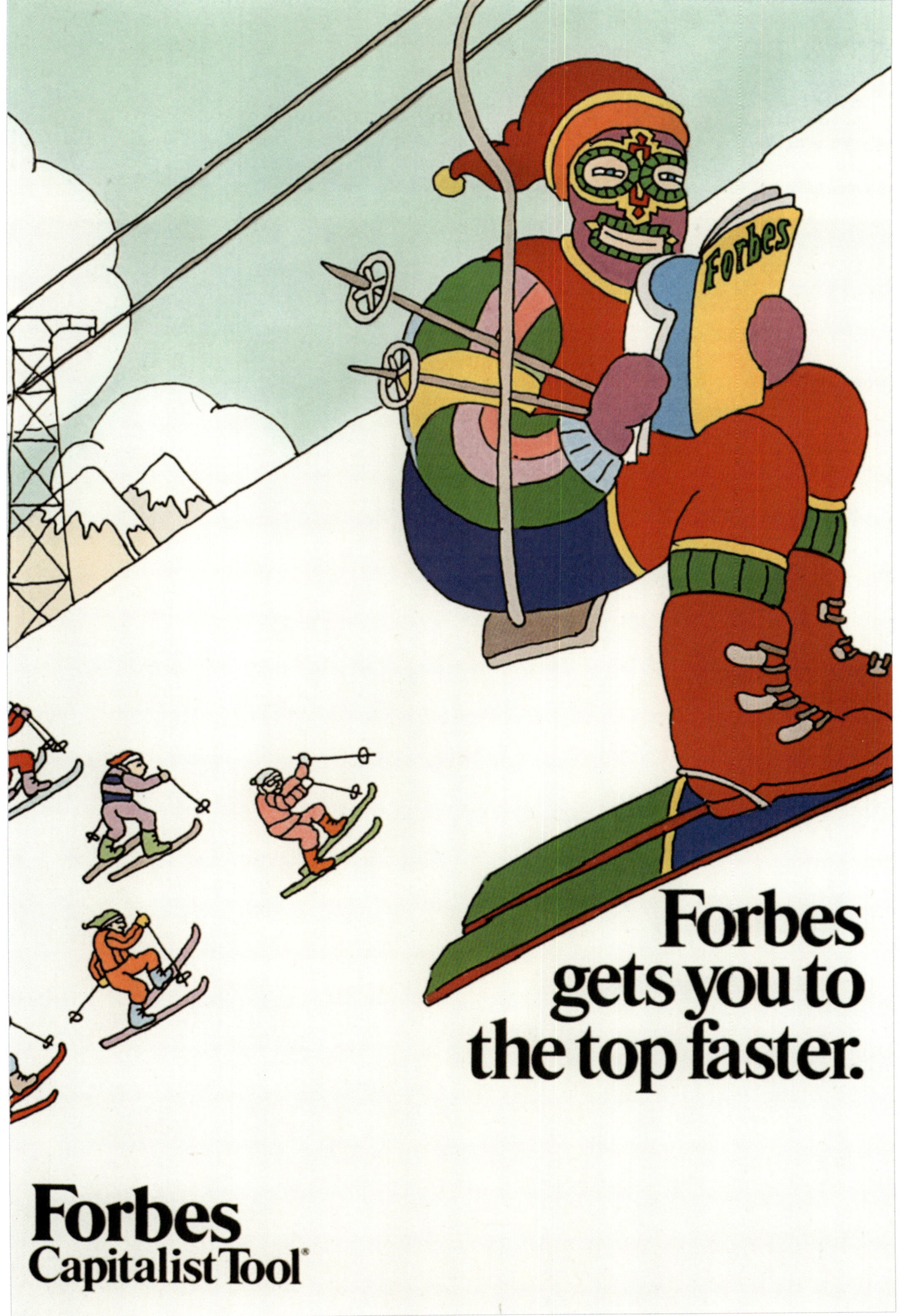

Pen and ink, color film, offset, 18" x 24", 1986

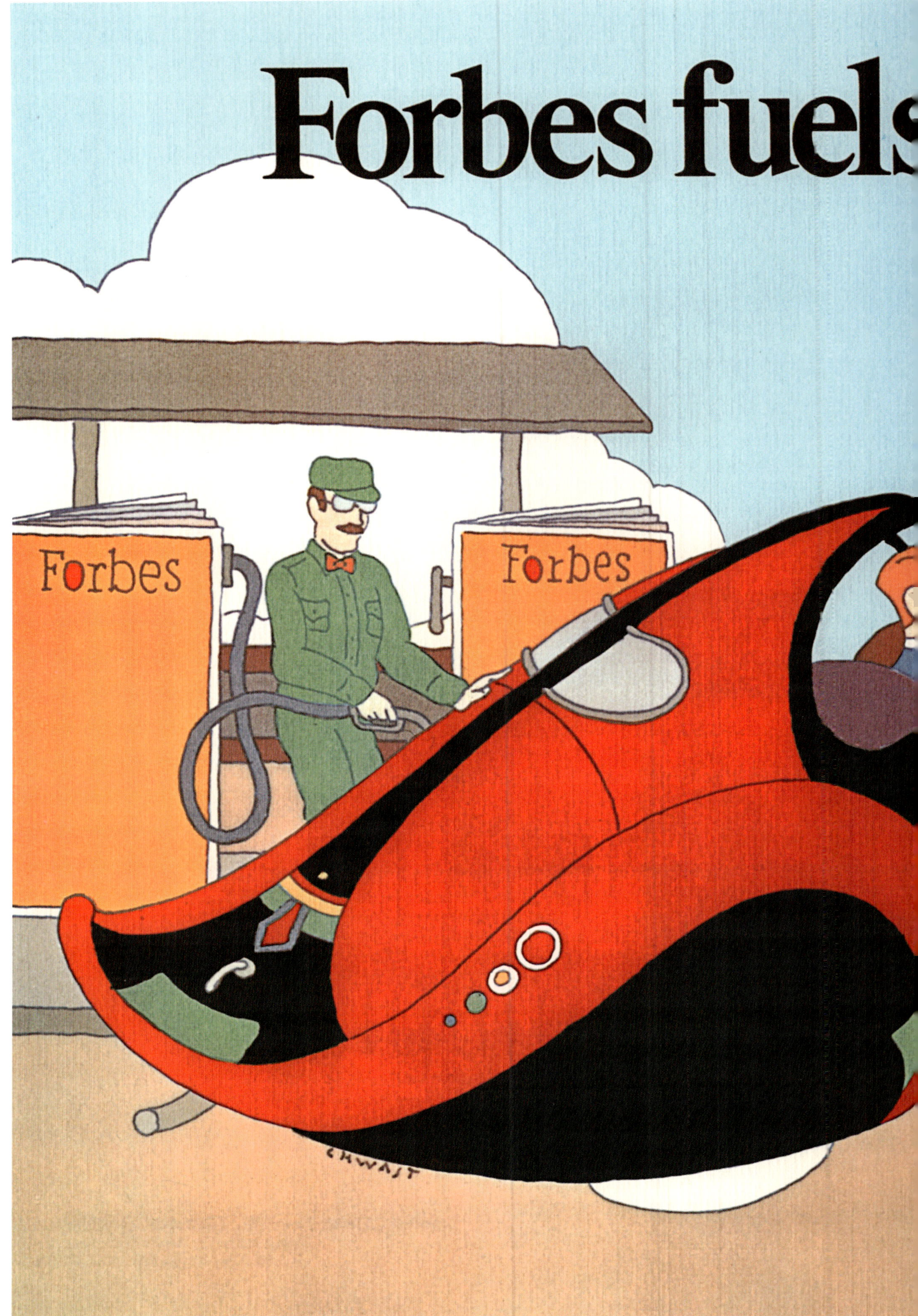

Pen and ink, color film, offset, 61" x 46", 1989

your drive.

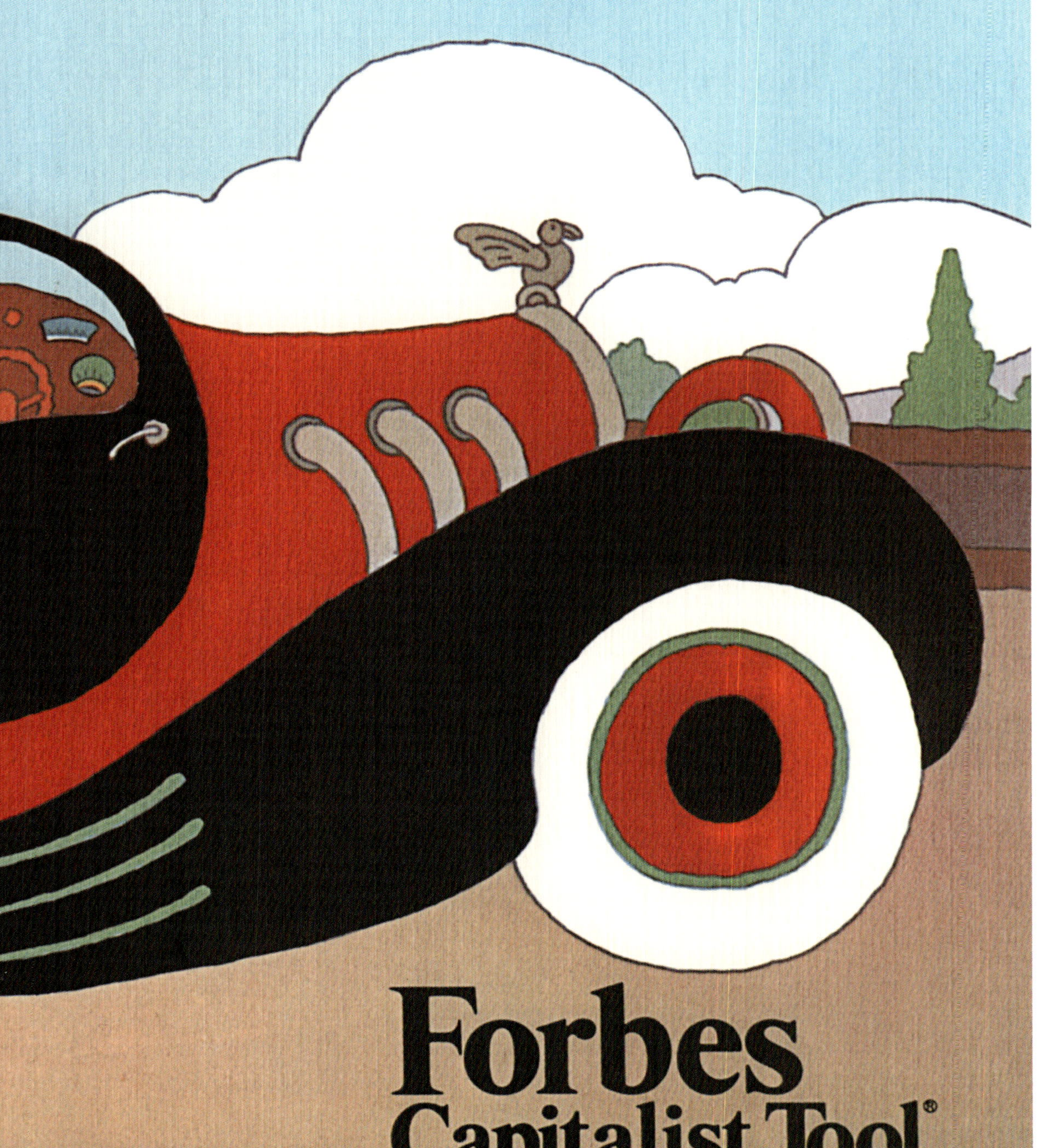

SERIGRAPHS (SILKSCREEN)

Below, right; and opposite: **YOU ARE WHAT YOU PRINT** and **COLOR.** Noblet Serigraphie, a fine art serigraph printer in New York, promoted the craft with these posters.

Below, left: **THE FACTORY.** A promotional poster for a Swedish serigraph printer.

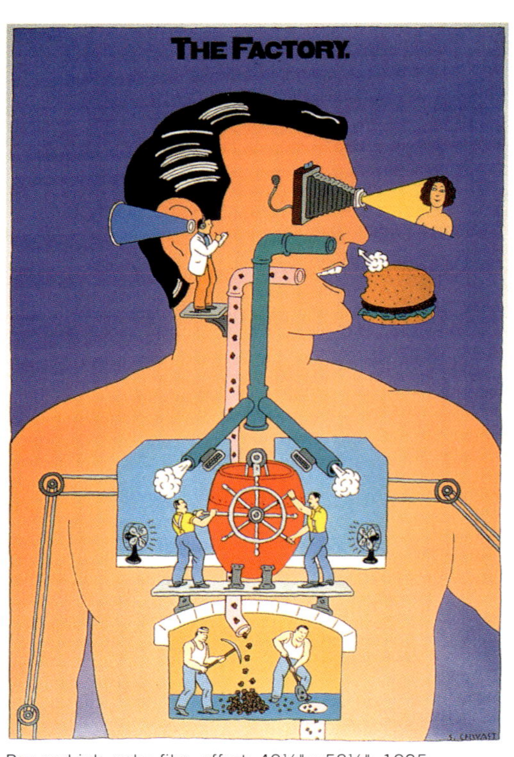

Pen and ink, color film, offset, 40½" x 58½", 1995

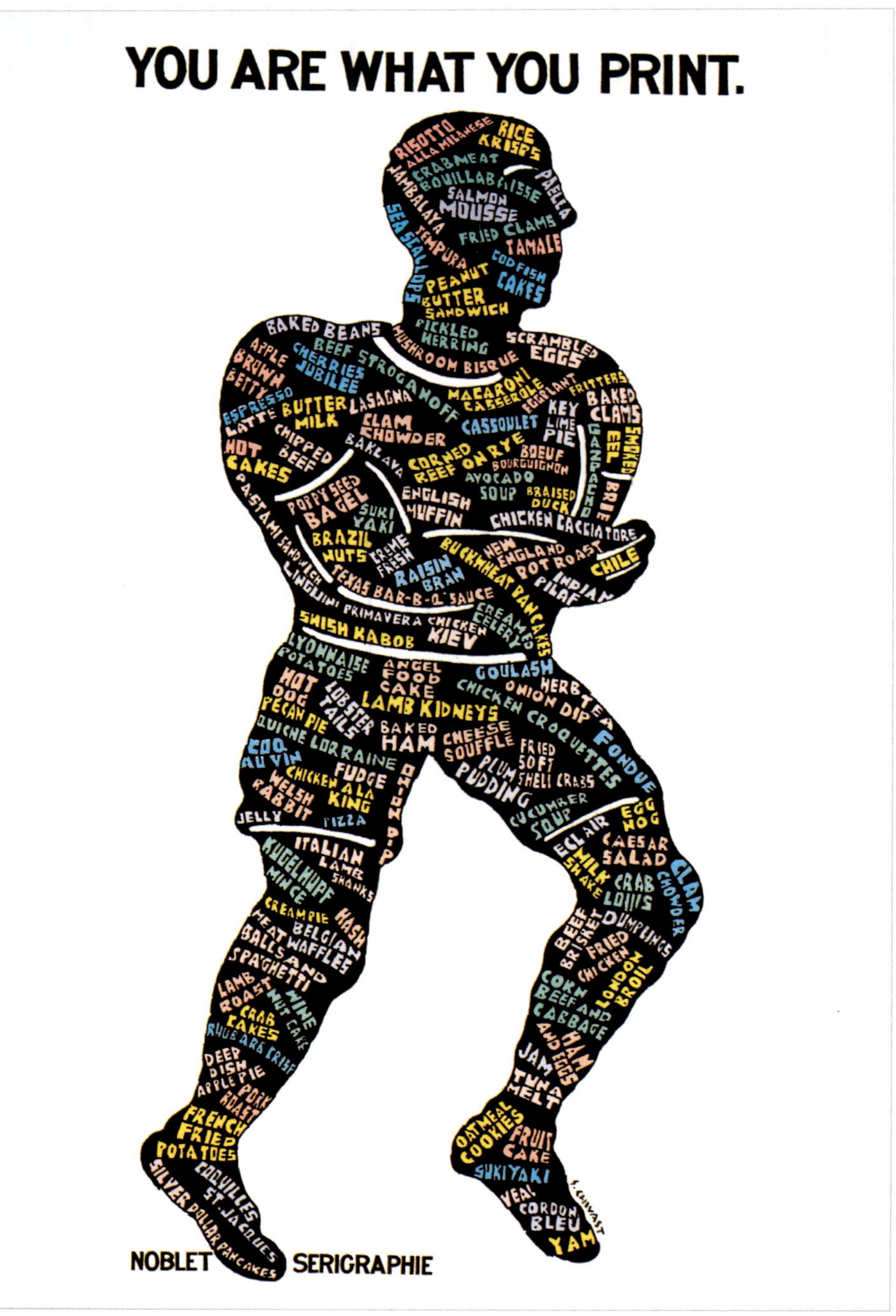

Serigraph, offset, 20" x 30", 1996

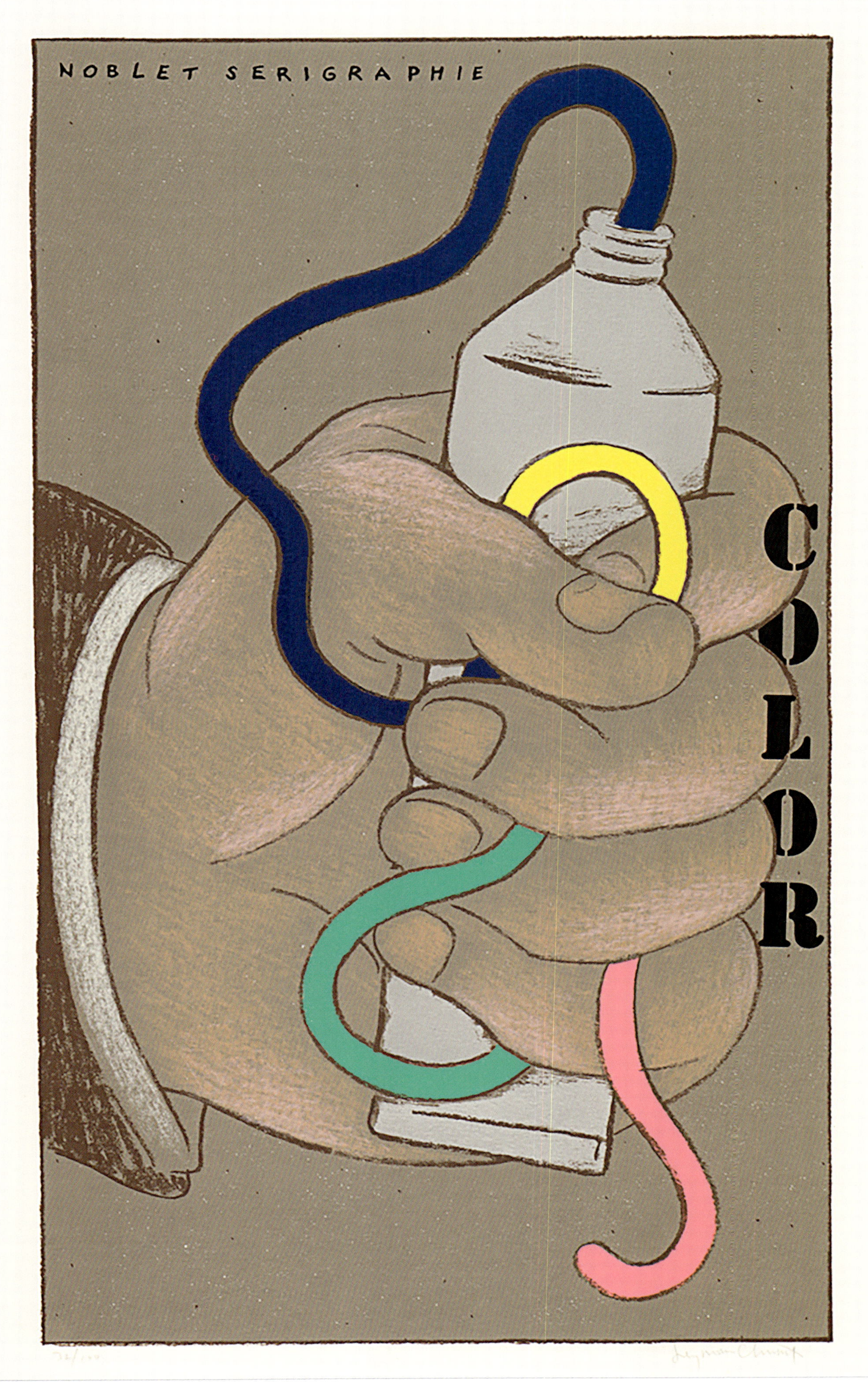

Serigraph, offset, 22" x 35", 1995

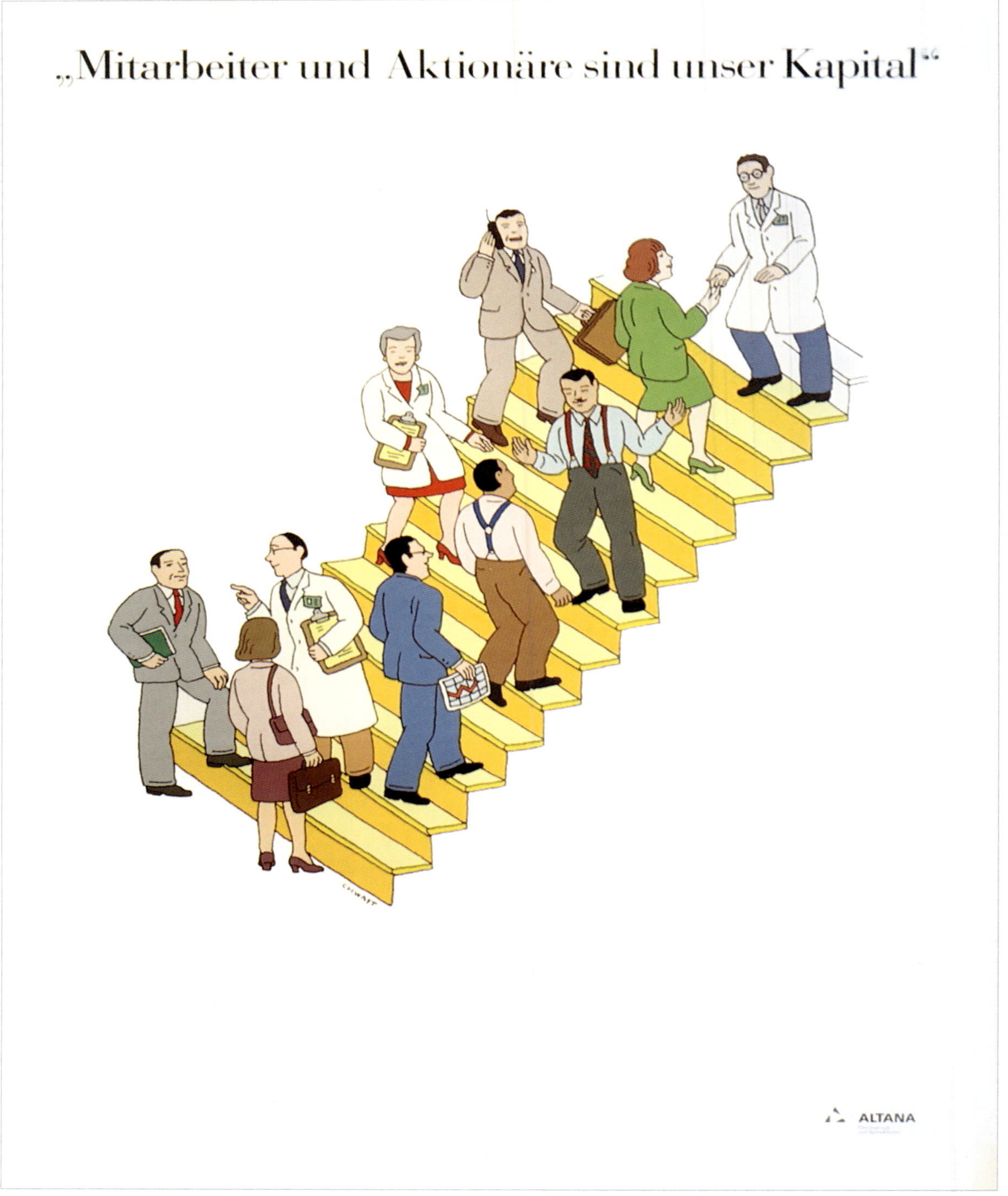

Pen and ink, color film, offset, 18" x 24", 1989

Above: **ALTANA.** Altana is a German pharmaceutical firm. The headline reads, "Employees and shareholders are our capital." The art director at the advertising agency designed the poster. My contribution was the illustration.

Opposite, top: **ELEKTRA.** Elektra was an animation studio. The traveling objects convey the idea that the studio is moving to a new location.

Opposite, below: **PERIDOT.** In the Peridot poster, clients are gleefully observing the progress of their commercial. This poster would be politically incorrect today. Drawing for animation used to be created on an animation stand. Twenty drawings were needed for each second of animation. Software later made the process much easier, with the animation stand obsolete.

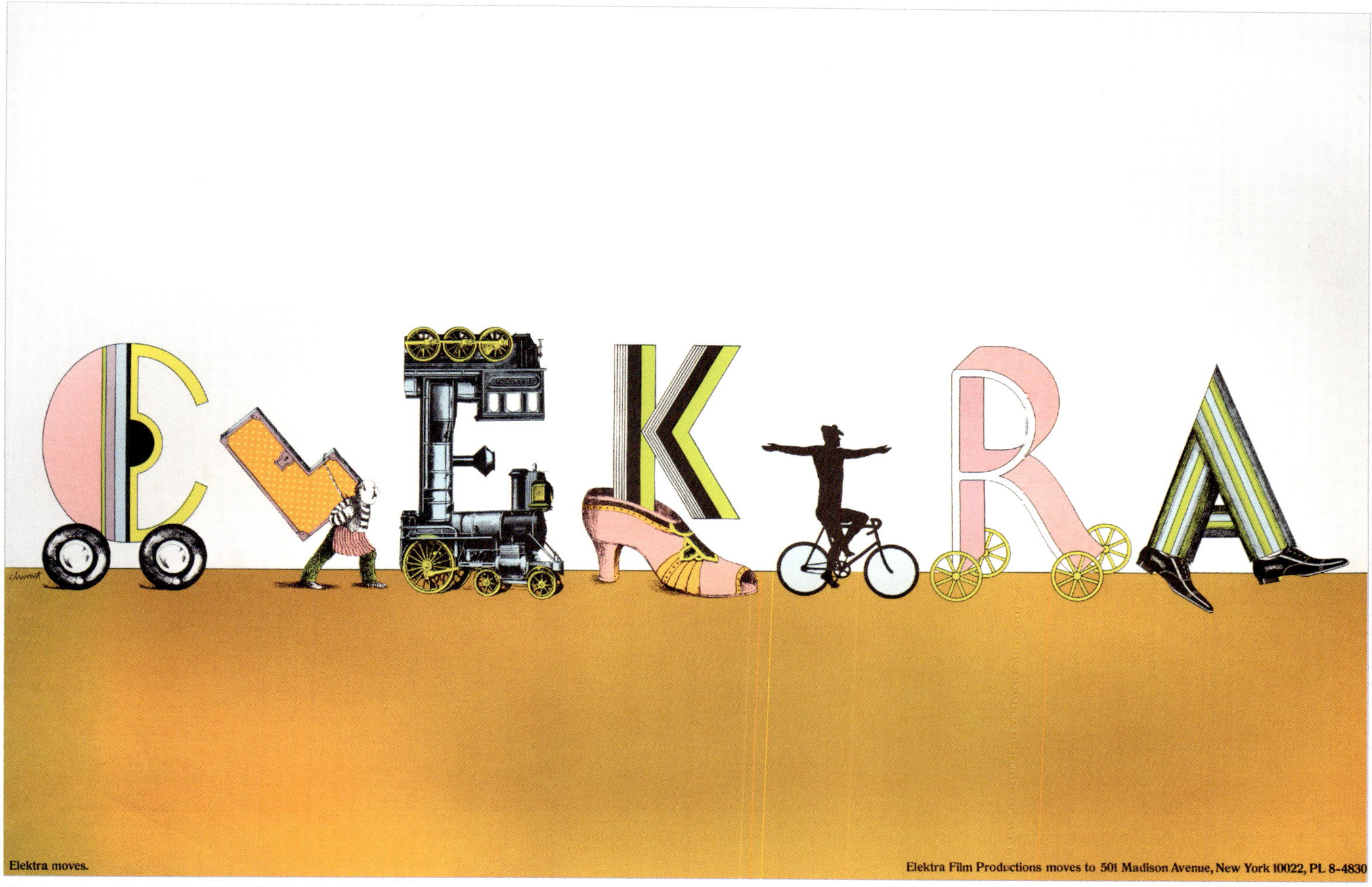

Mixed media, offset, 24" x 36", 1966

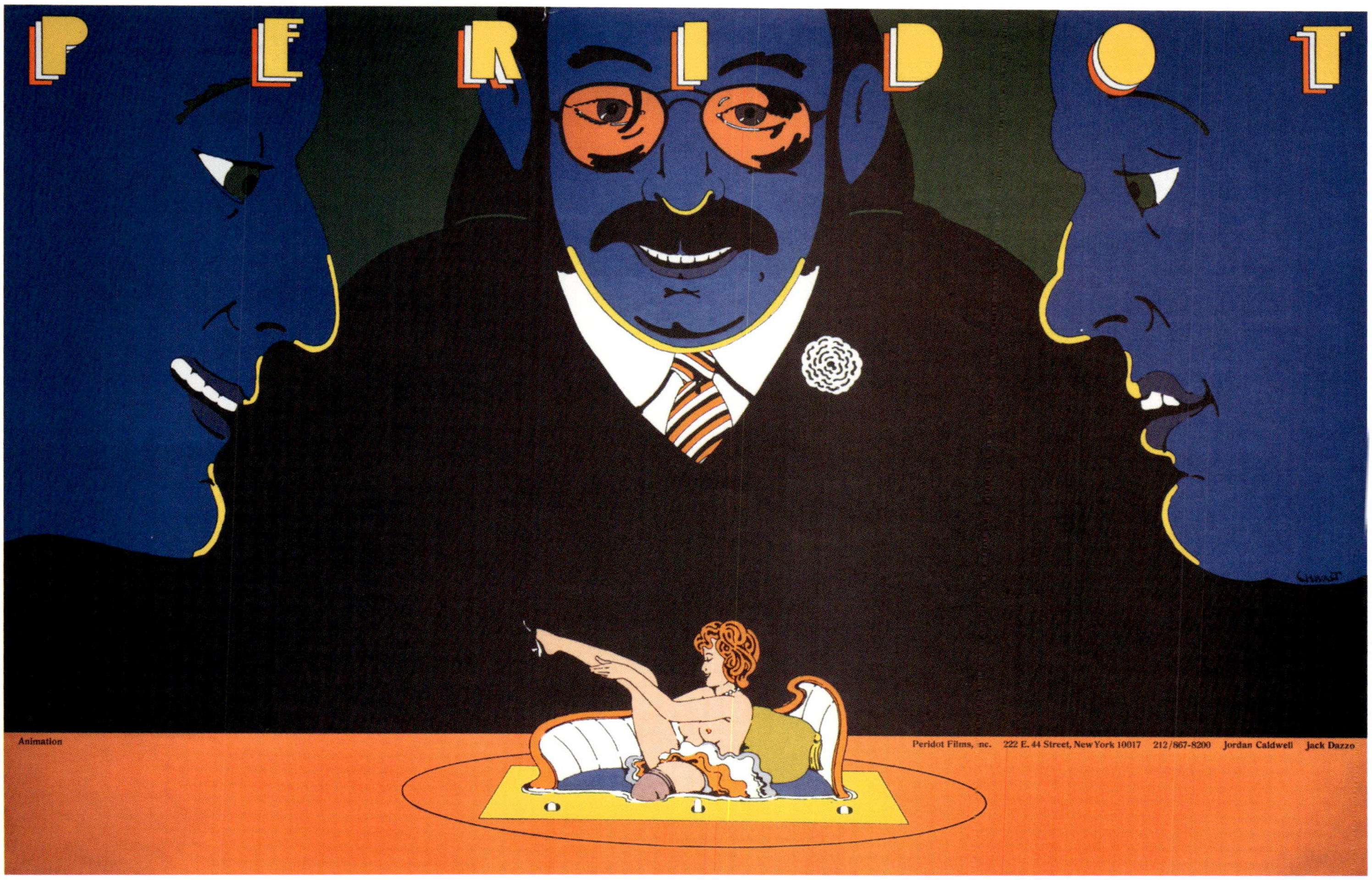

Pen and ink, matched color, offset, 24" x 36", 1969

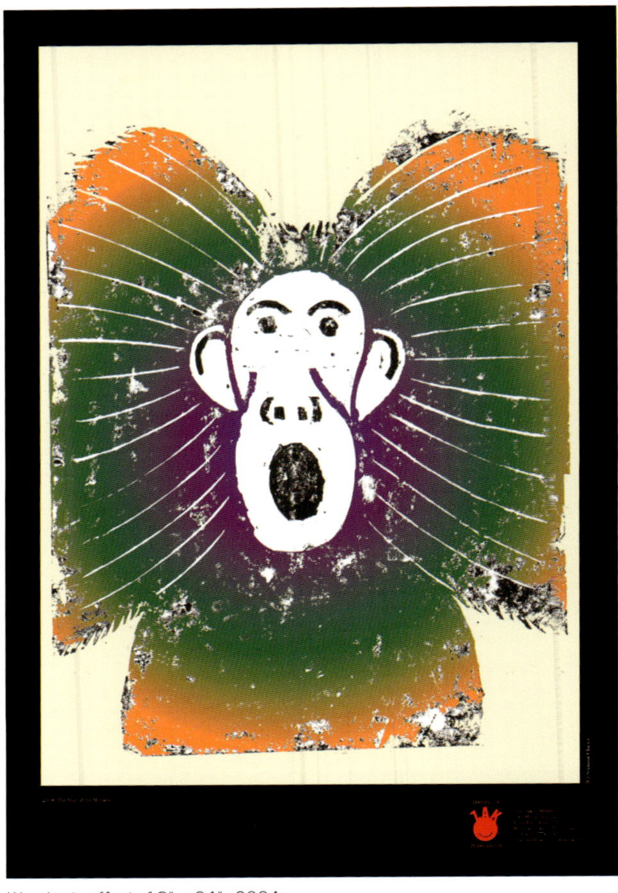
Woodcut, offset, 18" x 24", 2004

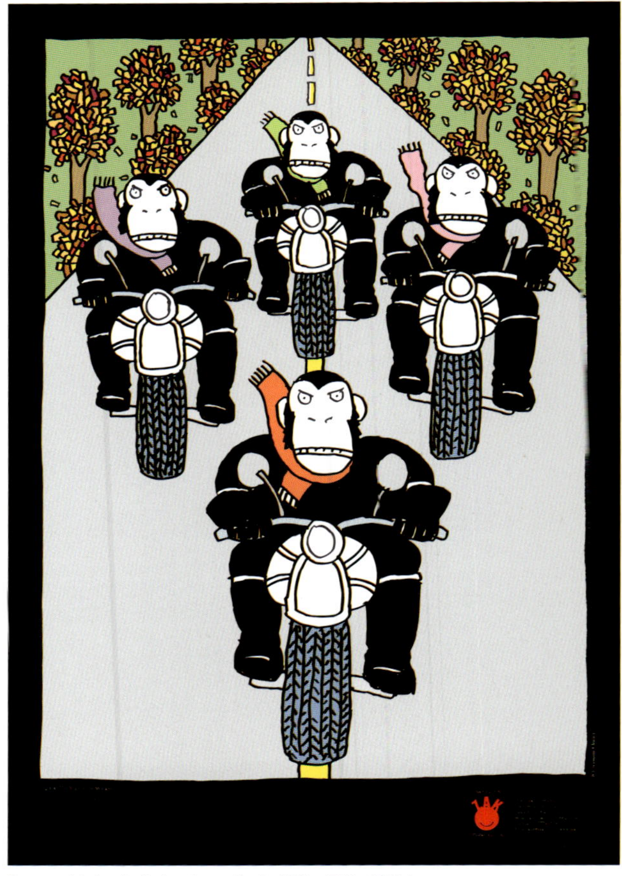
Pen and ink, digital color, offset, 18" x 24", 2004

THE YEAR OF THE MONKEY, 3 POSTERS
Kaz Imaeda is a Japanese entrepreneur. To promote his business, The Zak Company, he asked me to create three posters announcing the year of the monkey.

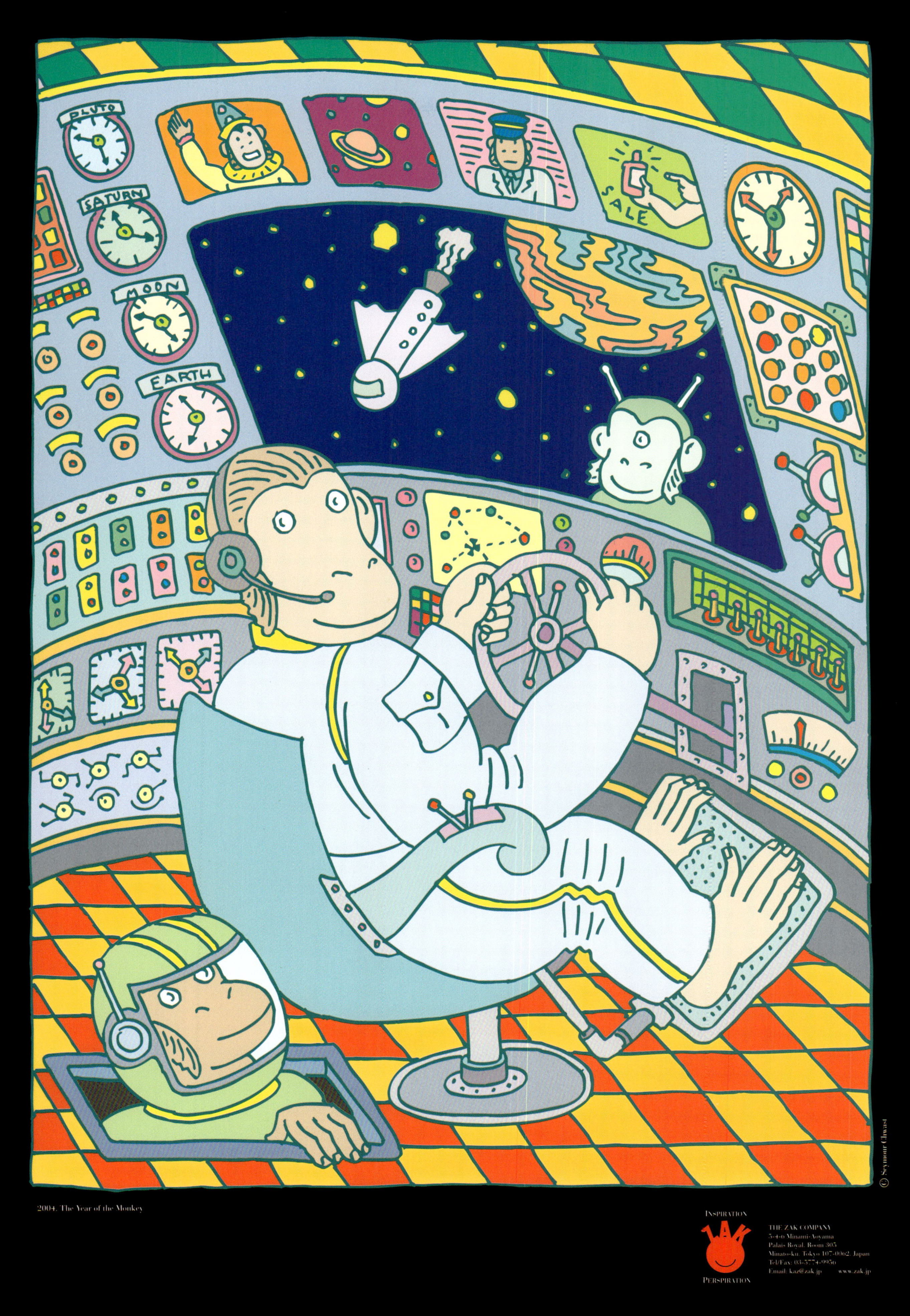

Pen and ink, digital color, offset, 18" x 24", 2004

PENNY PITCH
DECO MOTORCYCLE

Below and opposite: Penny Pitch was a game I invented. You don't hang this poster on the wall; you play it on the floor. This and the motorcycle were produced during the poster craze of the 1960s. The later poster contrasts the light-hearted and decorated motorcycle with the dark graphic image of its owner.

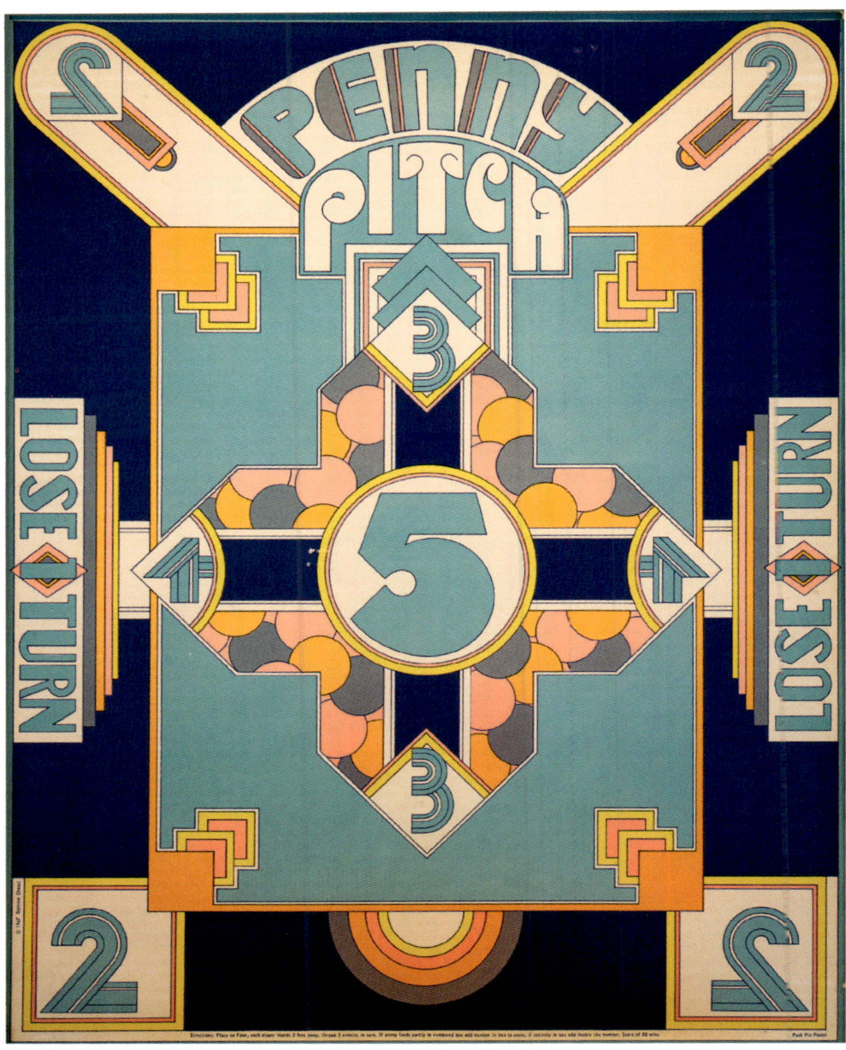

Mechanical art, offset, 24" x 36", 1967

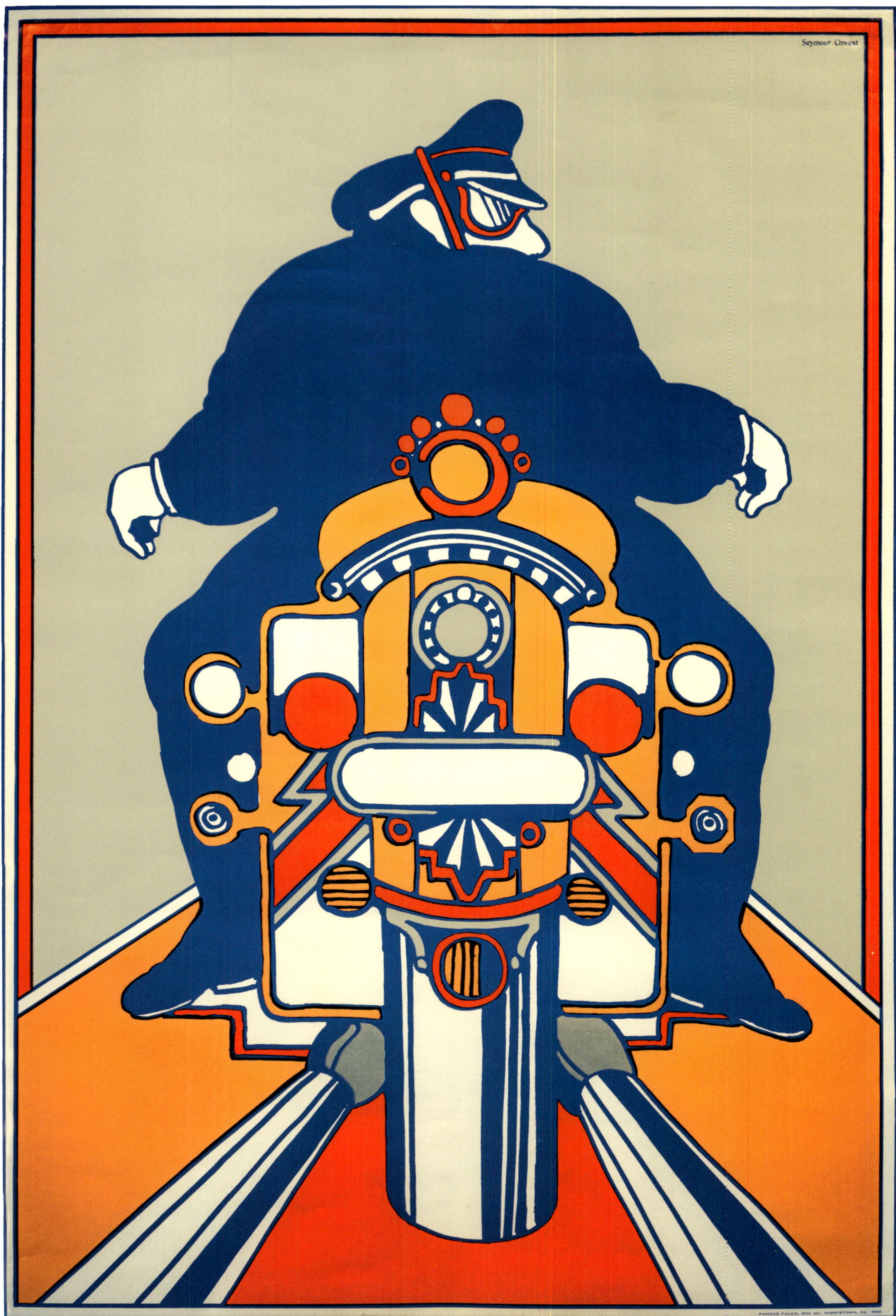

Mechanical art, offset, 24" x 36", 1967

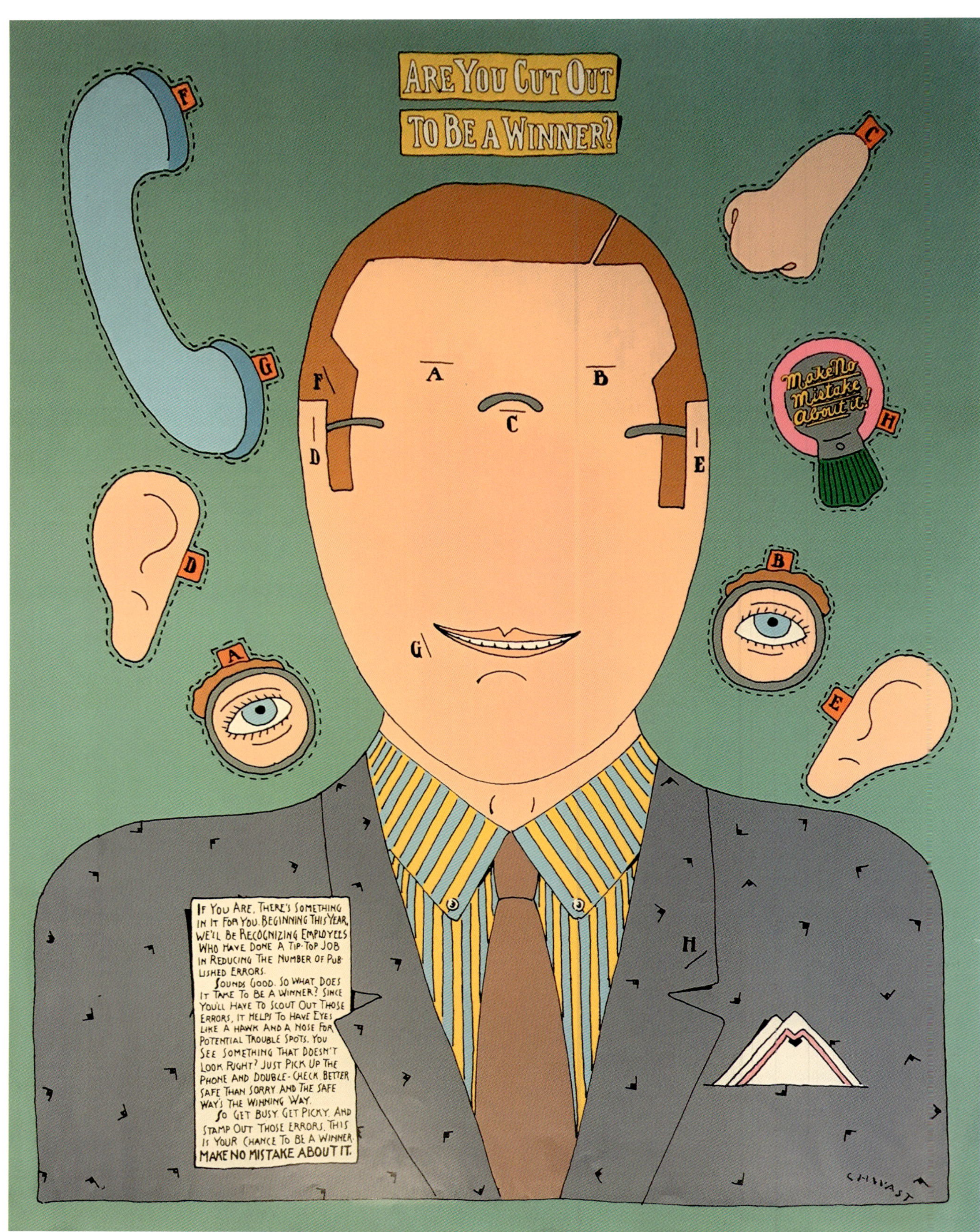

Hand lettered, pen and ink, color film, offset, 22" x 28", 1983

ARE YOU CUT OUT TO BE A WINNER

Opposite: The employees of the corporation were made aware of many costly mistakes. The winner of the contest was the one who found the most in the poster.

FILMSENSE

Below: Filmsense was a short-lived spin-off of Pushpin Studios. It produced animated films for our clients. I designed the alphabet-based forms on the poster for the Louvre, designed with Milton Glaser, page 123.

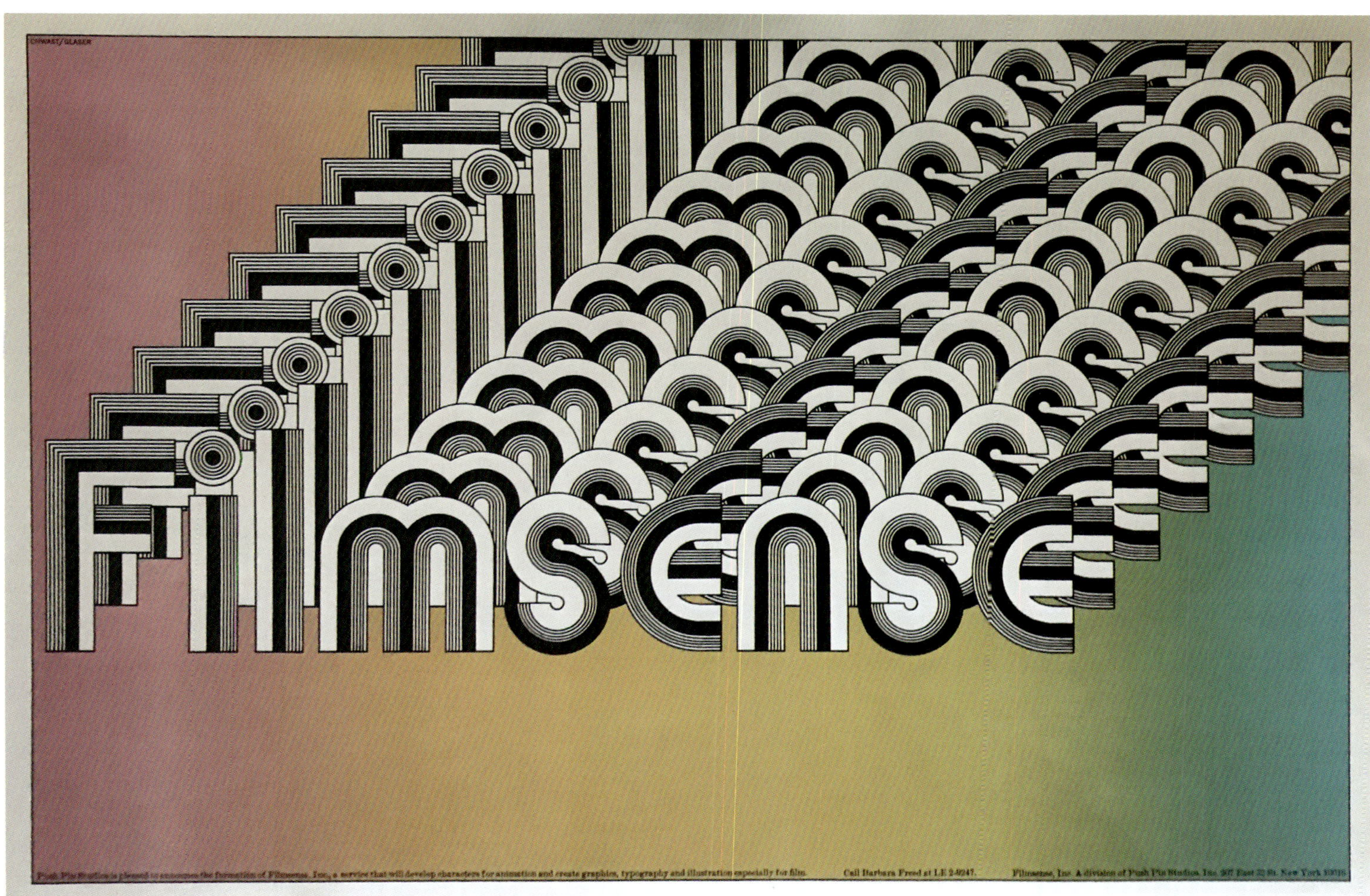

Mechanical art, four color process, offset, 18" x 24", 1973

PIONEER MOSS

Below and opposite: Pioneer Moss produced photo engravings for advertising agencies. There was no one style for the posters. The ad versions appeared in *The Push Pin Graphic*. The poster opposite used art from the 1920s. I did not design the logo.

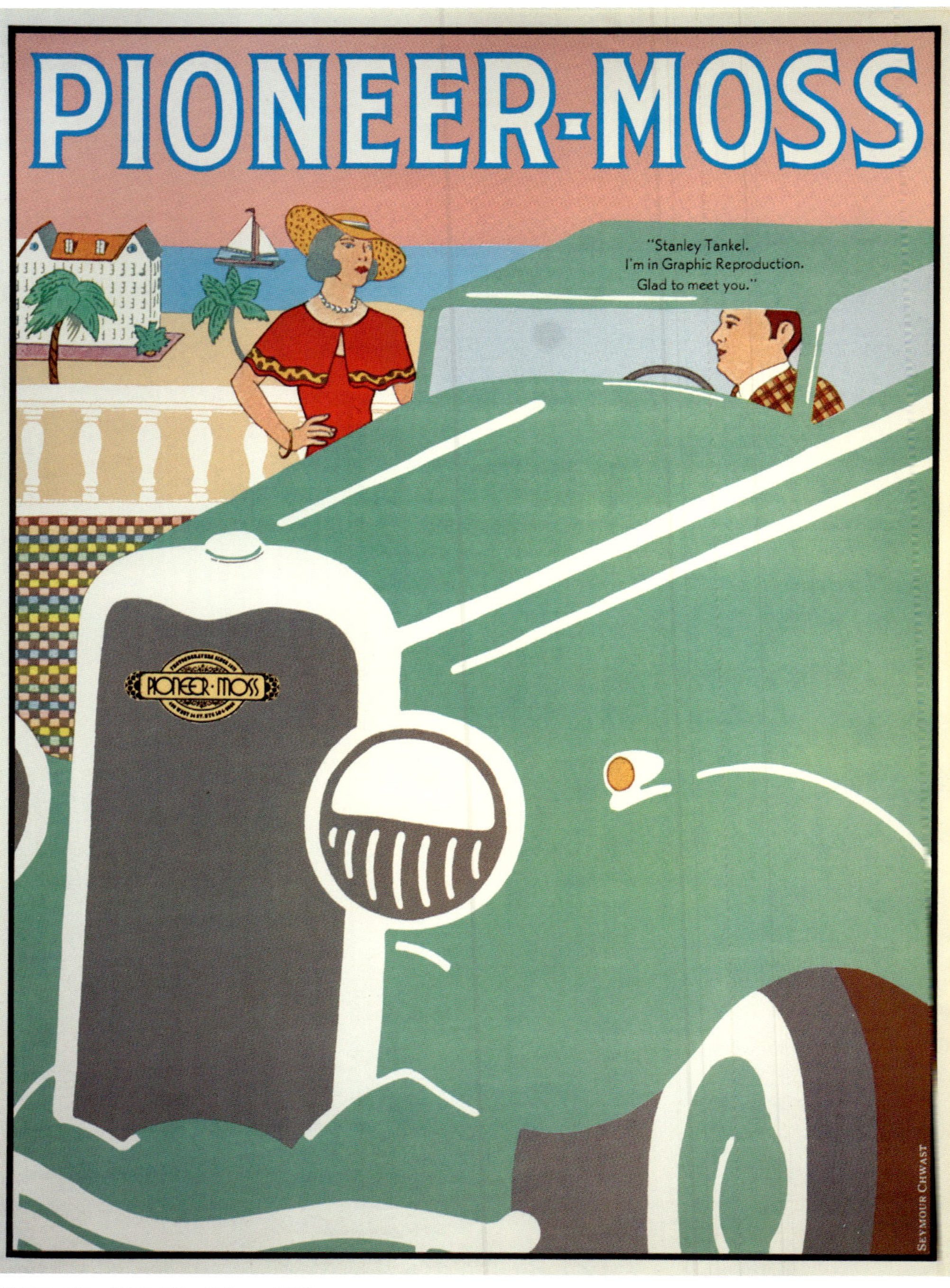

Mixed media, offset, 18" x 25", ca. 1971

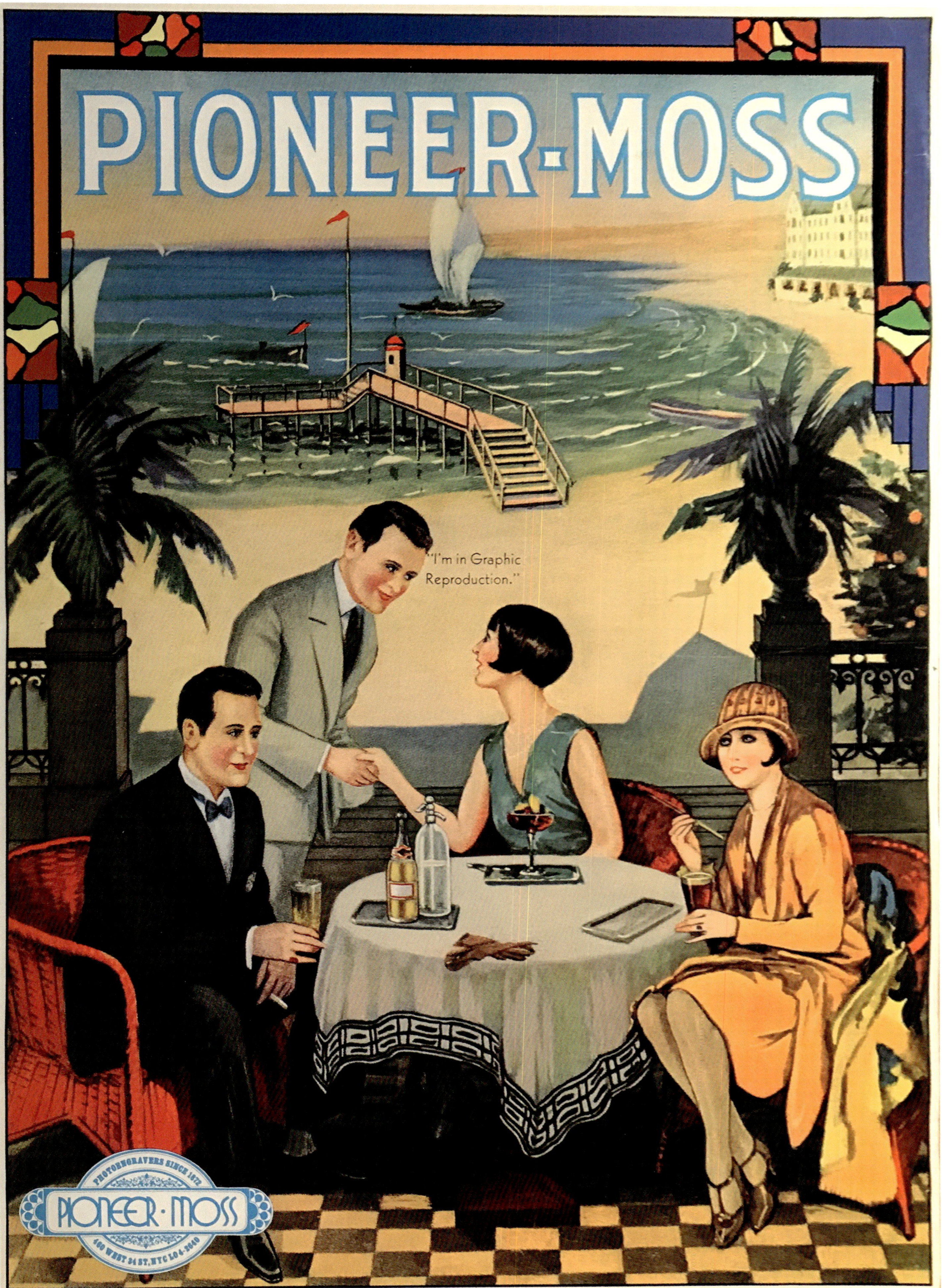

Collage, offset, 18" x 25", ca. 1971

CONNECTIONS

Designers and illustrators produced a campaign for Simpson Paper Company. The theme was "Connections." René Magritte's method of connecting incongruous elements inspired this poster.

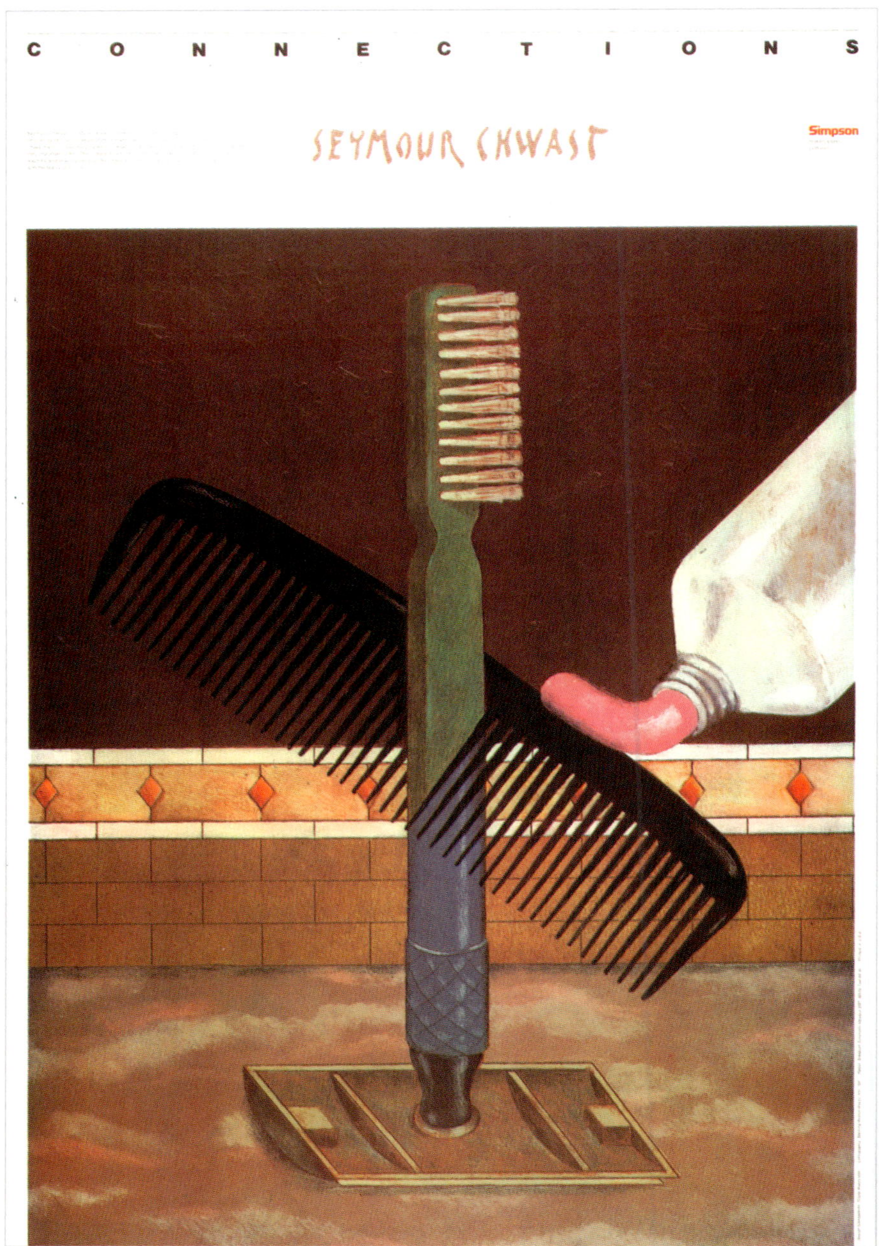

Acrylic on paper, offset, 20" x 28", ca. 1971

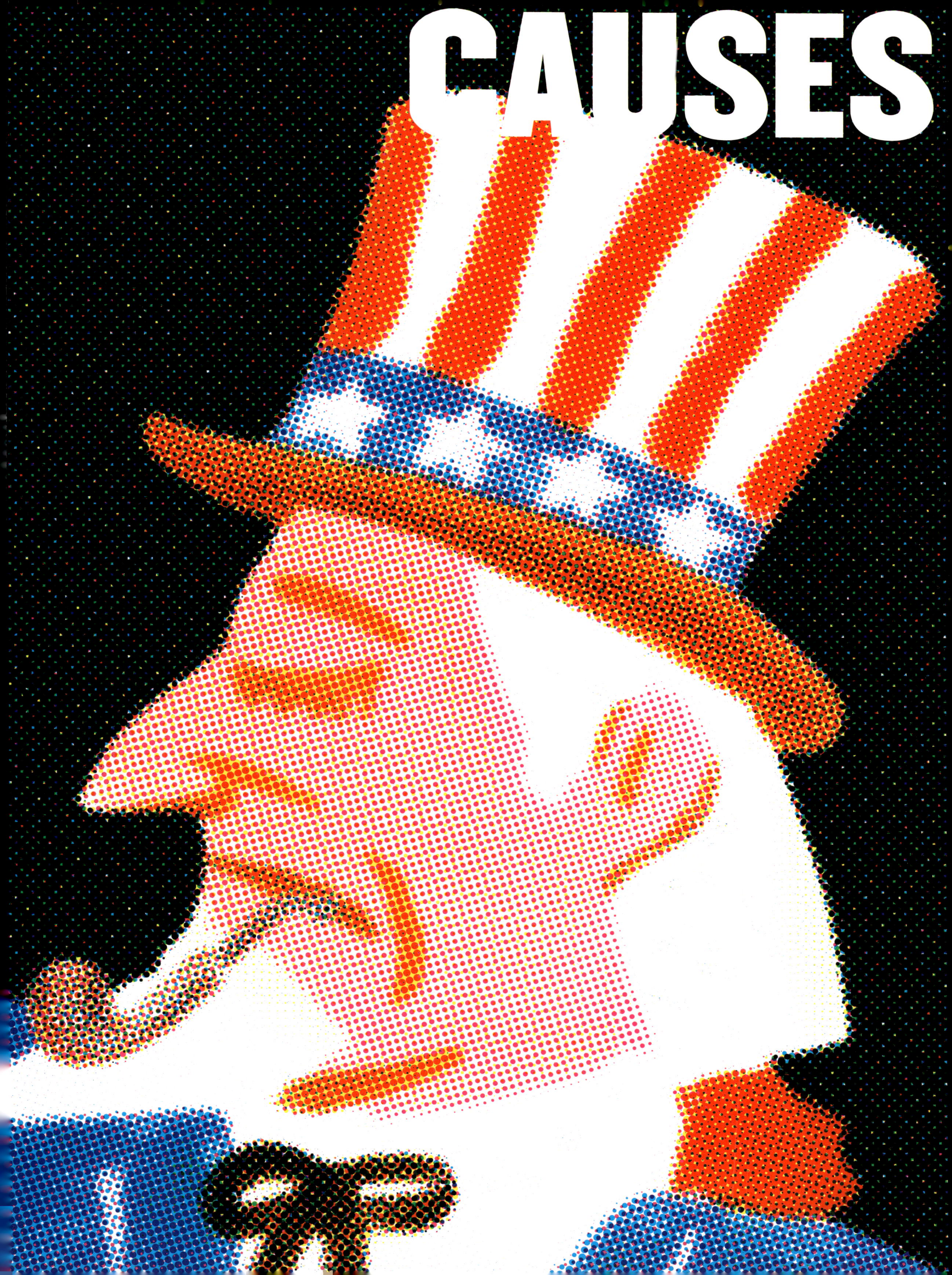
CAUSES

THE ENVIRONMENT

EARTH DAY 1990
EARTH DAY 1991

I've used the Statue of Liberty many times as a symbol of New York. It has become a cliché, but, alas, the city has too few symbols. The quest is to present it in a new context. The message of Earth Day has become more urgent since the eighties, when these posters were produced. We feel less safe with the changing climate.

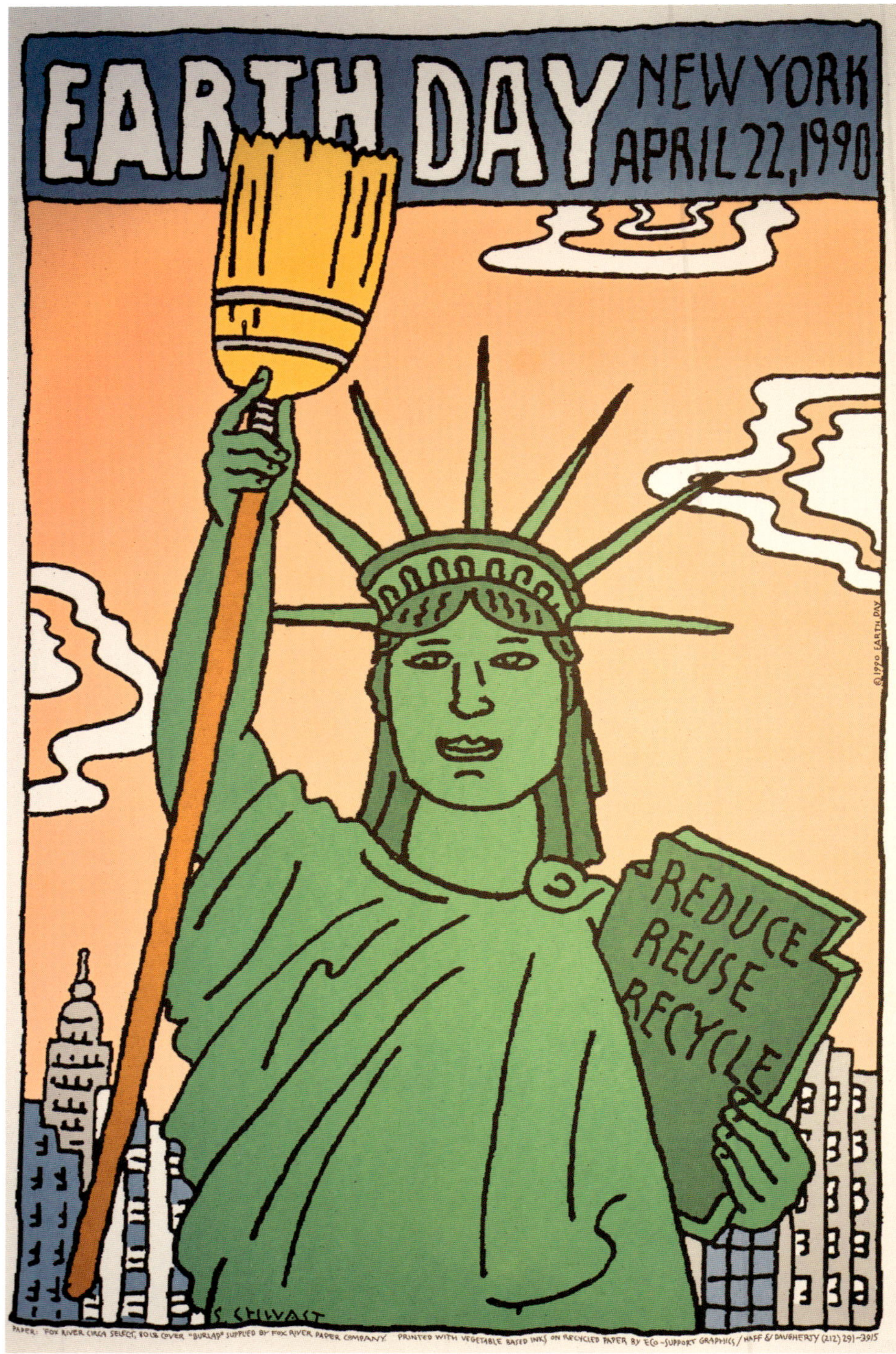

Pen and ink, color film, offset, 22" x 36", 1990

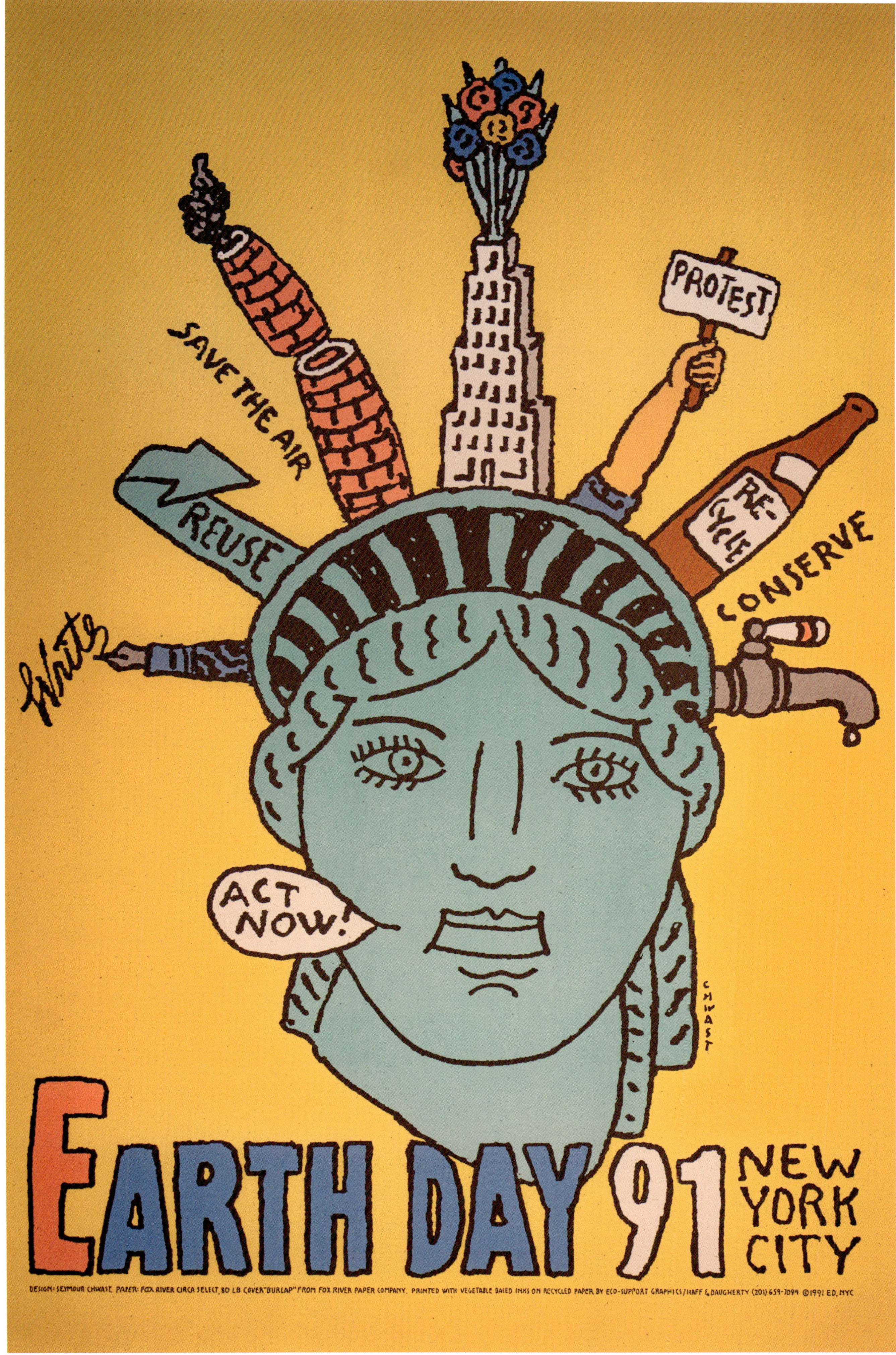

Pen and ink, color film, cffset, 22" x 36", 1991

Below: **CONCERTS FOR SAFE ENERGY.** An attempt to save the planet with music.

Opposite: **EARTH DAY 95.** Another Earth Day poster with a more graphic image, suggesting an uncomfortable future.

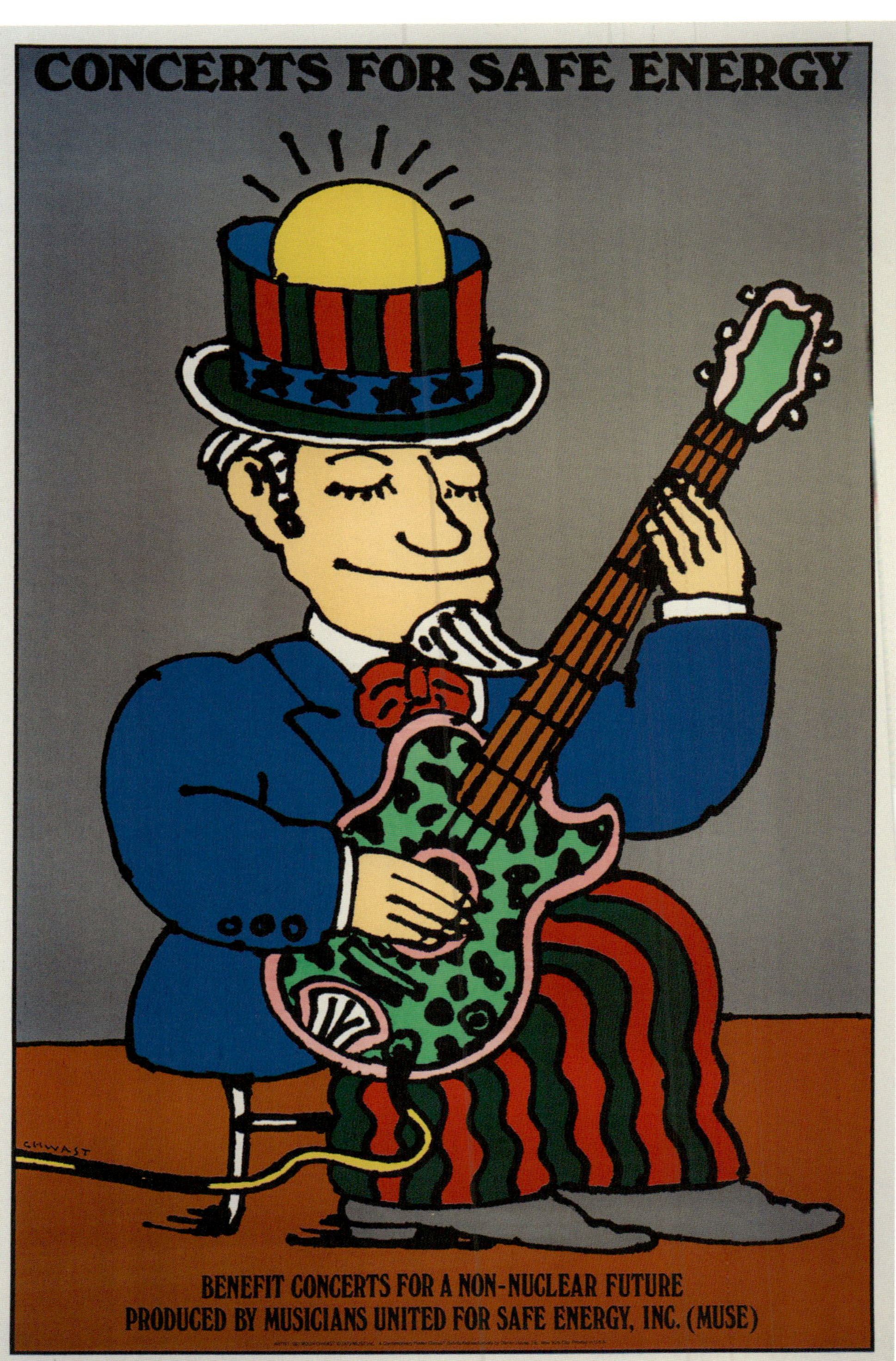

Pen and ink, separated color, offset, 20" x 36", 1978

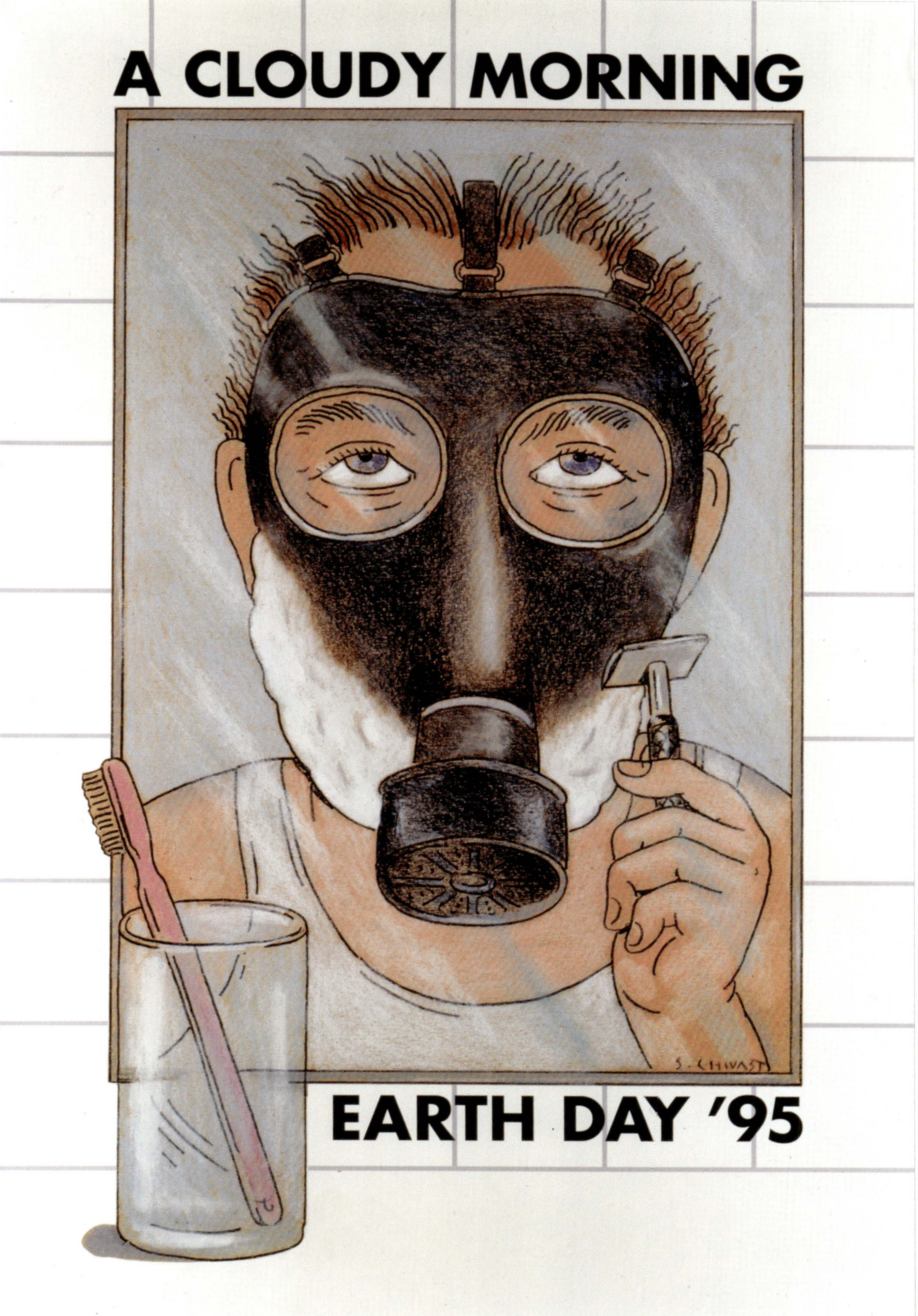

Pen and ink, colored pencil, offset, 22" x 36", 1991

GUN CONTROL

This page: **THEIR PROFIT OUR LOSS, GUNS KILL.** Guns are an integral part of our capitalist and democratic systems.

Opposite: **AMERICA'S SHAME.** This expressive style conveys a sense of urgency. The bullet holes in Uncle Sam are meant to shock us. Since the time when these posters were produced, ending gun violence has become essential.

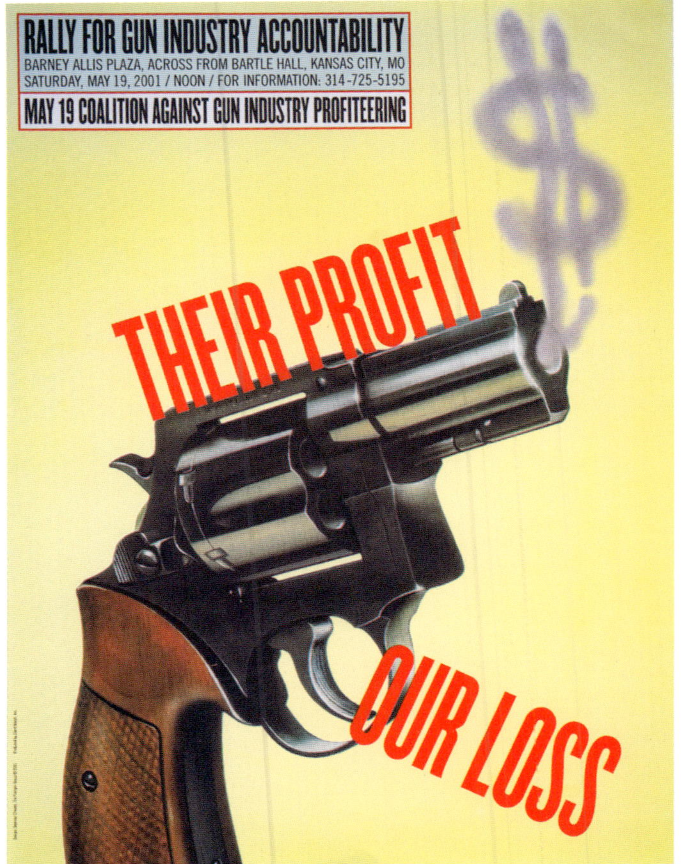

Collage, offset, 24" x 36", 2001

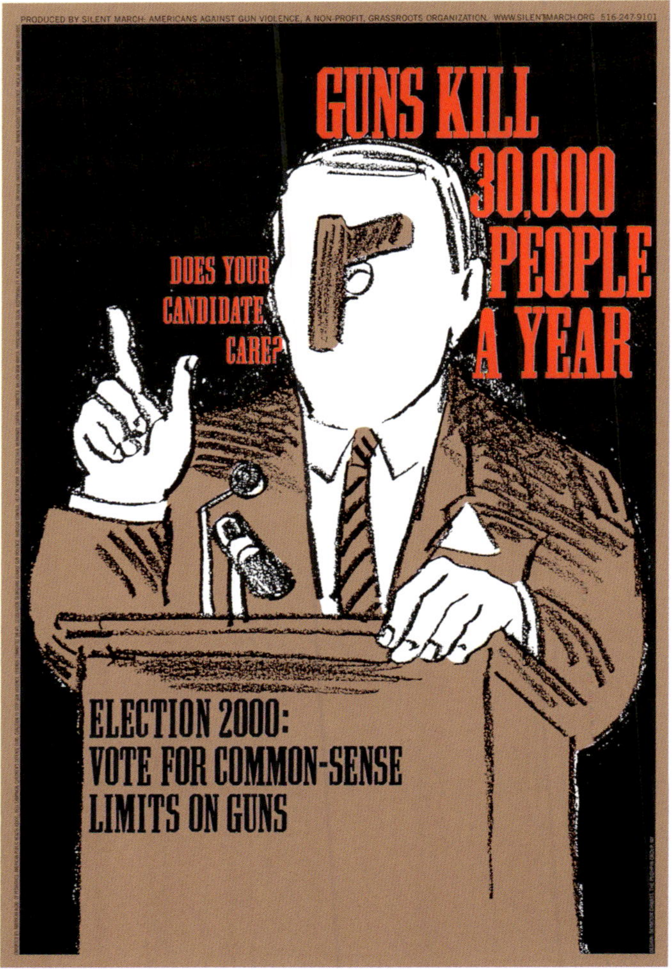

Pencil with digital color, offset, 24" x 36", 2000

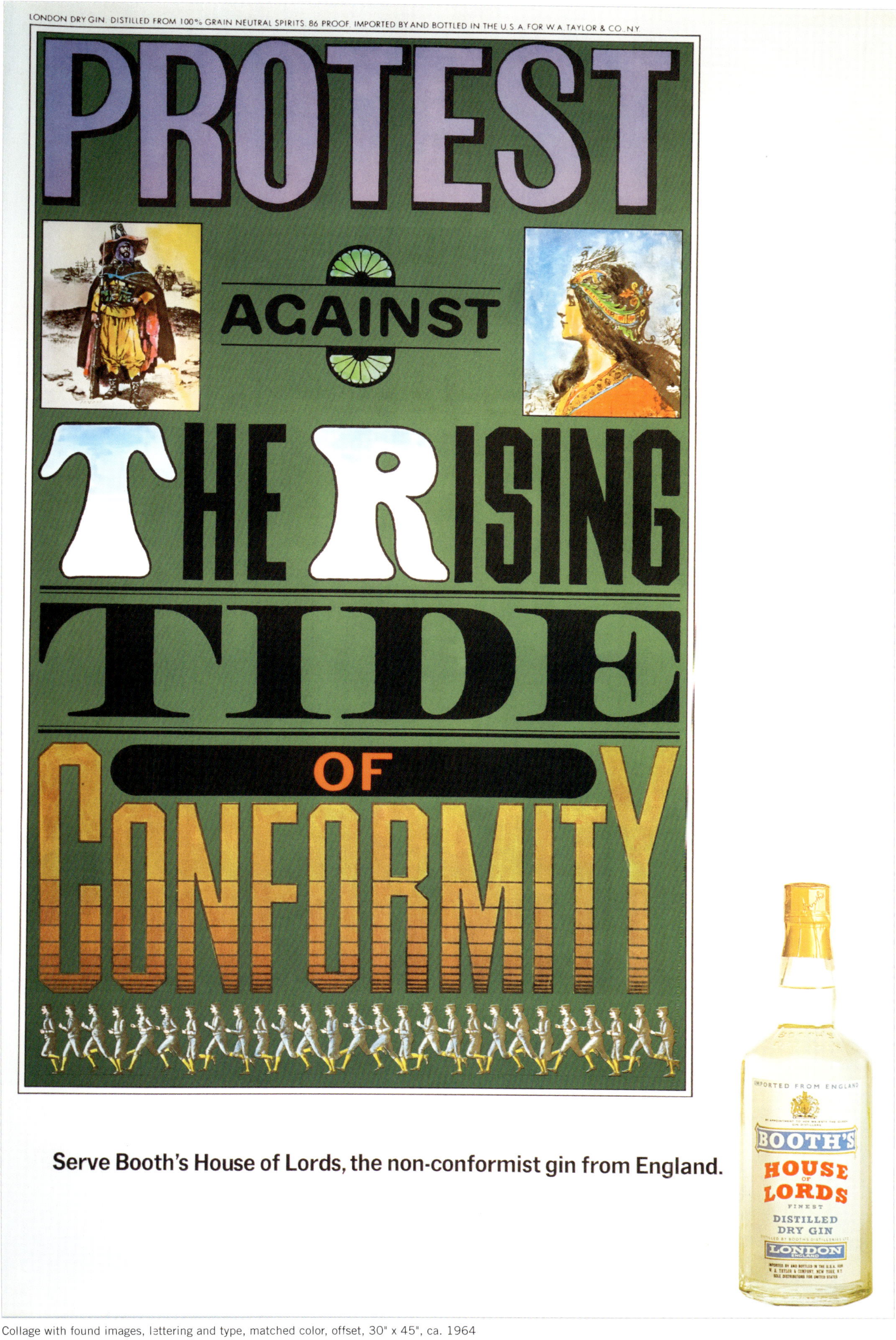

LONDON DRY GIN. DISTILLED FROM 100% GRAIN NEUTRAL SPIRITS. 86 PROOF. IMPORTED BY AND BOTTLED IN THE U.S.A. FOR W.A. TAYLOR & CO., N.Y.

PROTEST

AGAINST

THE RISING

TIDE

OF

CONFORMITY

Serve Booth's House of Lords, the non-conformist gin from England.

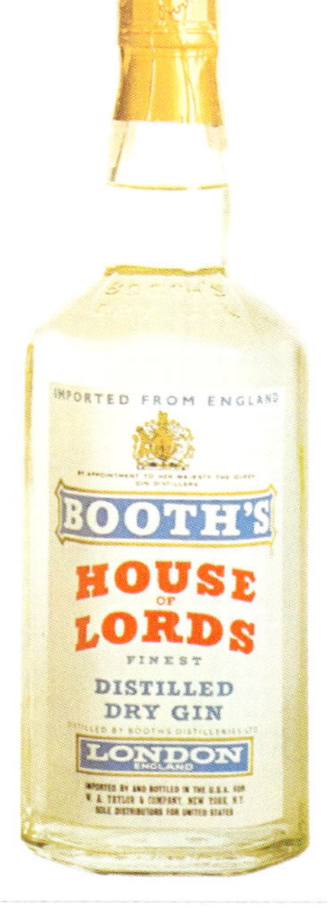

Collage with found images, lettering and type, matched color, offset, 30" x 45", ca. 1964

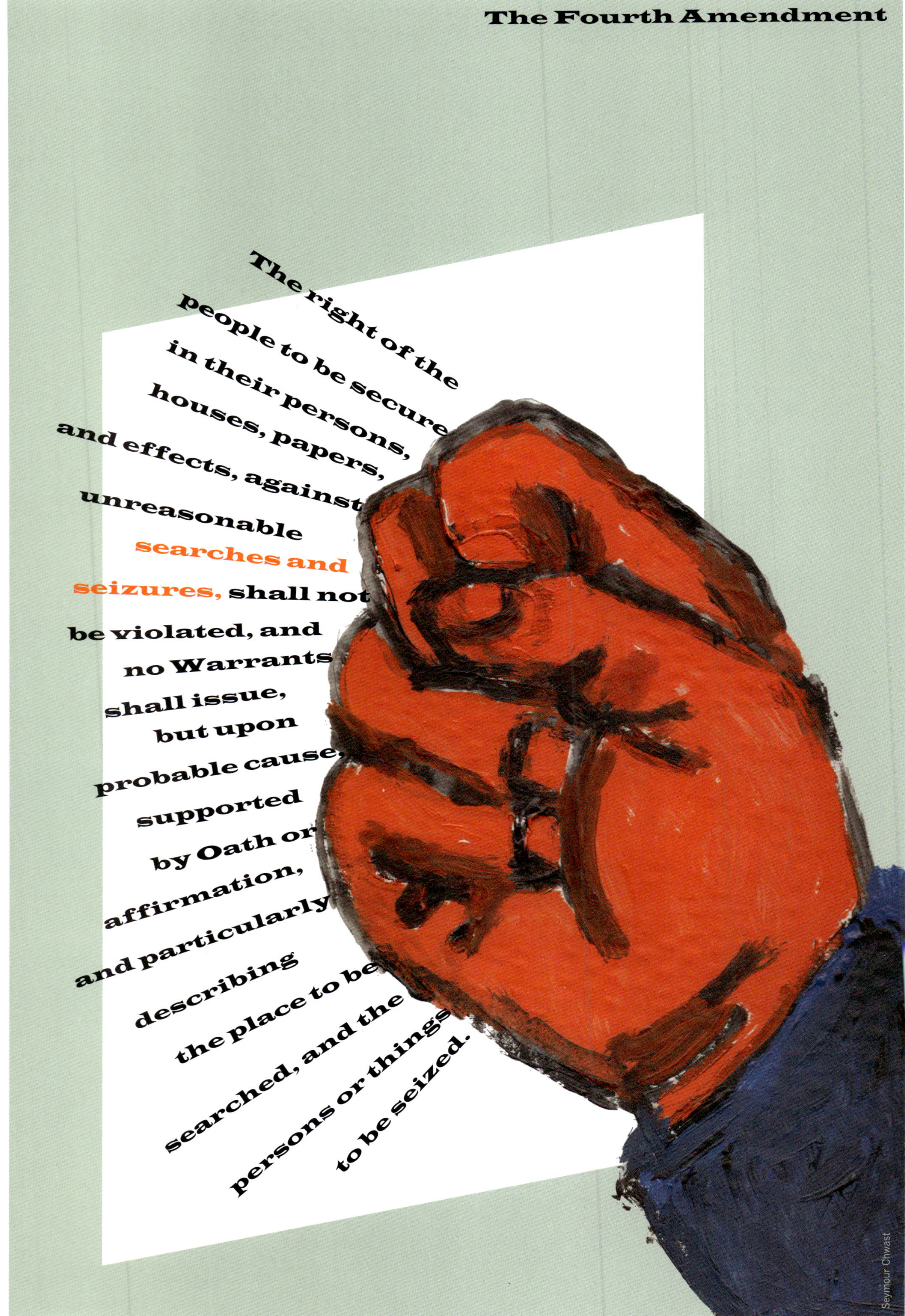

Brush and ink, digital color, digital printing, 36" x 60", 2017

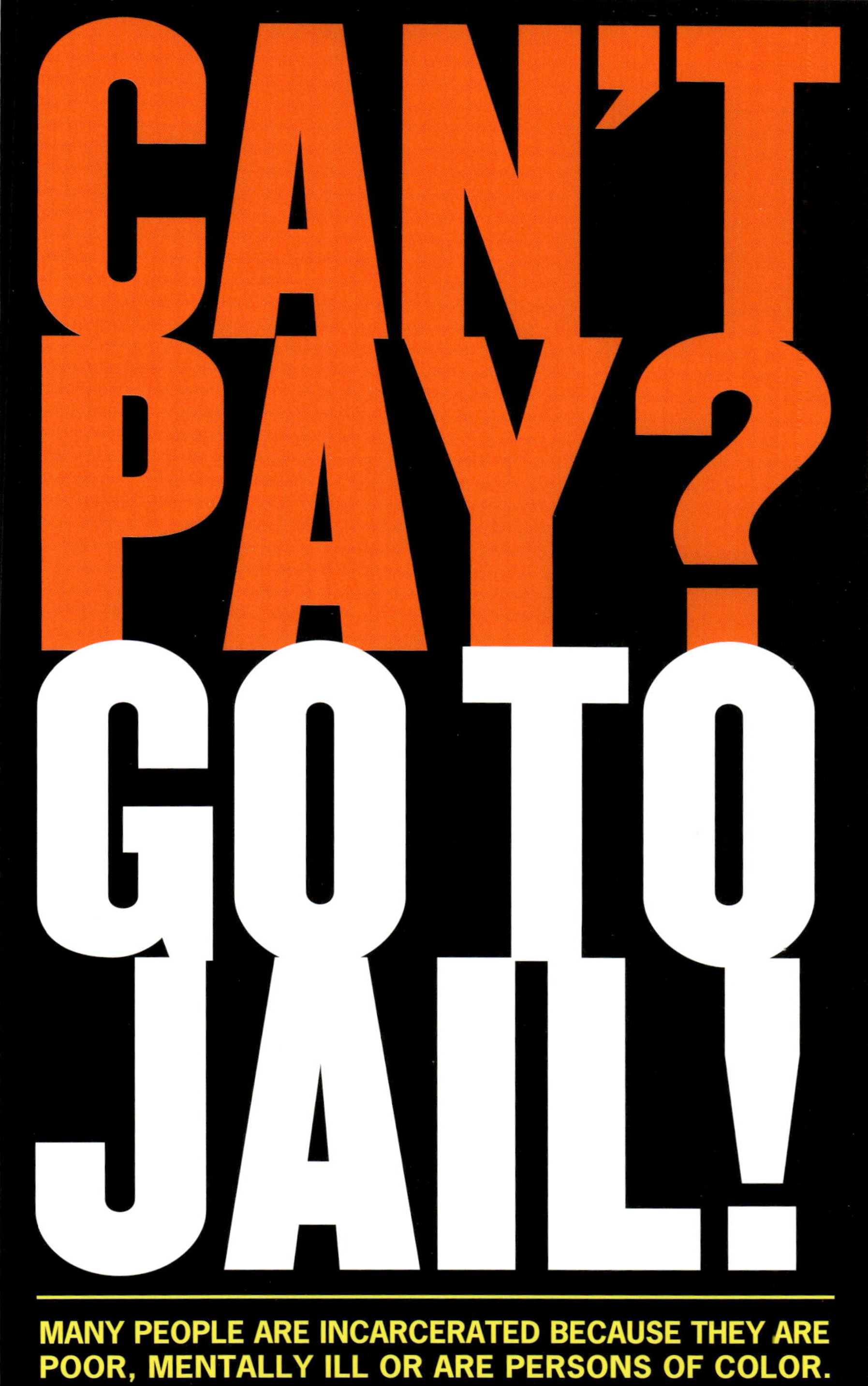

Vector art, digital printing, 36" x 60", 2017

JUSTICE

Above: **CAN'T PAY?** People with minor offenses spend time in jail because they can't raise bail. This poster promotes a change in the system and was created through the Amplify! project for the Vera Institute of Justice.

Opposite: **THE FOURTH AMENDMENT.** The Fourth Amendment to the Constitution prohibits "unreasonable searches and seizures." The creative branding and design agency ThoughtMatter, designer Mirko Ilic, and The Constitutional Sources Project *(ConSource)* collaborated to curate a poster exhibition to celebrate Constitution Day.

Below: **COMBAT COVID-19.** During the coronavirus pandemic, Poster House and *Print Magazine* sponsored the development of a series of posters by well-known designers. They advocated measures to prevent illness and calm society. The posters were shown in Times Square and distributed widely.

Opposite: **HUMAN RIGHTS NOW.** A poster for Amnesty International campaigns against abuses of human rights. My poster is meant to shed light on offenses around the world.

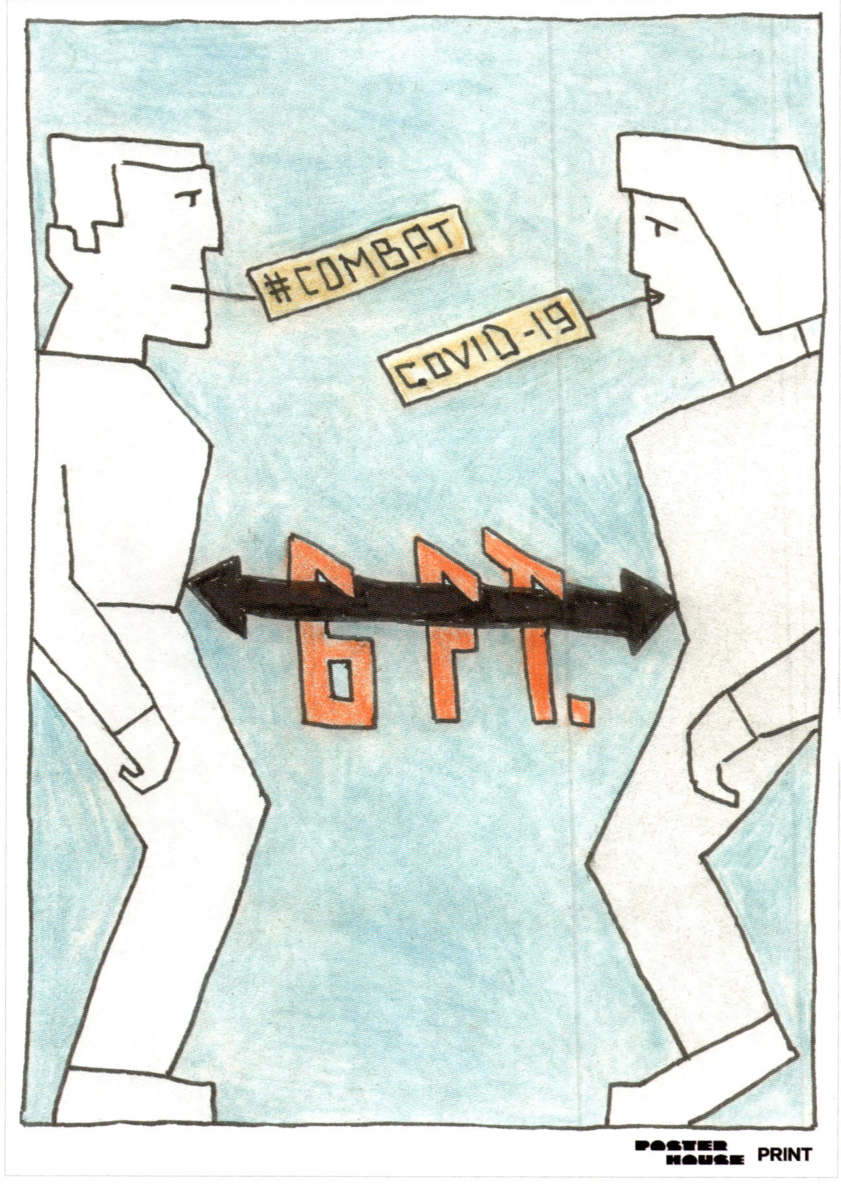

Pen and ink with colored pencil and digital color, hand lettering, digital printing, size variable, 2020

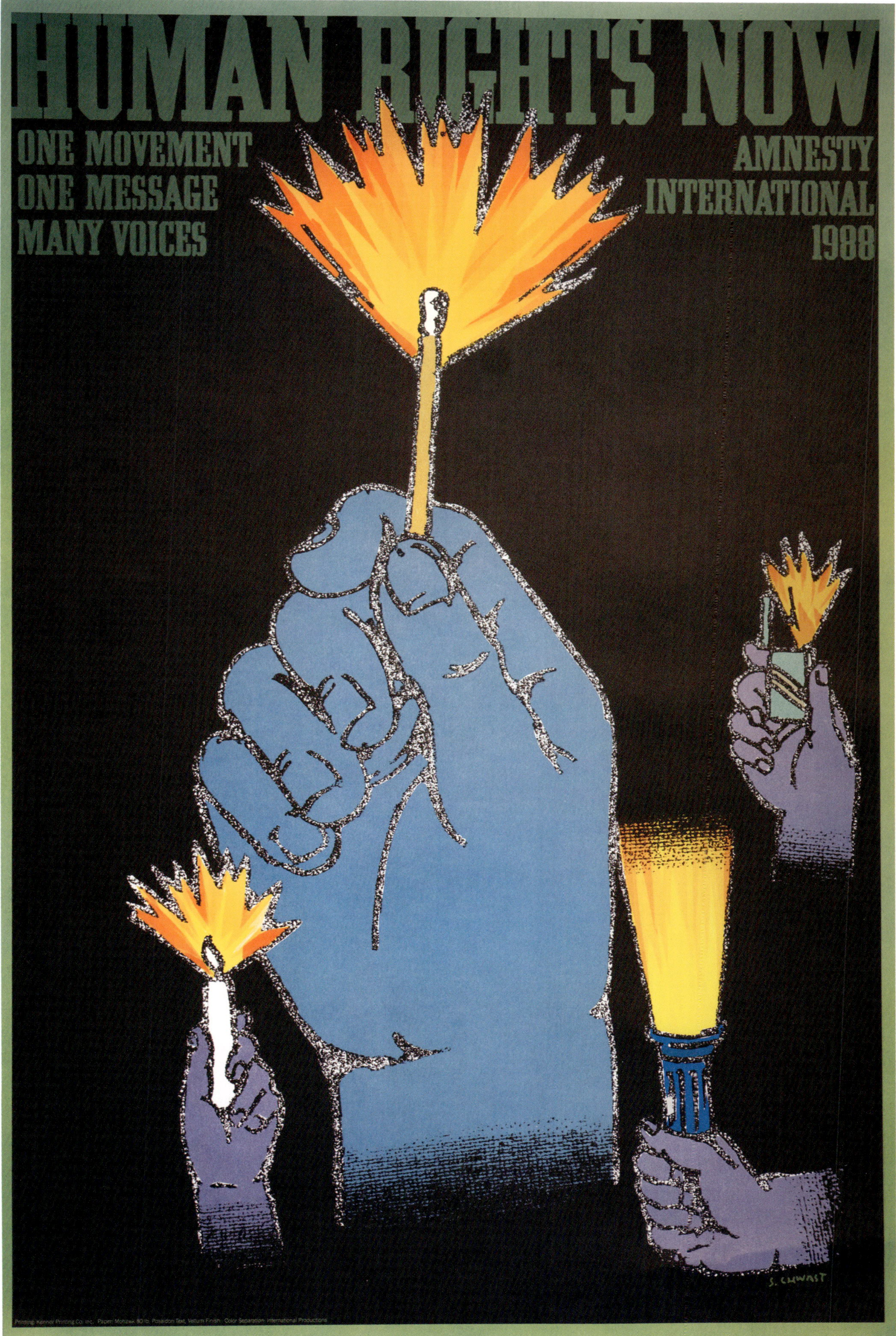

Marker and ink, digital color, offset, 24" x 36", 1988

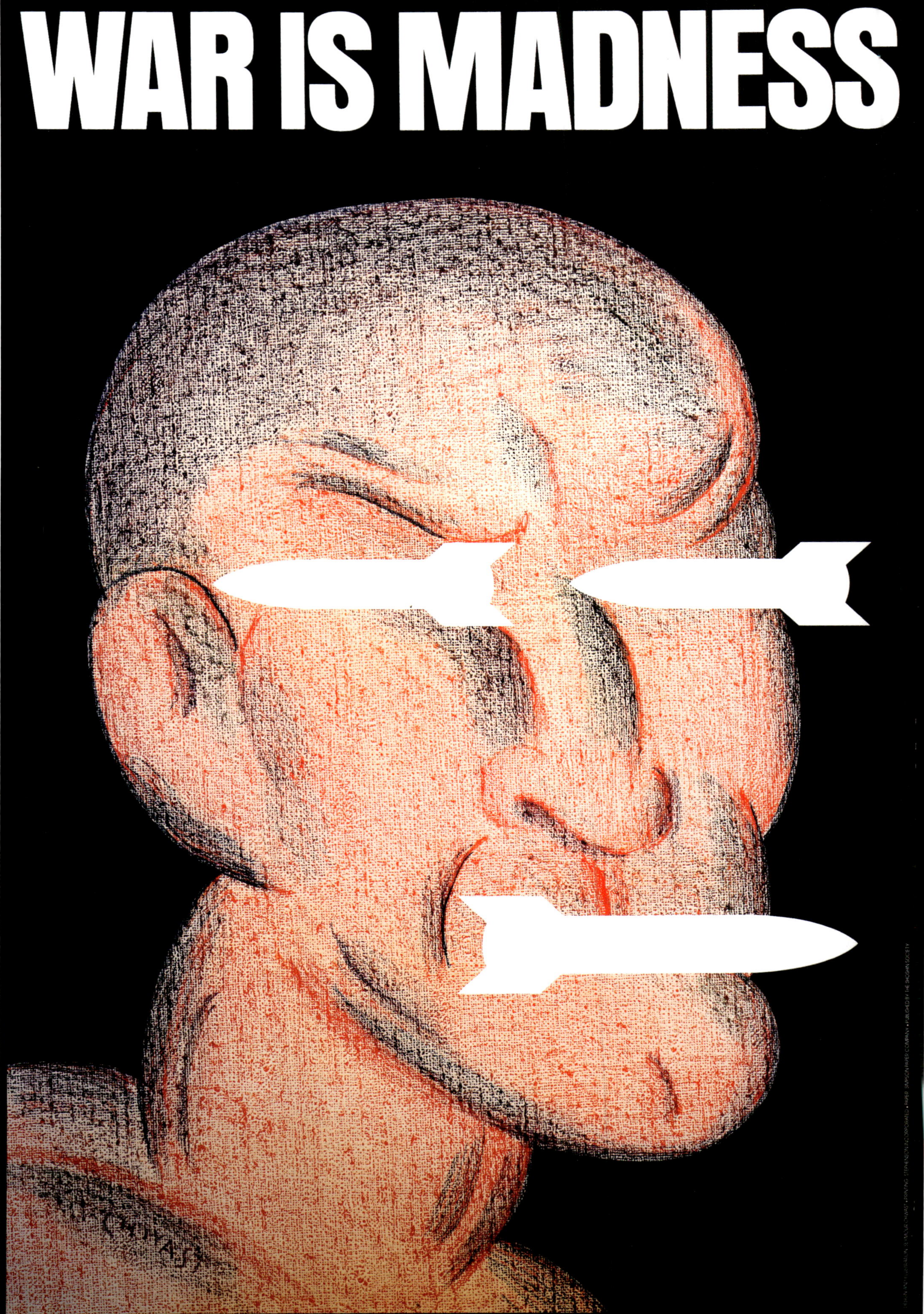

Crayon on canvas-style paper, offset, 24" x 36", 1986

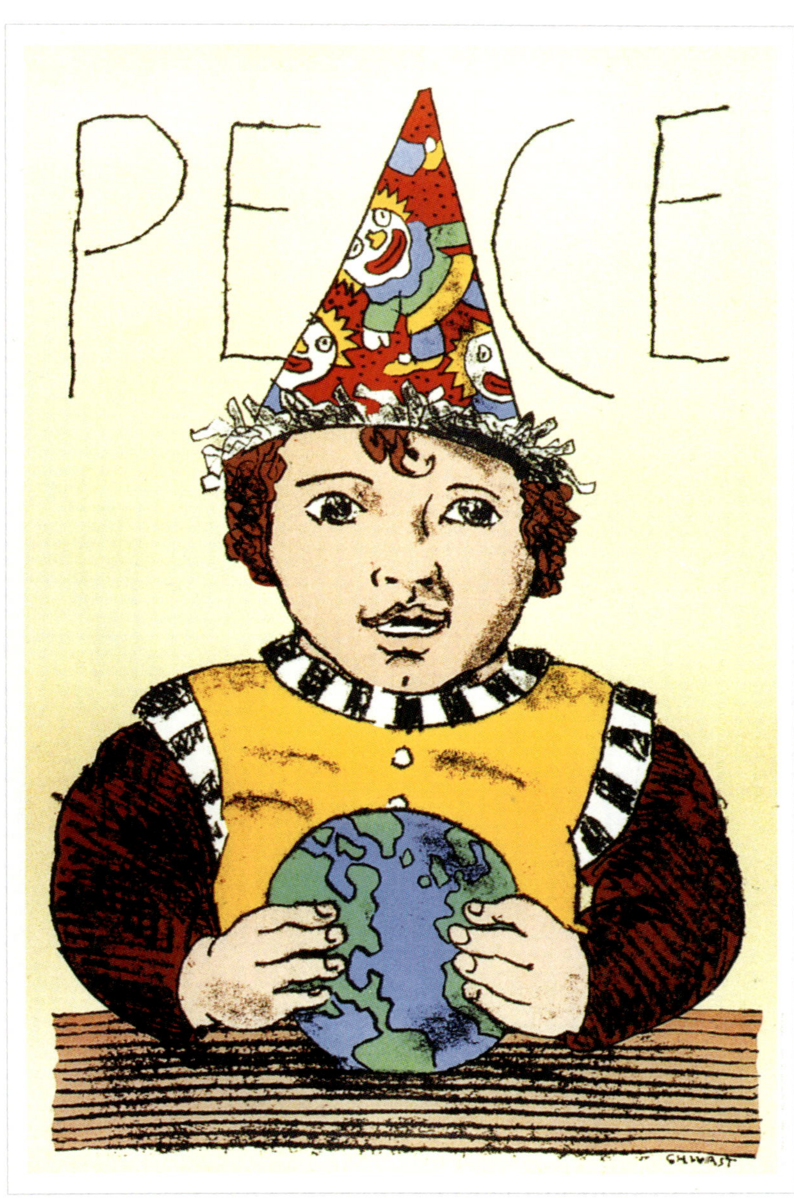

Monoprint on paper, color film, offset, 24" x 36", 1985

PEACE

WAR IS MADNESS
PEACE

The Shoshin Society, an international design organization based in Japan, sponsored peace posters. The Japanese, understandably, have a great interest in avoiding another war.

Right: **MARCH.** Thousands marched in many demonstrations during the Vietnam War.

Opposite: **END BAD BREATH.** *End Bad Breath* is a parody of advertising, but the message is a serious one. We were in the middle of an unpopular war and our planes were bombing Hanoi. America's might was pitted against a small country, a former French colony. It was a time when posters on the subjects of war and music were cheap and sold in shops dedicated to posters. The blue art was a print from my woodcut.

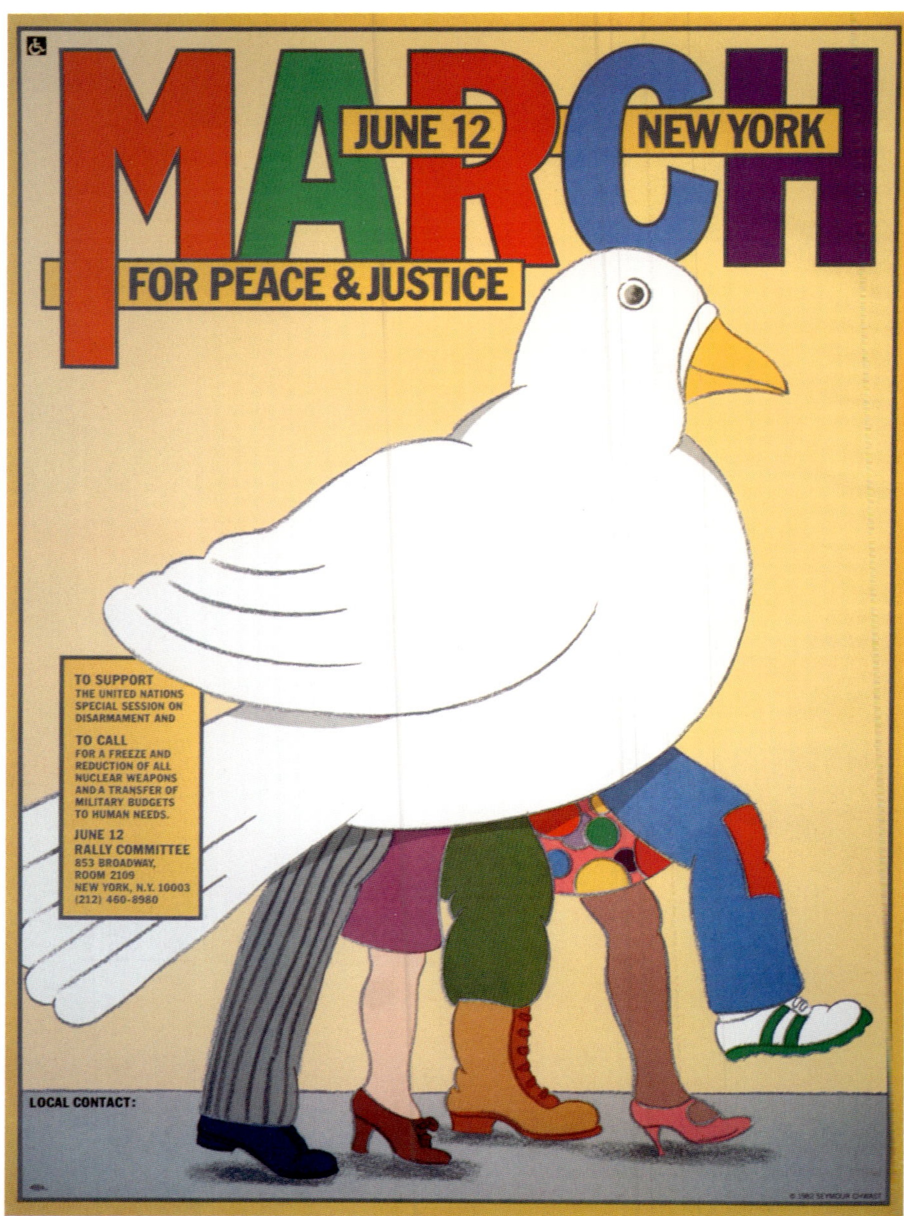

Pen and ink, pencil, color film, offset, 18" x 24", 1989

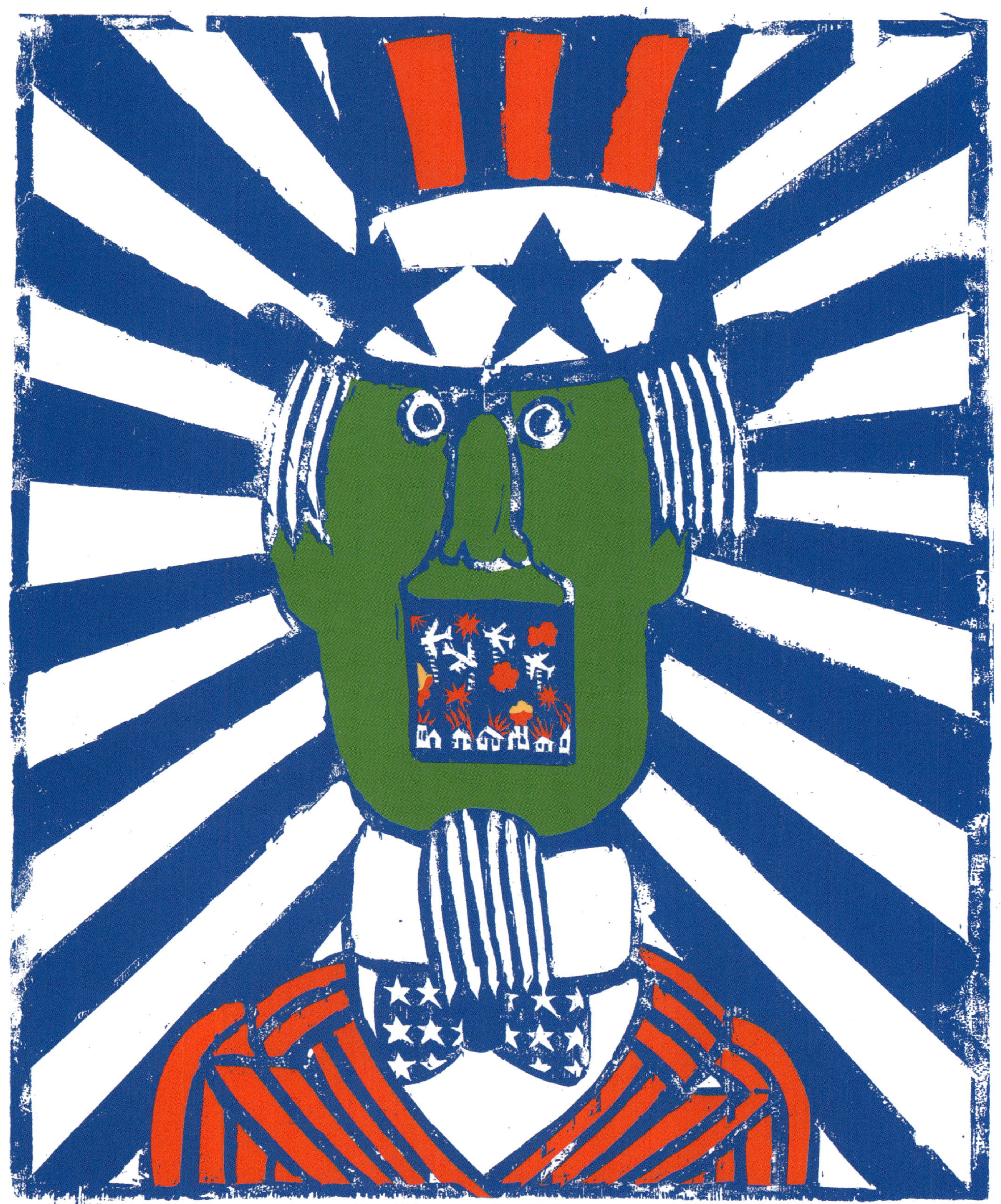

Linocut on paper, flat matched color, offset, 24" x 36", 1968

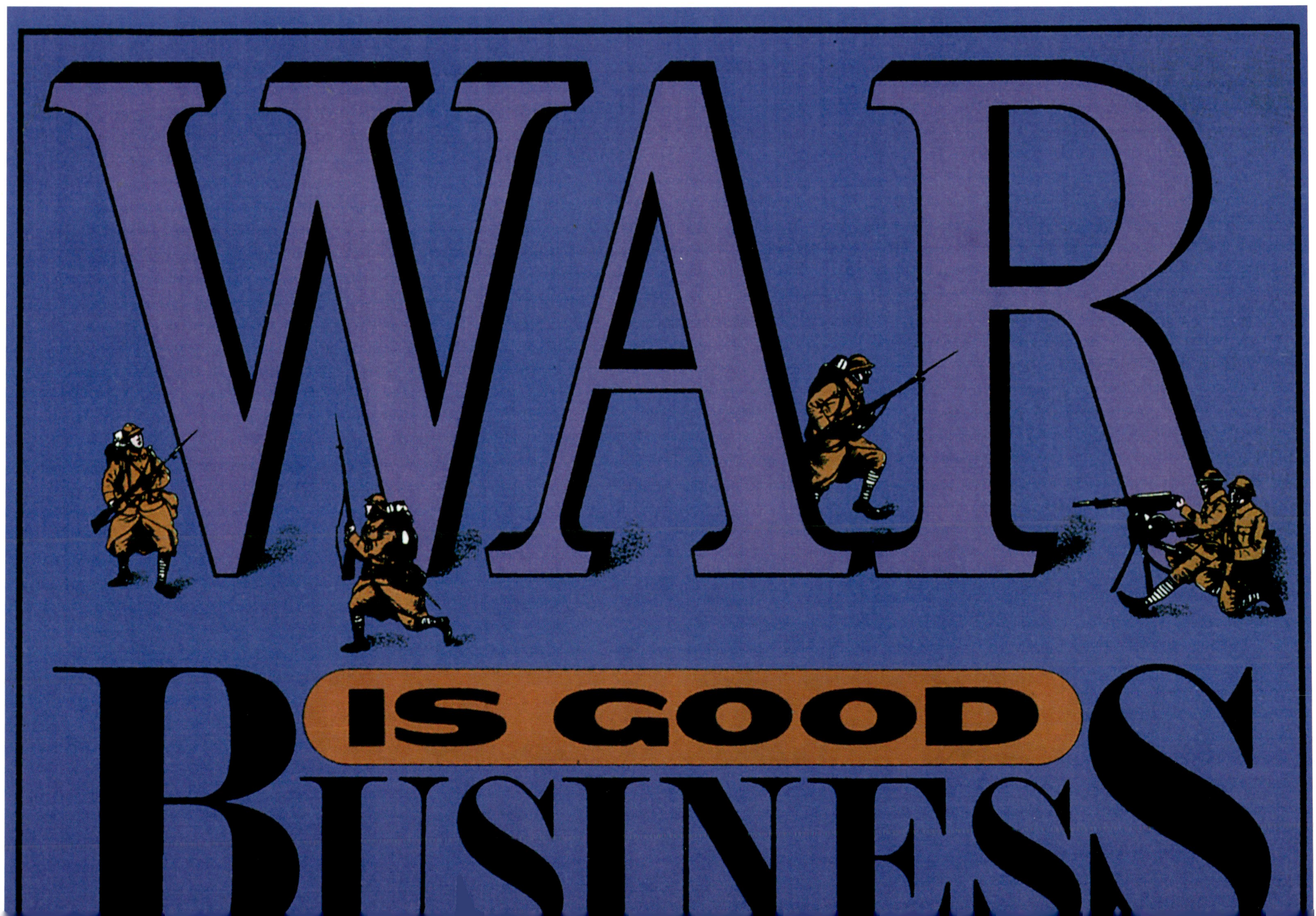
WAR
IS GOOD
BUSINESS

WAR IS GOOD BUSINESS. The Vietnam war was raging. I found this slogan on a button that was popular along with antiwar posters.

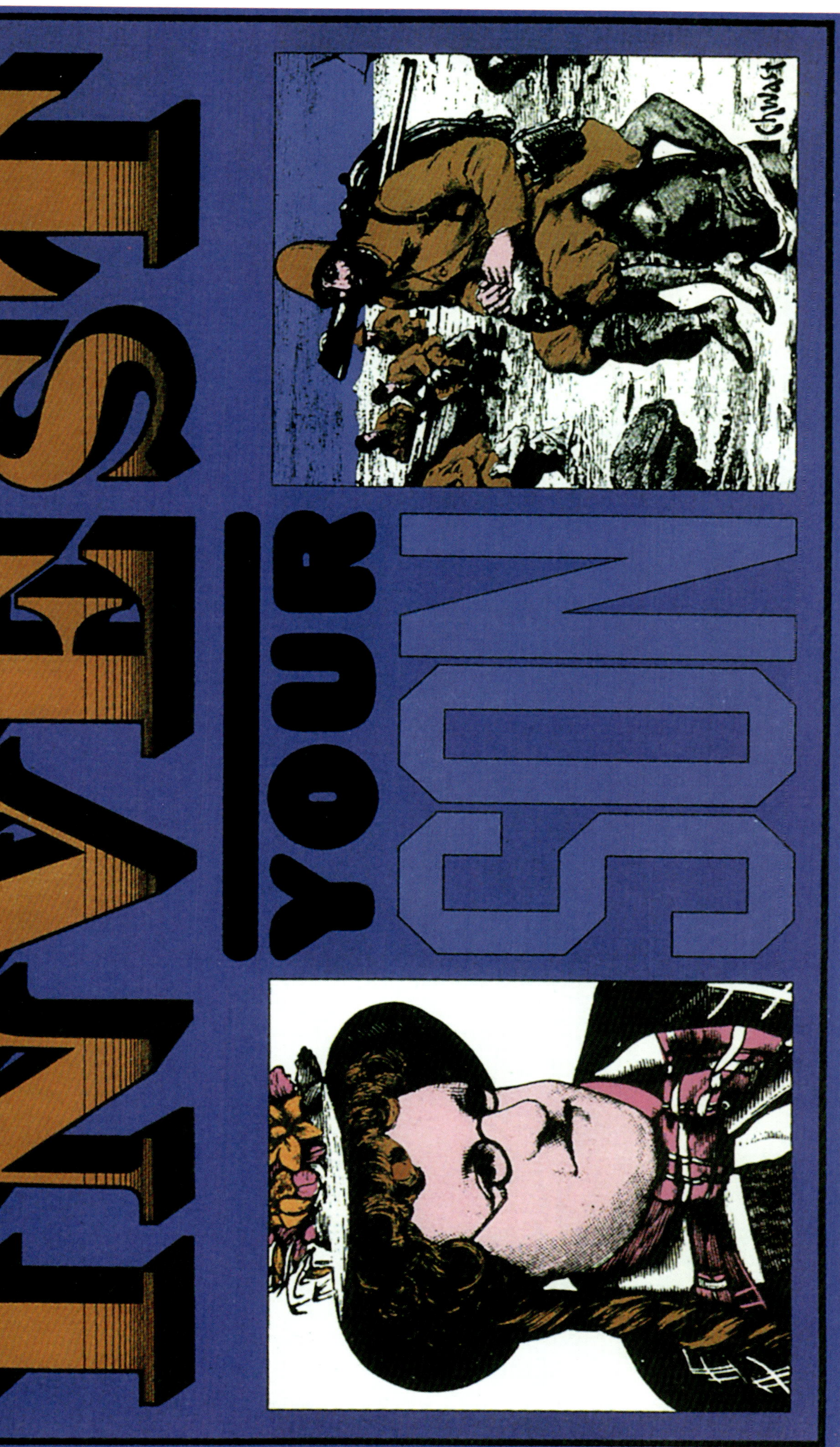

Collage with found images, color film, offset, 24" x 36", 1968

NO GO. This poster was done for the Hague Appeal for Peace at the United Nations.

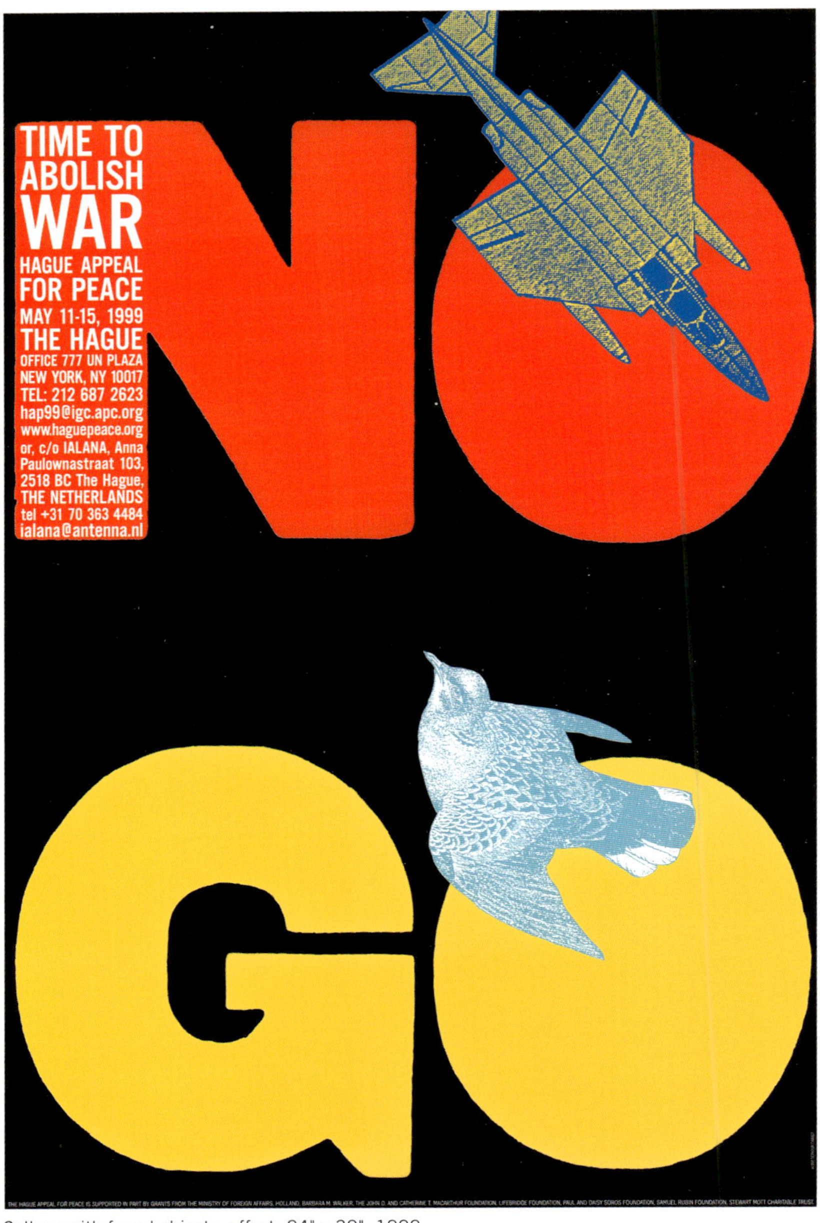

Collage with found objects, offset, 24" x 39", 1999

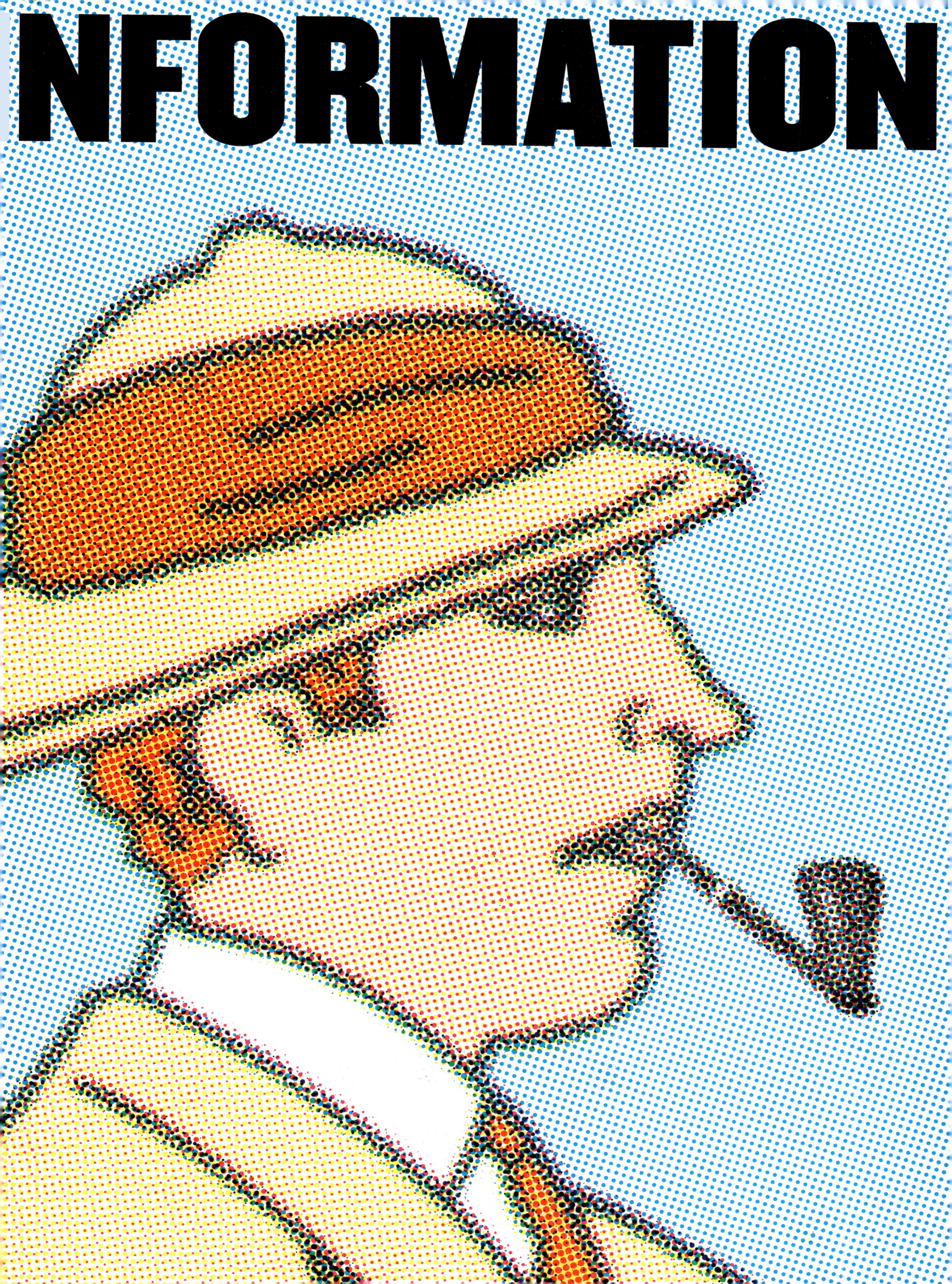
NFORMATION

STROKE
CHOLESTEROL
DEPRESSION

For twenty-five years I've been helping Paul Tracey, a medical educator, inform people with diabetes about treatment. The posters hang in medical facilities. I also design handouts for anyone to print. He is especially interested in informing low-literacy patients. My simple drawings are easy to follow.

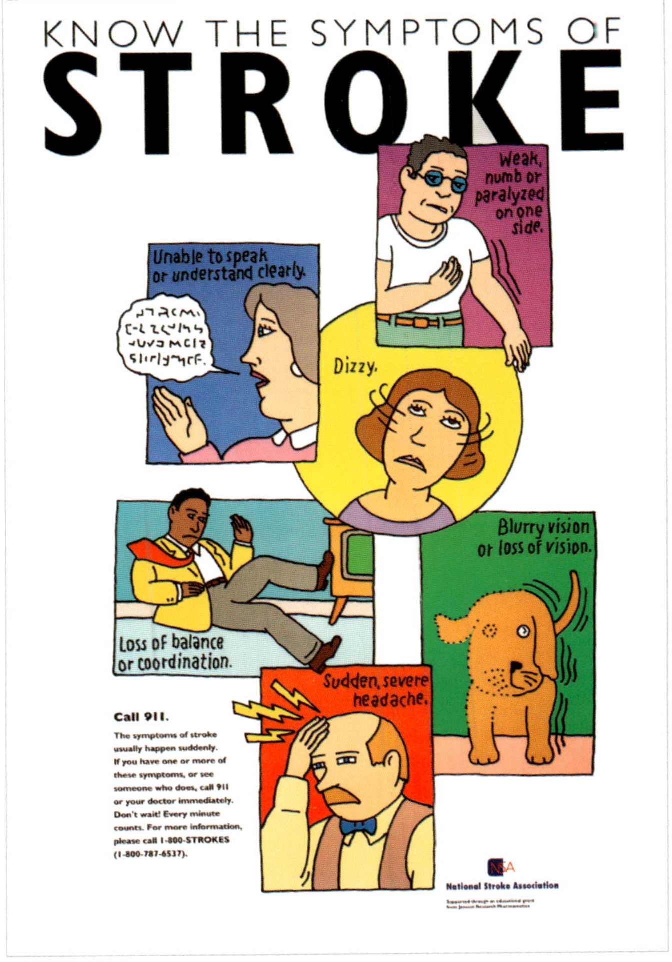

Marker and ink with digital color, offset, 24" x 36", ca. 1995

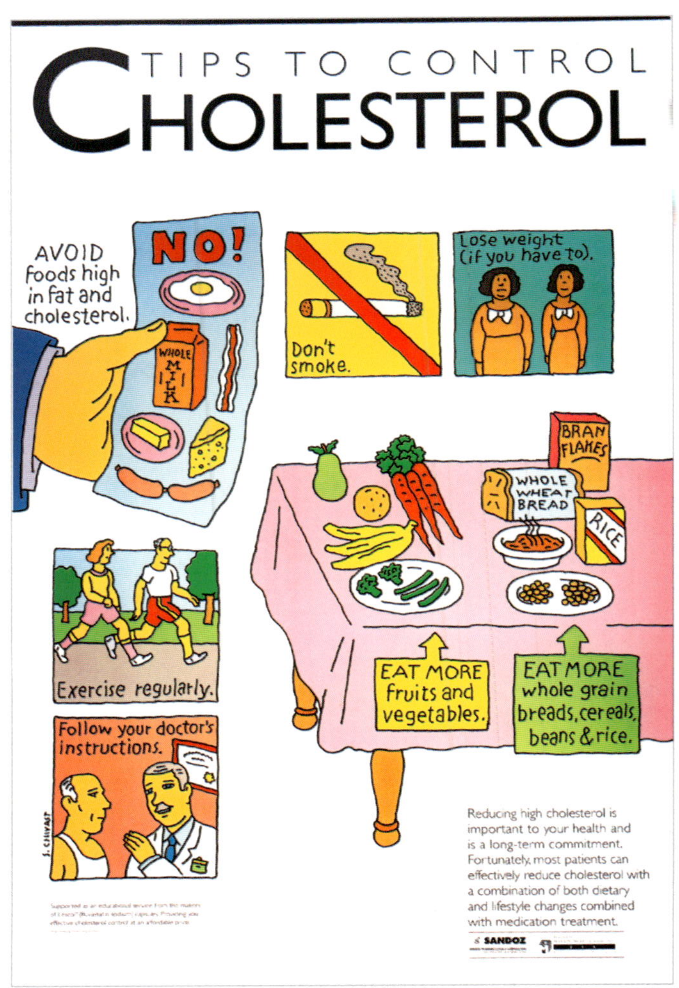

Marker and ink with digital color, offset, 24" x 36", ca. 1995

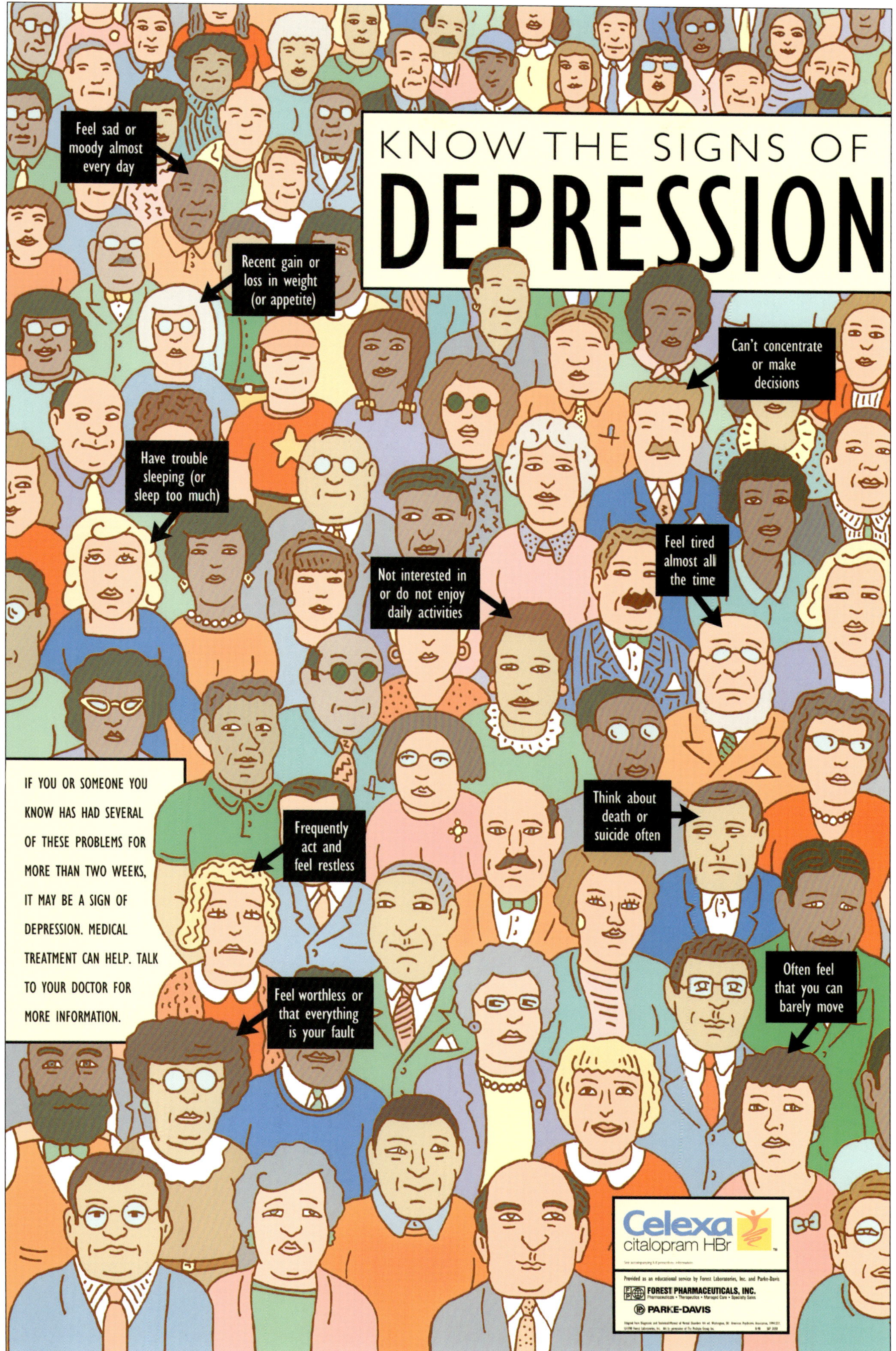

Marker and ink with digital color, offset, 24" x 36", ca. 1995

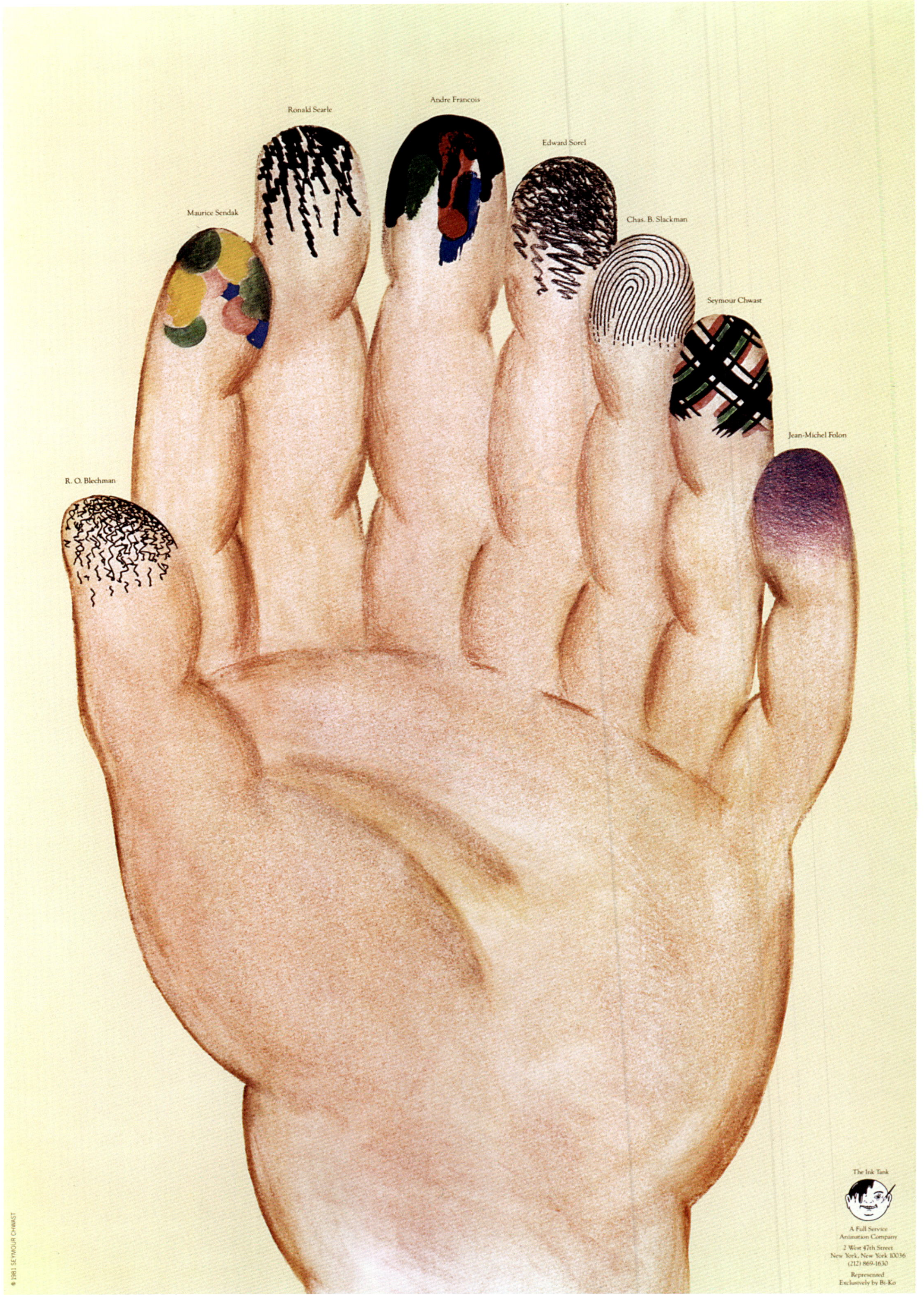

Mixed media hand-drawn with colored pencil, flat color background, offset, 24" x 36", ca. 1982

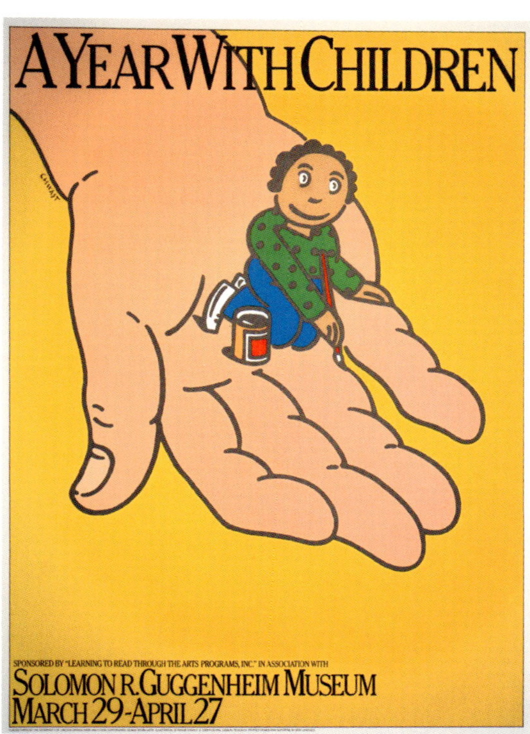

Marker and ink, flat matched color, offset, 24" x 36", ca. 1983

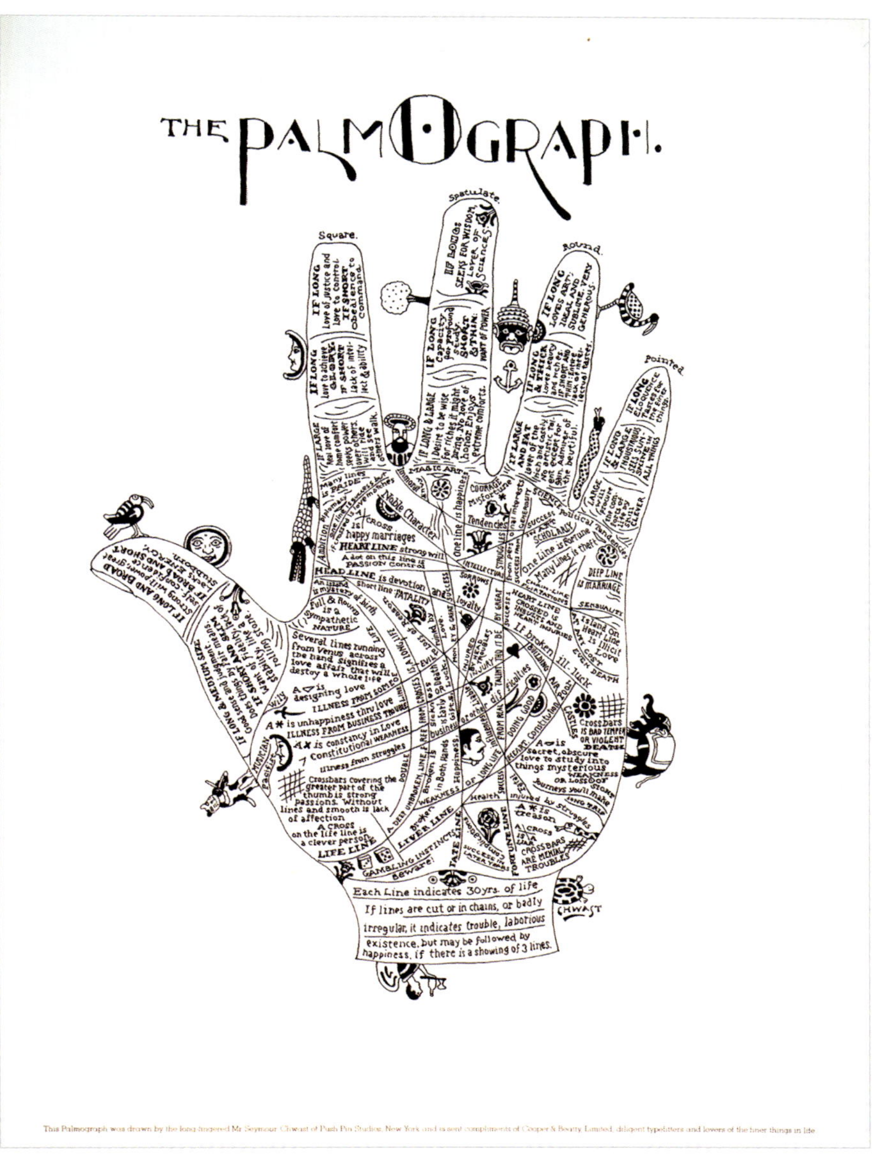

Pen and ink, hand lettering, offset, 24" x 36", ca. 1995

Above: **A YEAR WITH CHILDREN.** The nurturing oversized hand is a foil for the vulnerable (by the nature of the size) kid. He doesn't get lost, however, due to the strong colors of his outfit and the weaker colors around him.

Below: **THE PALMOGRAPH.** Palmistry is part of nineteenth-century quackery. Phrenology heads offer the same misinformation, and they are fun to render and illustrate.

Opposite: **THE INK TANK.** The ink-stained fingers represent different illustrators offering their animation services. R. O. Blechman, the director of The Ink Tank, is naturally on the thumb.

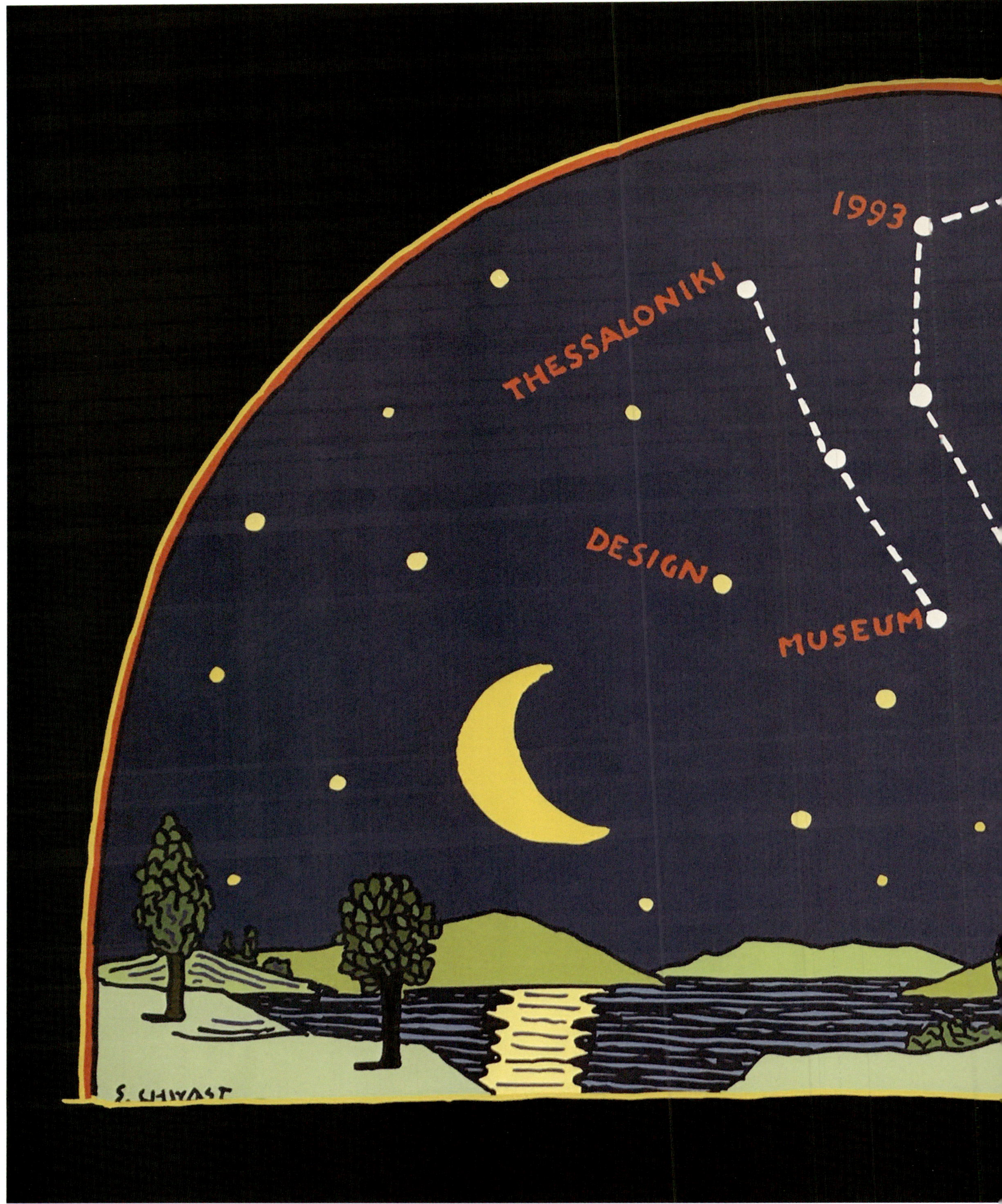

Pen and ink, hand lettering, digital color, offset, 27" x 19", 2003

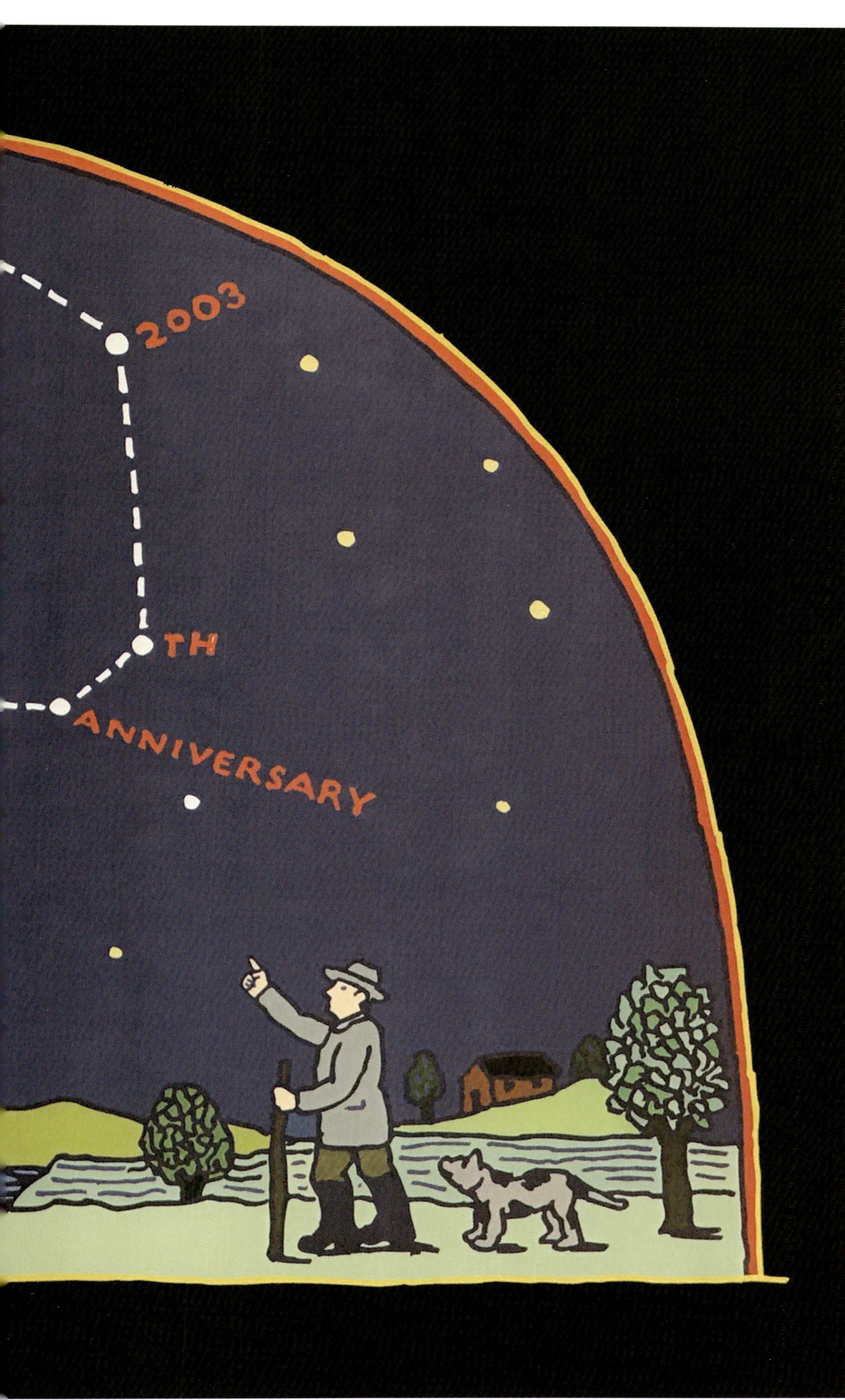

THESSALONIKI DESIGN MUSEUM. This poster celebrates the tenth anniversary of the first design museum in Greece.

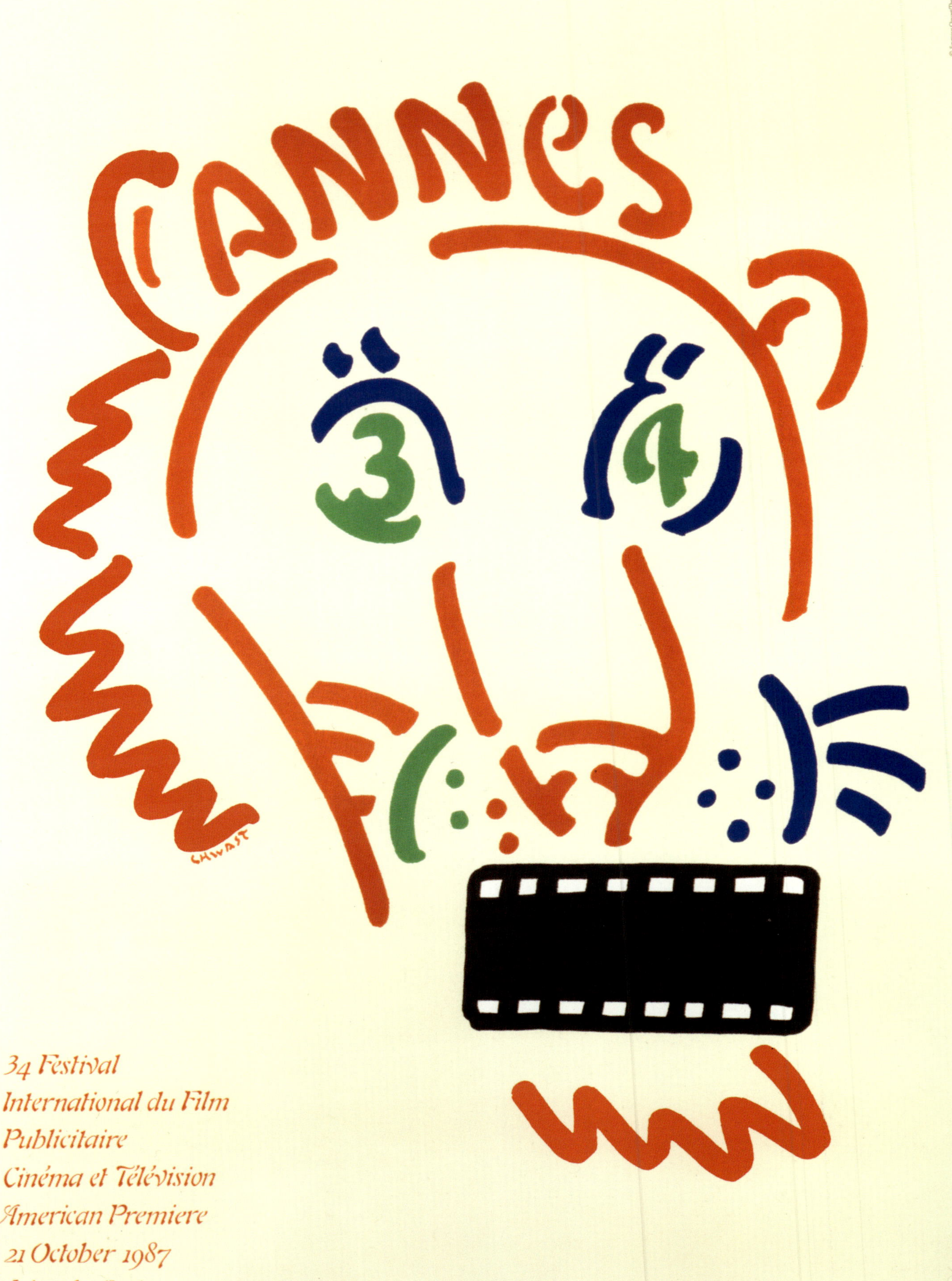

Marker and black ink converted to color, offset, 24" x 36", 1987

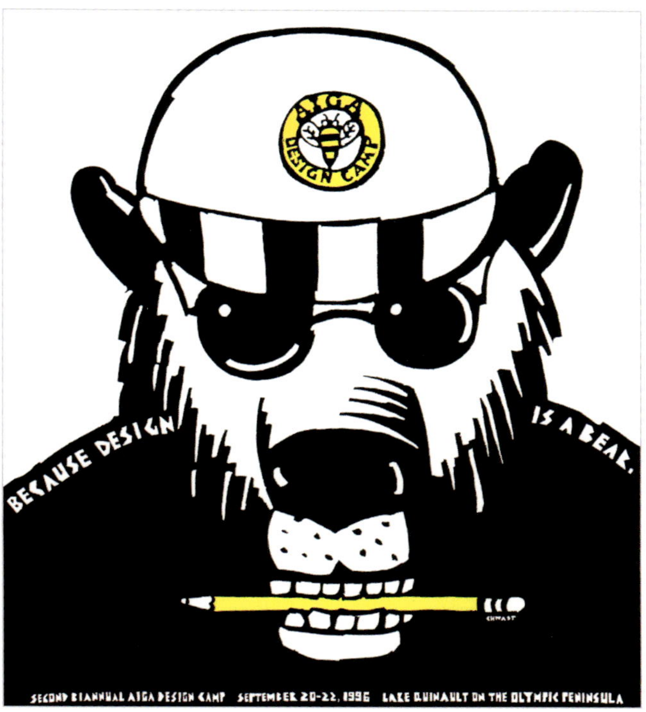

Black marker, color film, offset, 24" x 27", 1996

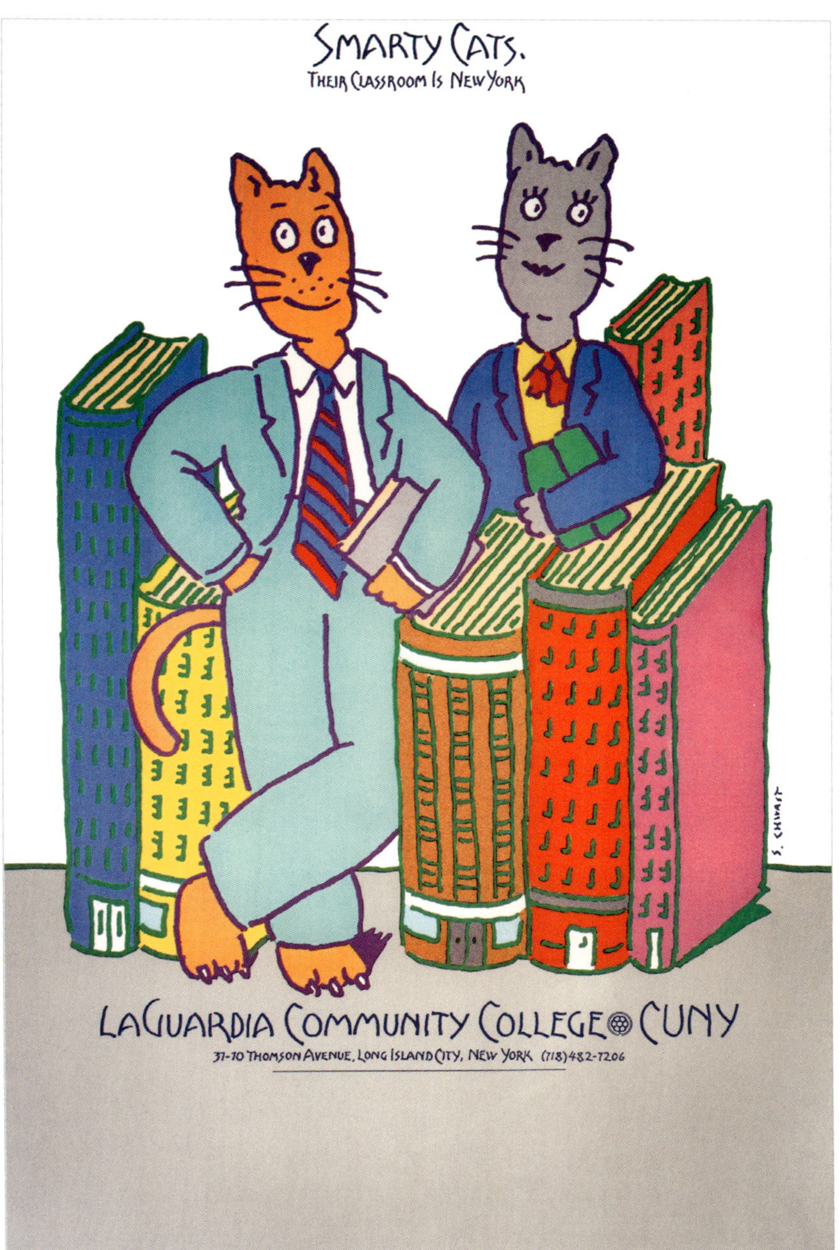

Marker and ink, color film, offset, 23" x 35", ca. 1983

Above: **DESIGN CAMP.** The bear, as a mascot for a design "camp" in Washington State, is designed to excite or frighten the designers who attend.

Below: **SMARTY CATS.** An aspirational poster for students.

Opposite: **CANNES.** The Cannes Film Festival was previously held in Venice, where the city's icon is the lion. The lion was kept when the festival moved to Cannes.

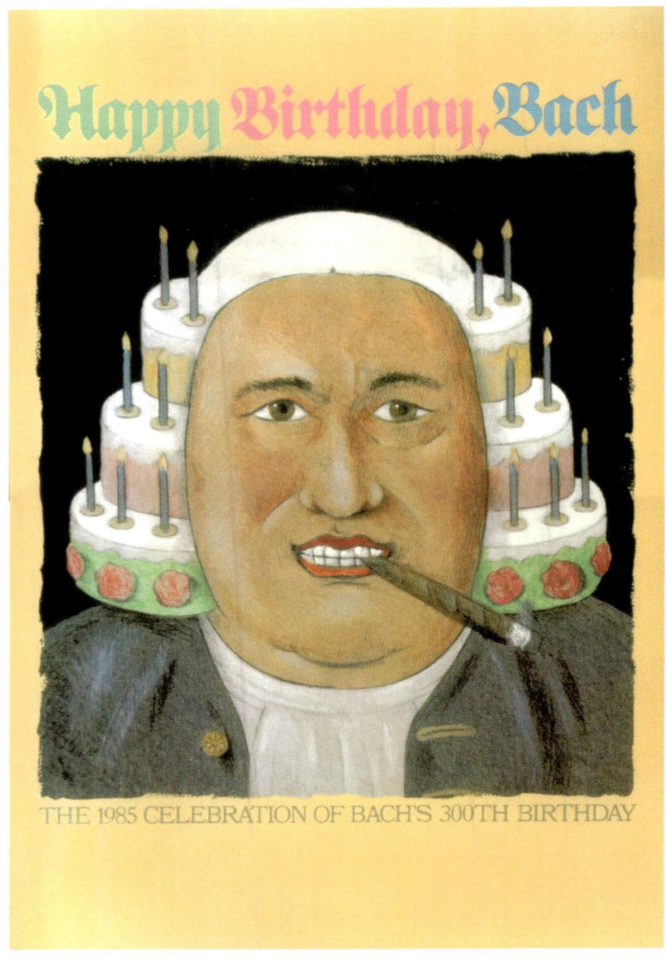

Acrylic and colored pencil on board, offset, 18" x 24", 1985

Right, above: **HAPPY BIRTHDAY BACH.** This supports the book that irreverently has a portrait of Bach for every year since his birth in 1685.

Right, below: **PUCCINI FESTIVAL.** My view of Puccini was that of a dandy surrounded by a bevy of beauties from his operas. The period was Victorian, as was the lettering and type.

Opposite: **BASIE GETZ.** One of the tricks I perform in solving graphic design problems is combining two or more objects in one image. While Basie and Getz do not totally integrate, it's close enough for my purpose.

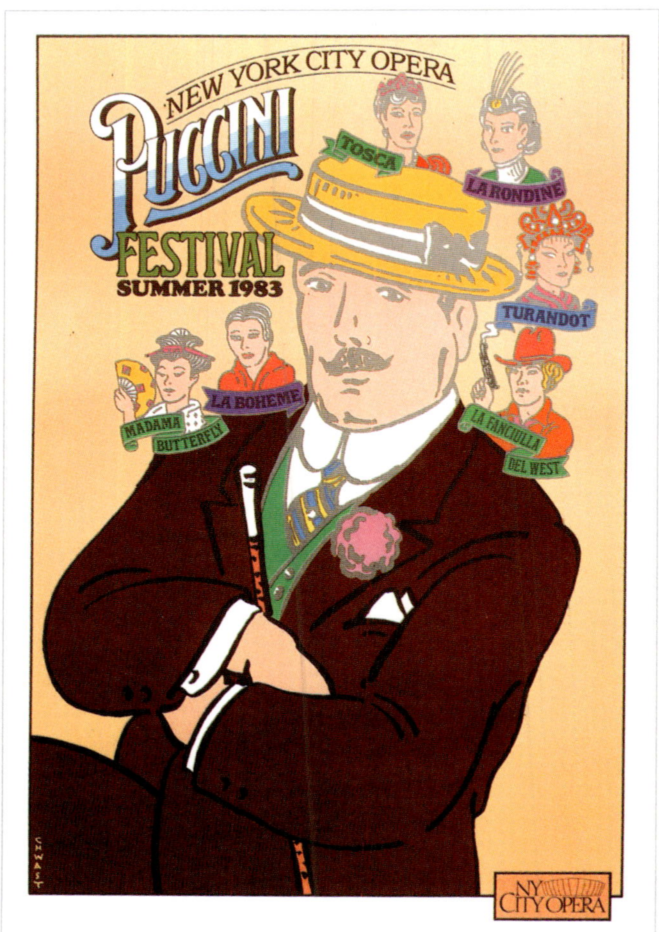

Brush and ink with flat color, offset, 16" x 24", 1983

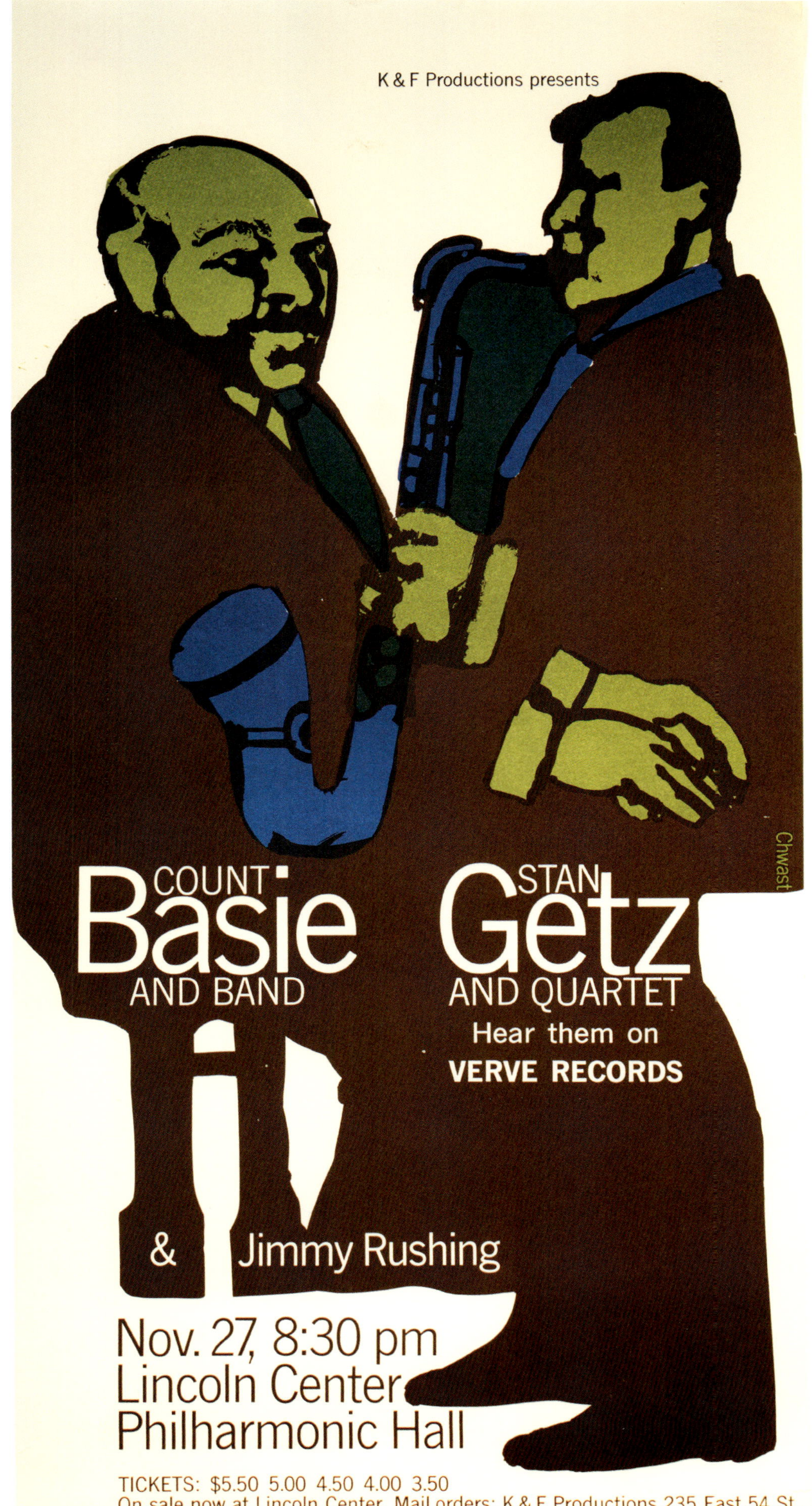

Brush and ink with flat color, offset, 18" x 36", ca. 1964

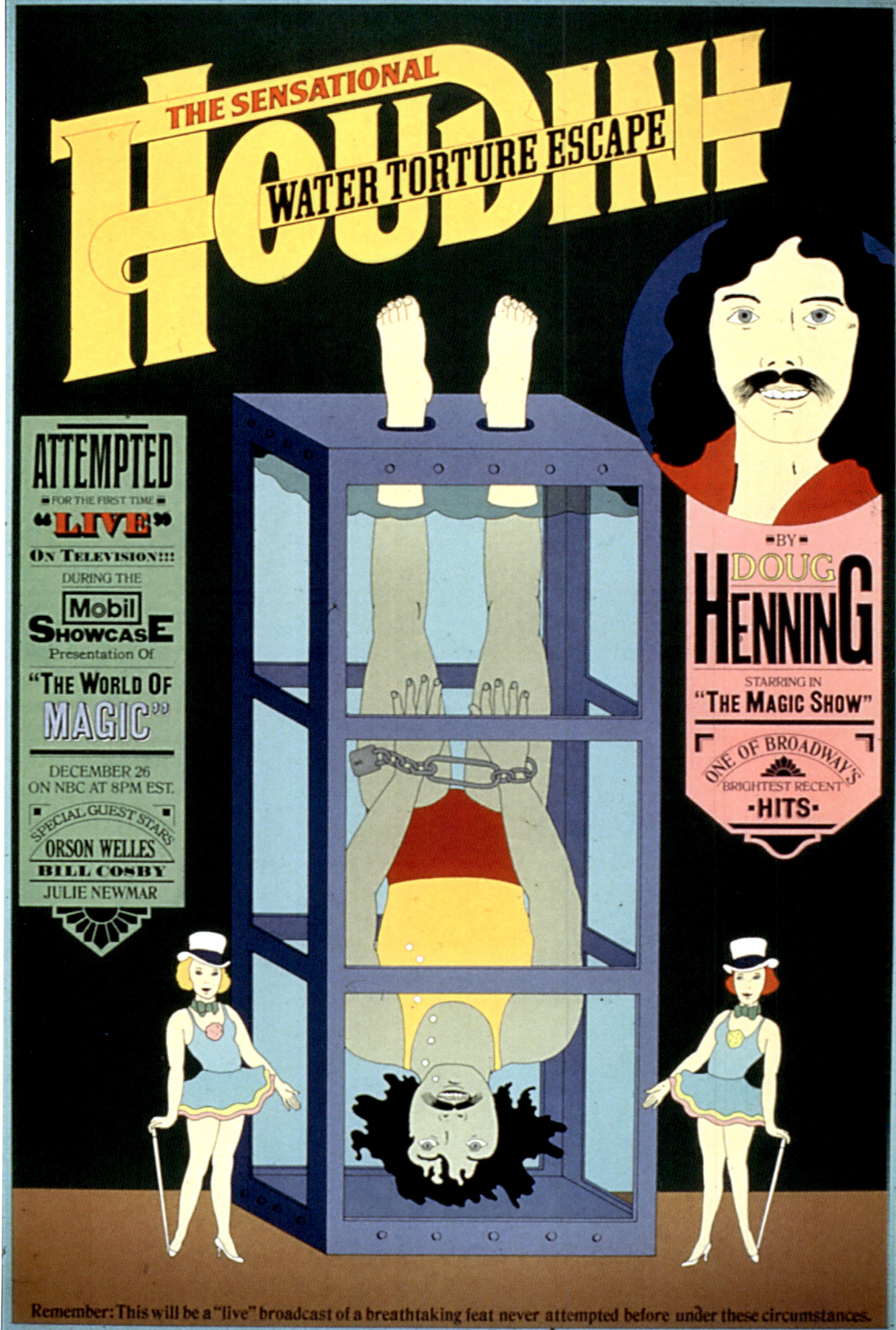

Pen and ink, color film, offset, 30" x 46.5", ca. 1975

MOBIL

Several designers were involved in promoting Mobil Oil's Masterpiece Theaters productions. The posters were intended to impress lawmakers with the cultural value of an oil company that had a negative image. The British productions were of the highest quality.

Below: **NOEL COWARD.** Noel Coward, the Grand Master of British theater, presents his stories with the finest actors of stage and screen. This art deco style fits his time and personality.

Opposite: **HOUDINI.** The Houdini announcement is in the style of Victorian magic posters with all its promise of excitement.

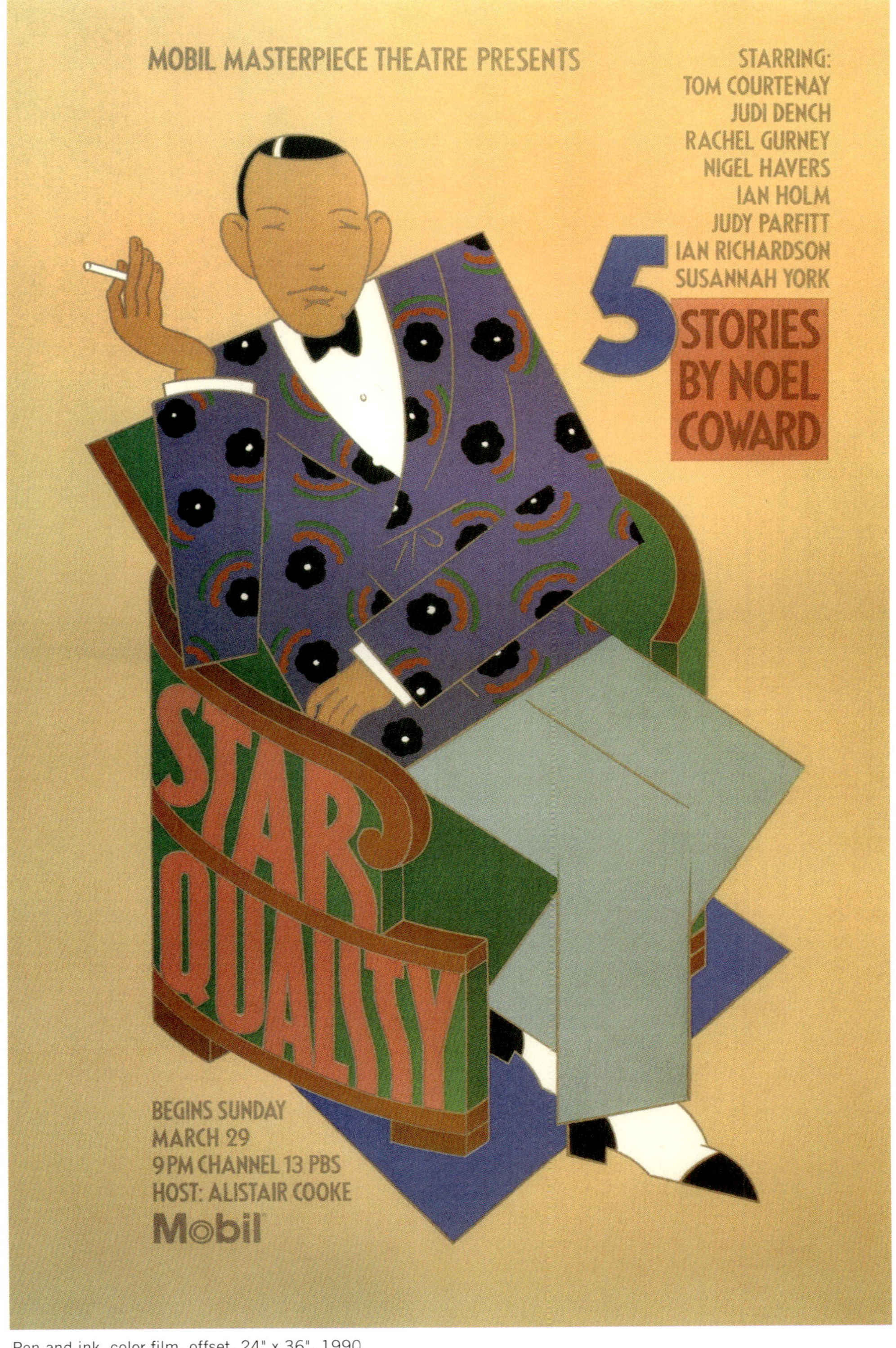

Pen and ink, color film, offset, 24" x 36", 1990

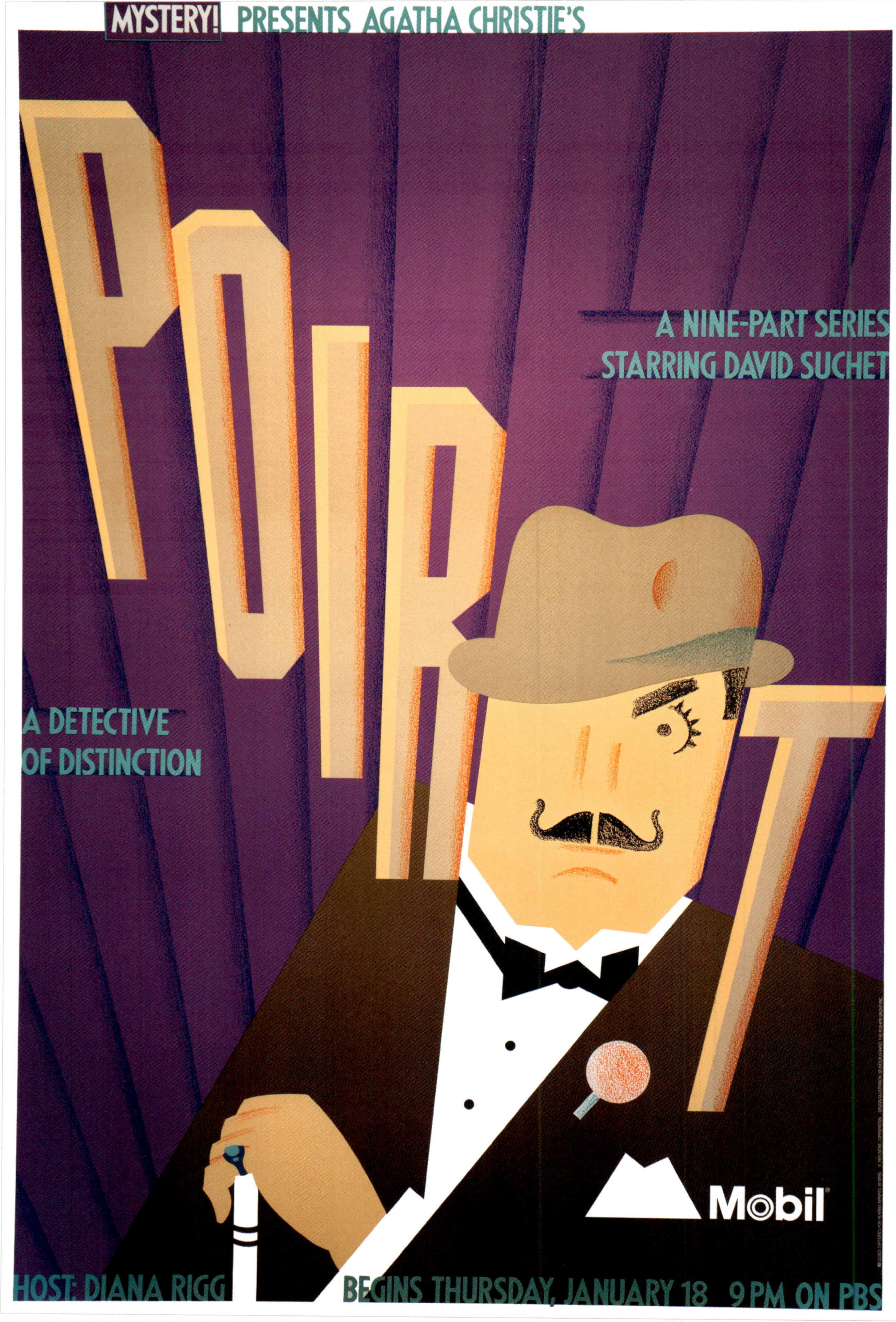

Color film, hand lettering, offset, 24" x 36", ca. 1979

Opposite: **POIROT.** Hercule Poirot is the Agatha Christie dapper Belgian detective.

Below: **SCOOP.** Evelyn Waugh's novel was about the gardening columnist for a newspaper who interfered with a revolution in Africa.

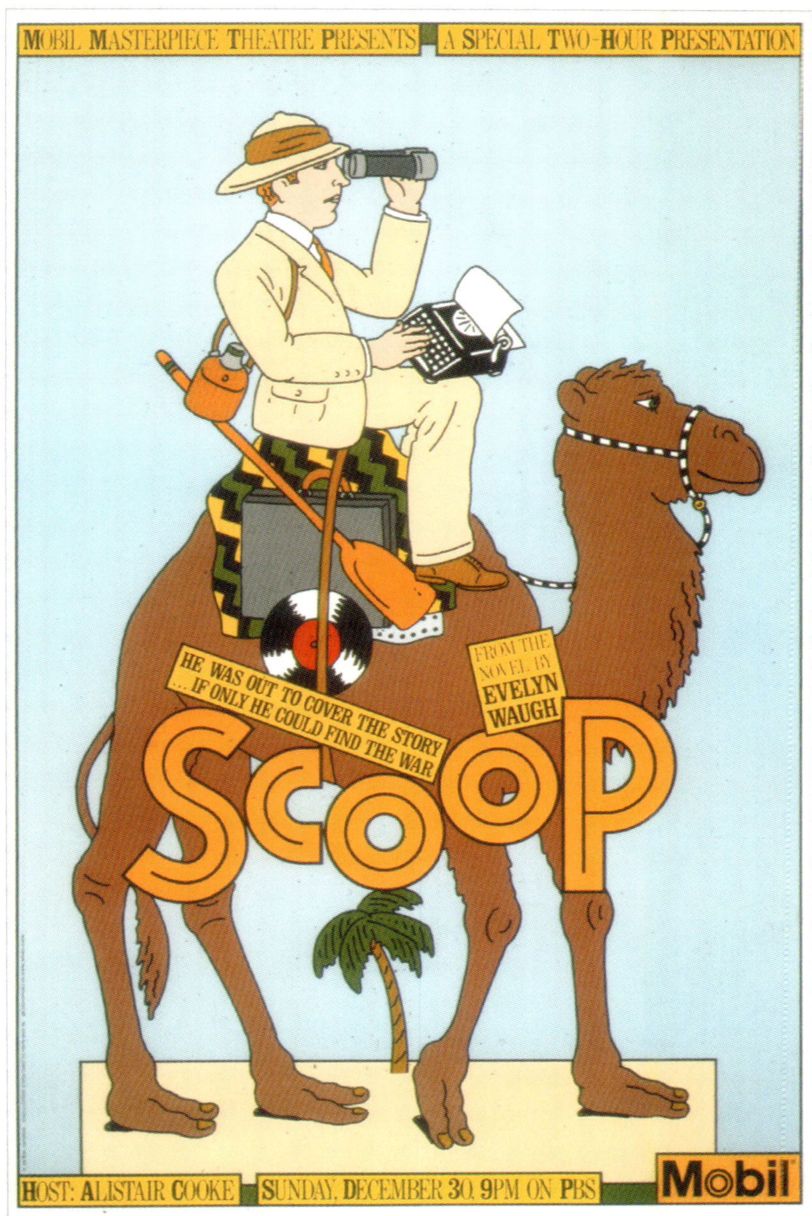

Pen and ink, color film, offset, 30" x 46.5", ca. 1984

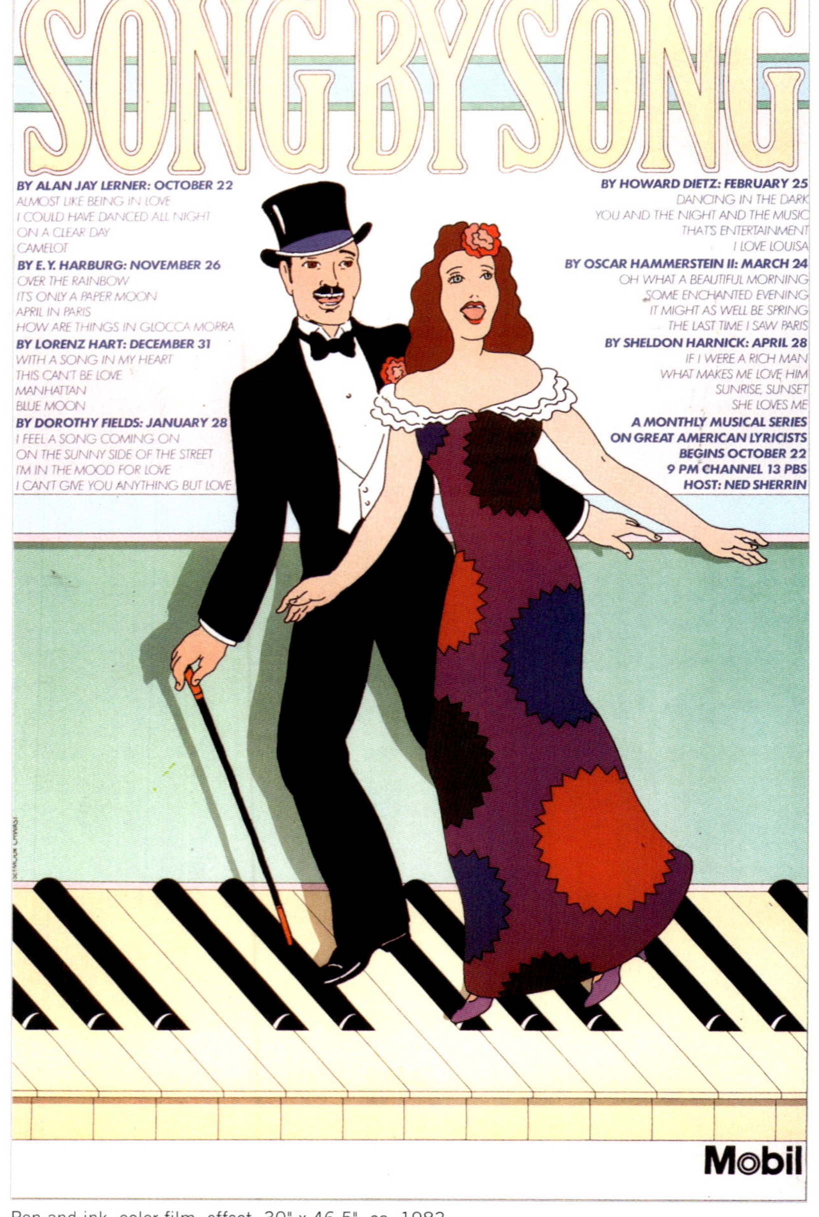

Pen and ink, color film, offset, 30" x 46.5", ca. 1983

Left: **SONG BY SONG.** A century-old sheet music cover (The Ragtime Goblin Man) had him dancing on piano keys. Adapting that idea was the easy part. It looks easy, but the tough job was getting the two columns of type to line up.

Opposite: **NICHOLAS NICKLEBY.** Charles Dickens's *Nicholas Nickleby* was a British film production with colorful characters creating a burden for poor Nick. The graphic solution came from an 1821 political cartoon showing people perched on a ladder. I put a ladder on Nick's shoulders, suggesting his role in dealing with those characters.

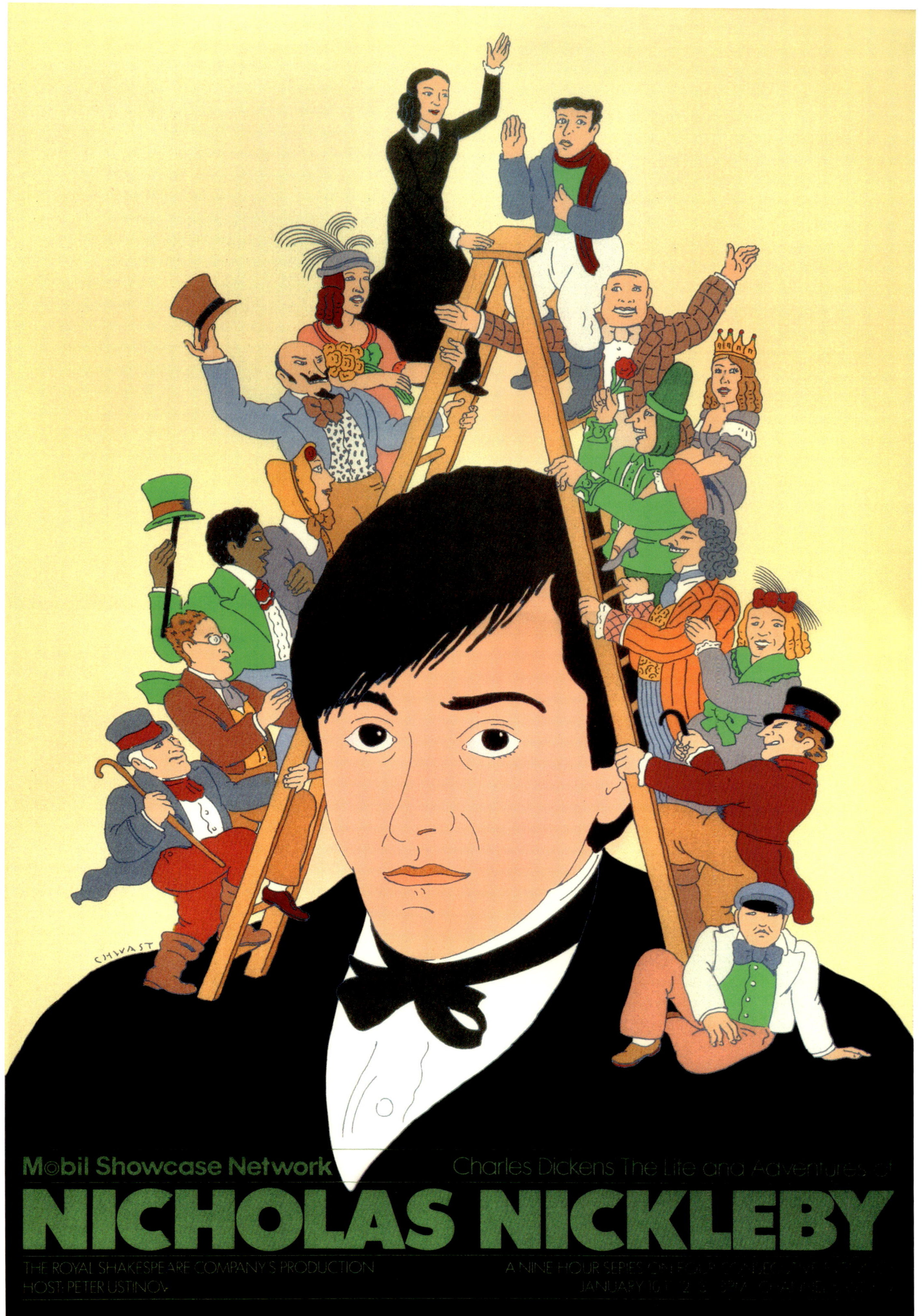

Pen and ink, color film, offset, 30" x 46.5", ca. 1983

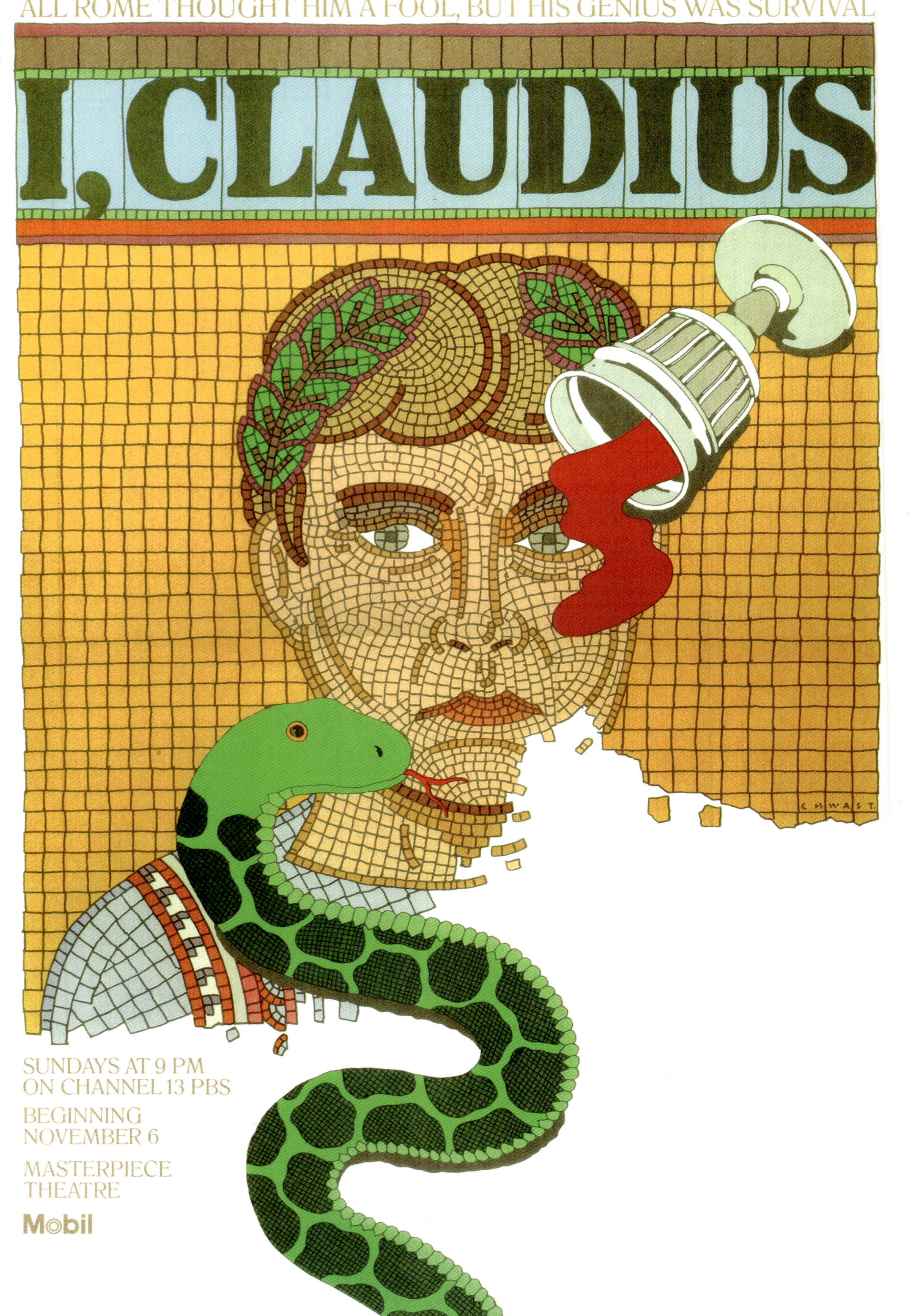

Pen and ink, color film, offset, 30" x 46.5", ca. 1976

Below, left: **RUMPOLE OF THE BAILEY.** *Rumpole of the Bailey* is a British TV series. He is an aging London barrister who surprises everyone with his brilliance and charm.

Below, right: **JEEVES & WOOSTER.** P. G. Woodmere wrote a series of novels about a feckless ne'er-do-well and his clever butler.

Opposite: **I, CLAUDIUS.** I couldn't improve the idea of the mosaic tiles that was used for the opening titles to the film production. The live snake of the film's titles was rendered, and I added a goblet with wine/blood spilling out. While the look was the same as seen with mosaic tiles in New York City subways, my art was in outline filled in with fifteen spot colors. Each sheet had to pass through the press four times.

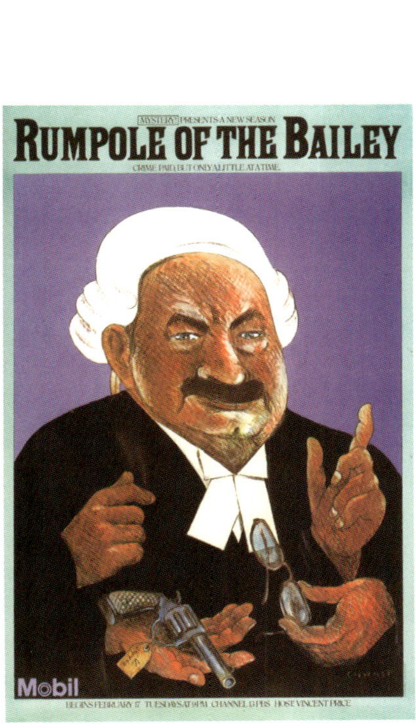

Acrylic and colored pencil on board, offset, 30" x 46.5", ca. 1980

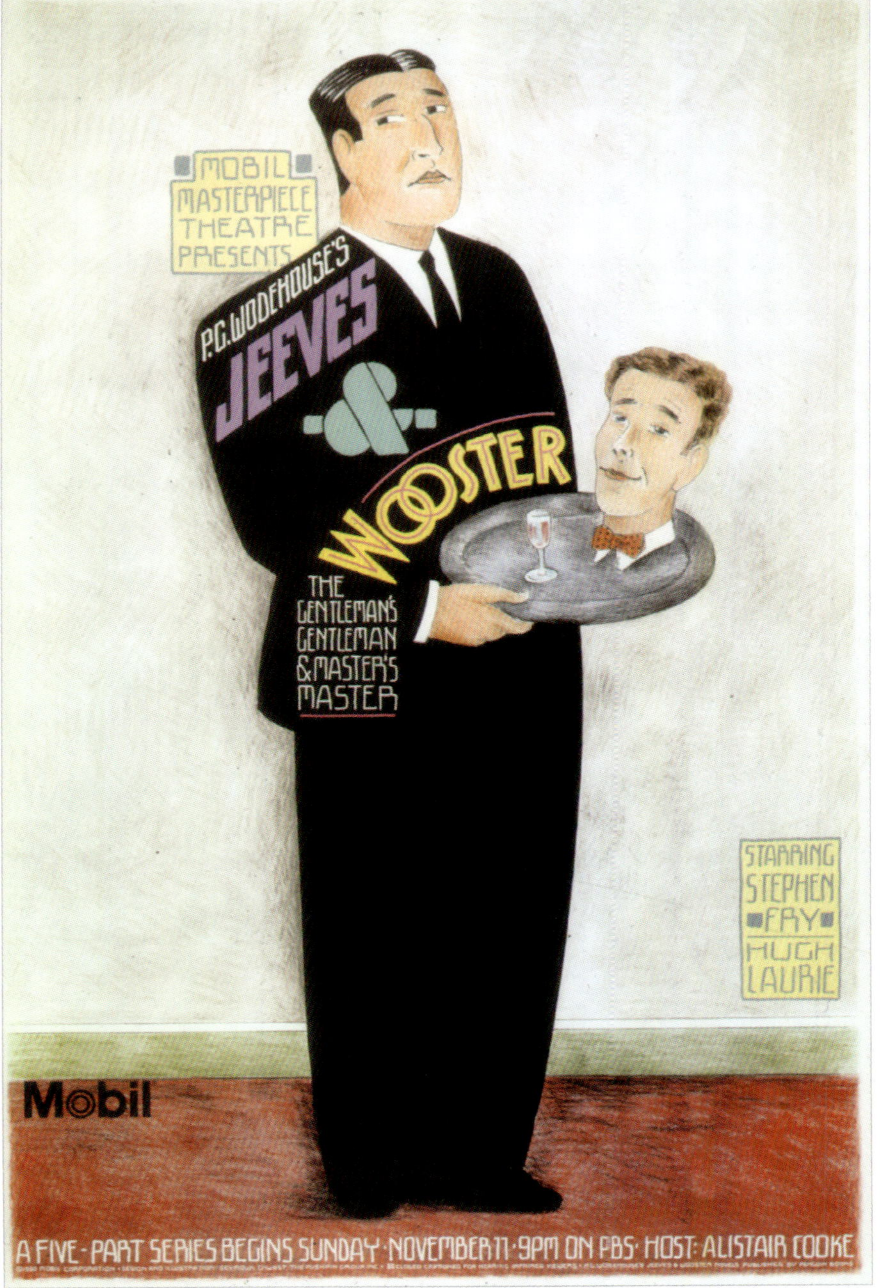

Pen and ink with colored pencil, offset, 24" x 36", ca. 1980

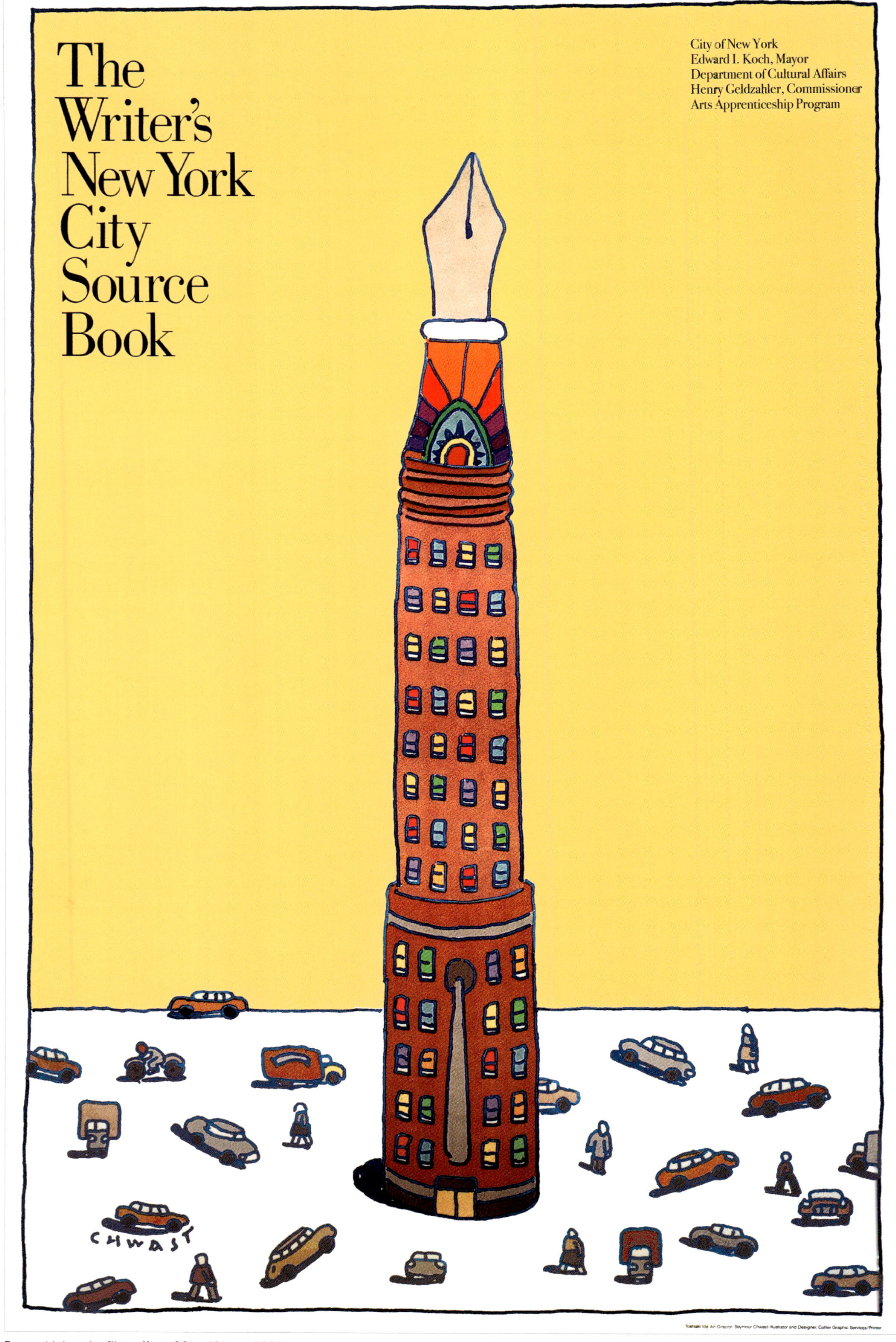

Pen and ink, color film, offset, 26" x 40", ca. 1985

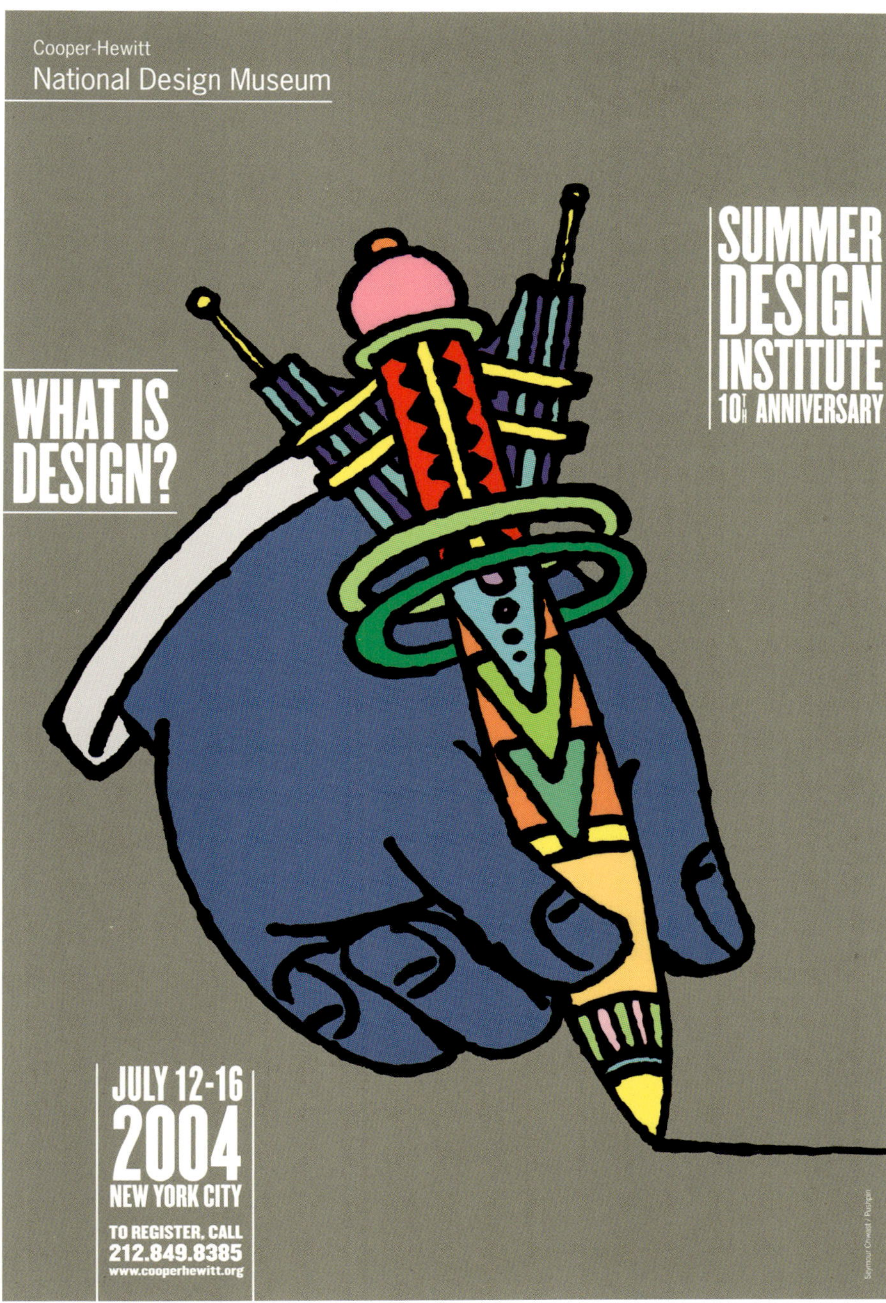

Marker and ink, digital color, offset, 24" x 36", 2004

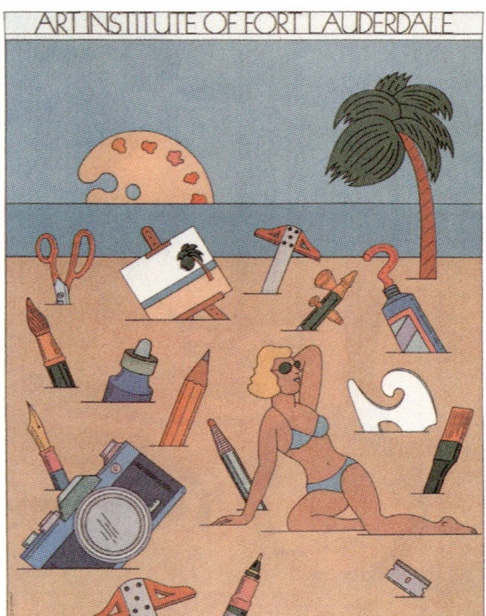

Pen and ink, color film, offset, 16" x 21", ca. 1980

Left: **WHAT IS DESIGN.** Cooper Hewitt, The National Design Museum, is the first in New York. This Buck Rogers pen tells us to look forward to the future in design.

Below: **ART INSTITUTE OF FORT LAUDERDALE.** Serious and some not-so-serious art students attend the Art Institute of Fort Lauderdale. The computer eliminated the need for many of these art materials.

Opposite: **THE WRITER'S NEW YORK CITY SOURCE BOOK.** New York City offered a book for writers in their search for information, with one image representing "writers" with a pen and "New York" with a skyscraper. It is a little too close to the work of my idol, Saul Steinberg, for which I apologize.

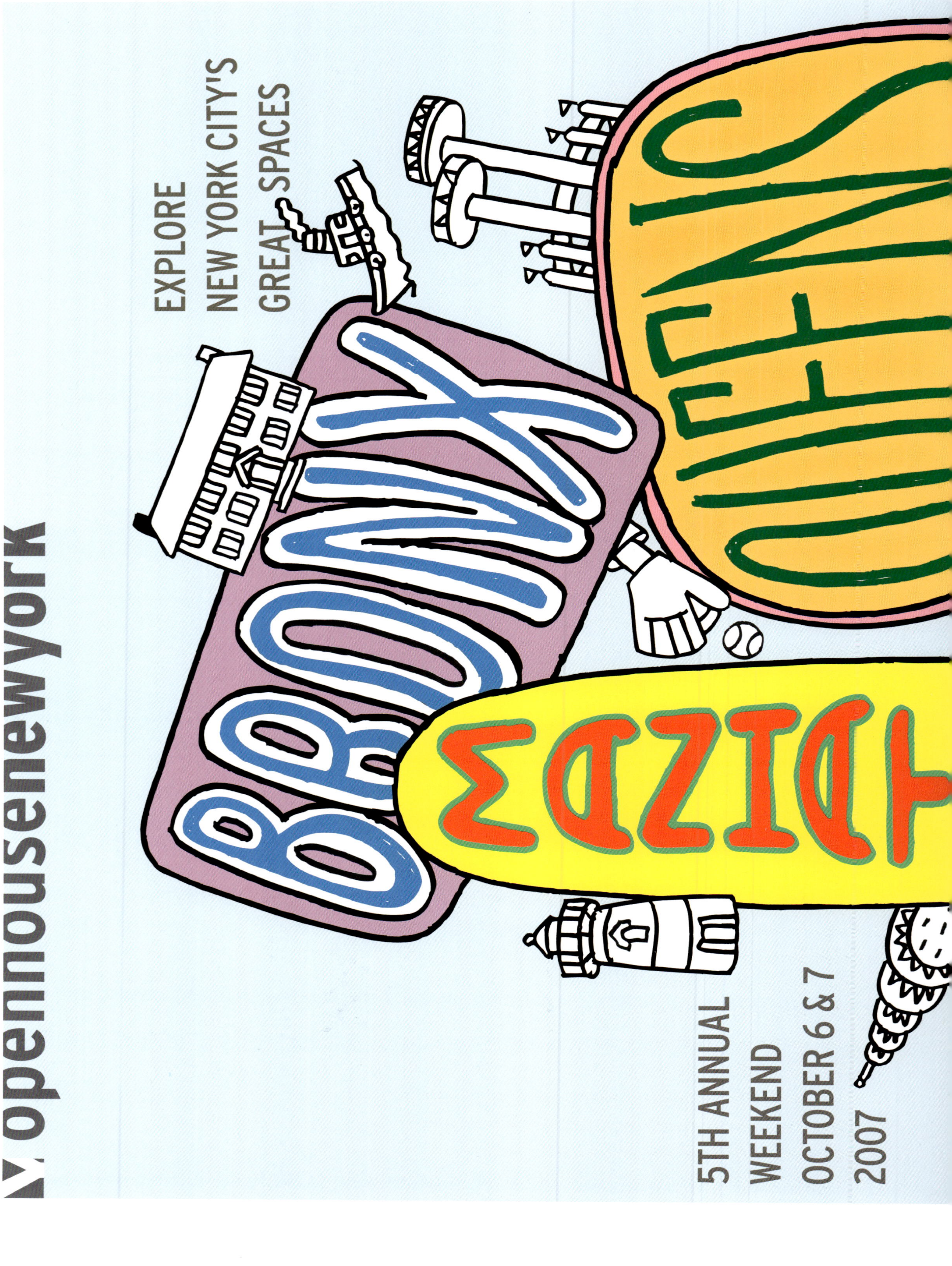

openhousenewyork

BRONX

EXPLORE
NEW YORK CITY'S
GREAT SPACES

MANHAT

QUEENS

5TH ANNUAL
WEEKEND
OCTOBER 6 & 7
2007

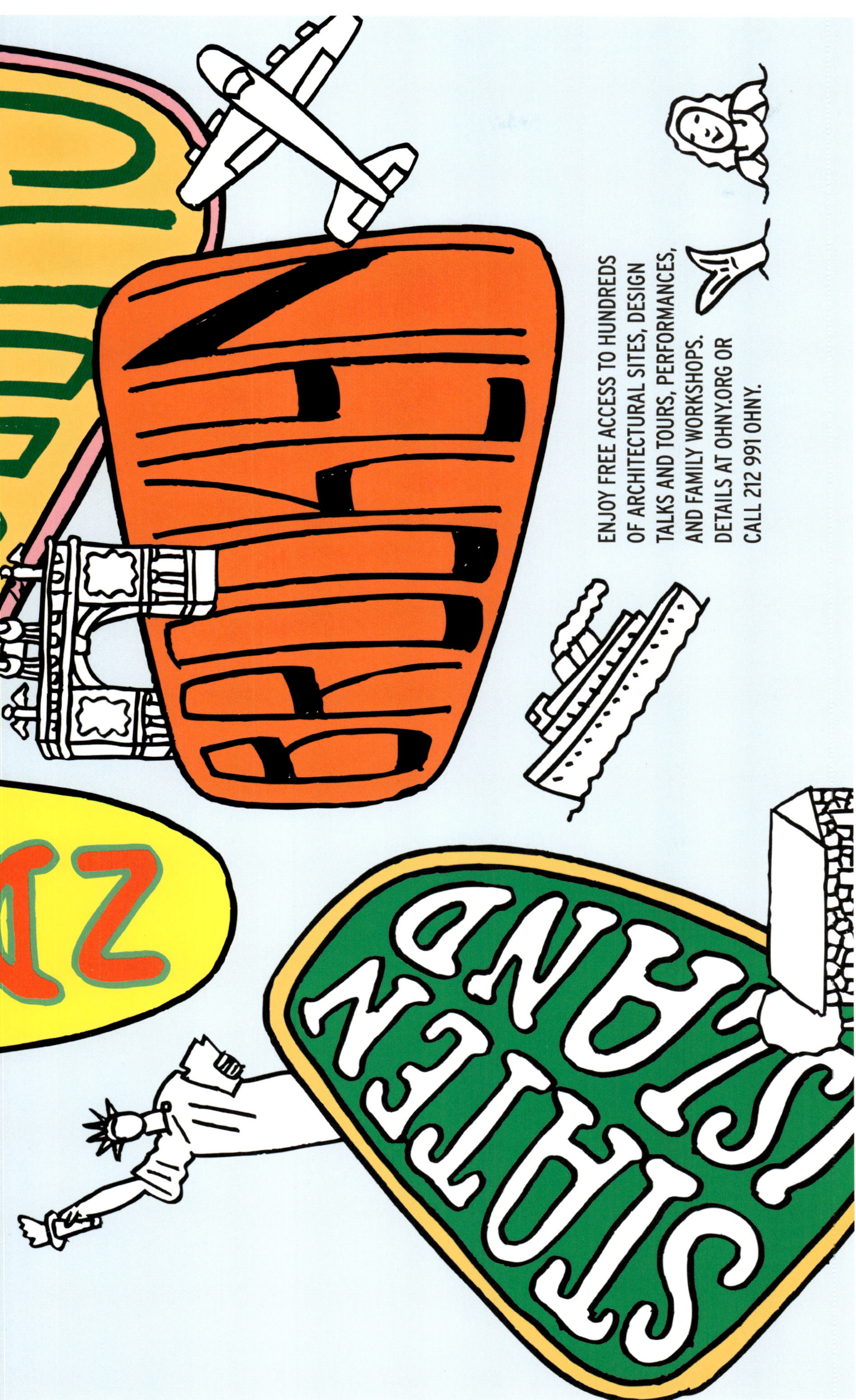

Marker and ink, digital color, offset, 11" x 22", 2007

OPENHOUSENEWYORK. Open House organizes tours for the public to discover architecturally important and exciting locations. I have always looked for new ways to represent New York. Molding the shape of the city is one way.

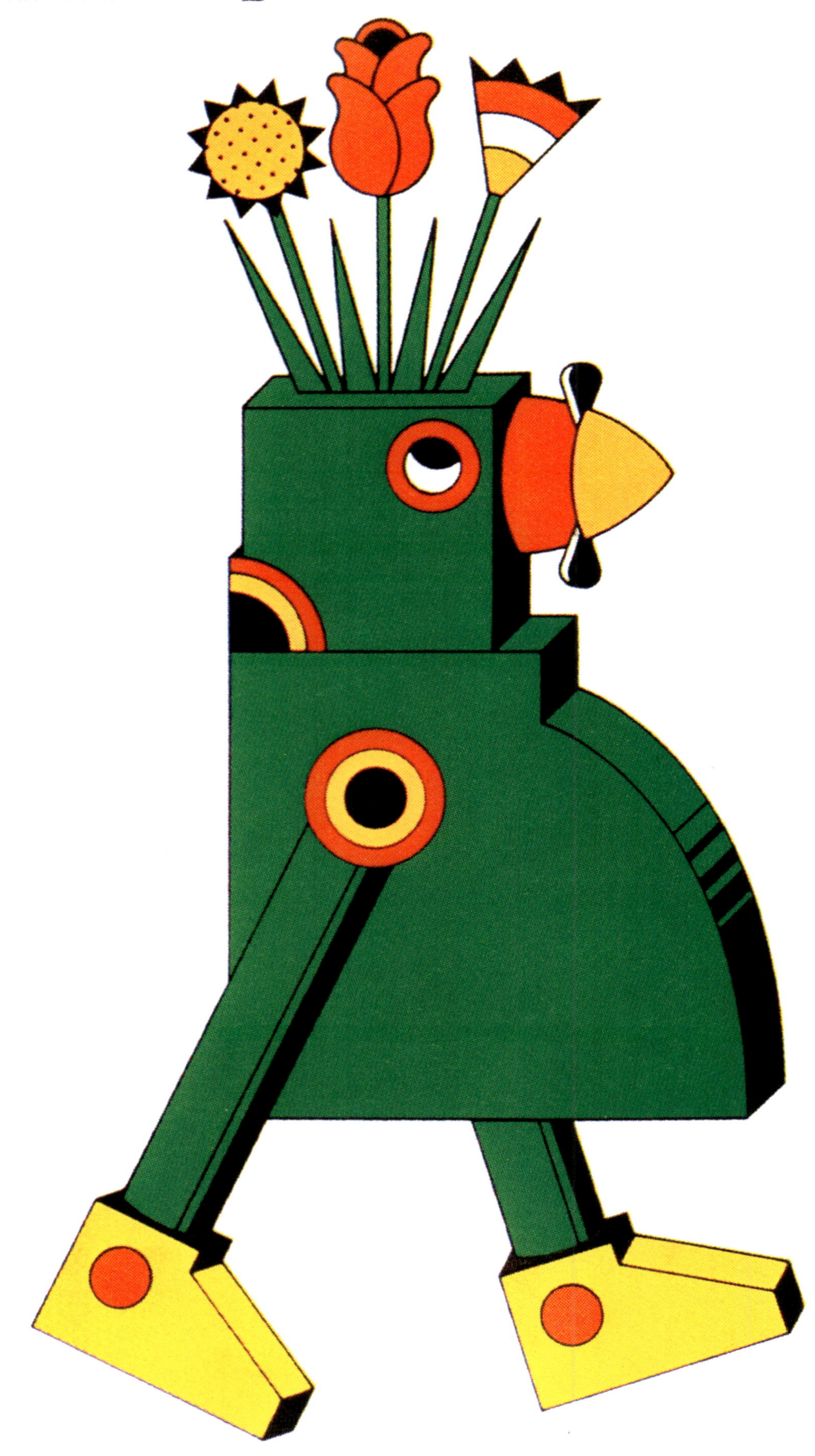

Pen and ink, mechanical art, color separations, offset, 24" x 36", ca. 1980

Below, left: **MOONRIDE.** The poster promotes the book about a boy who takes a ride on the moon.

Below, right: **IT'S NEVER TOO EARLY.** LaGuardia College in New York offers classes to young children.

Opposite: **THE BROOKLYN CHILDREN'S MUSEUM.** Technology, nature, and humanity are offered by the Brooklyn Children's Museum. This logo/mascot reflects this. As a physical object he can make himself useful. A wastebasket is an example.

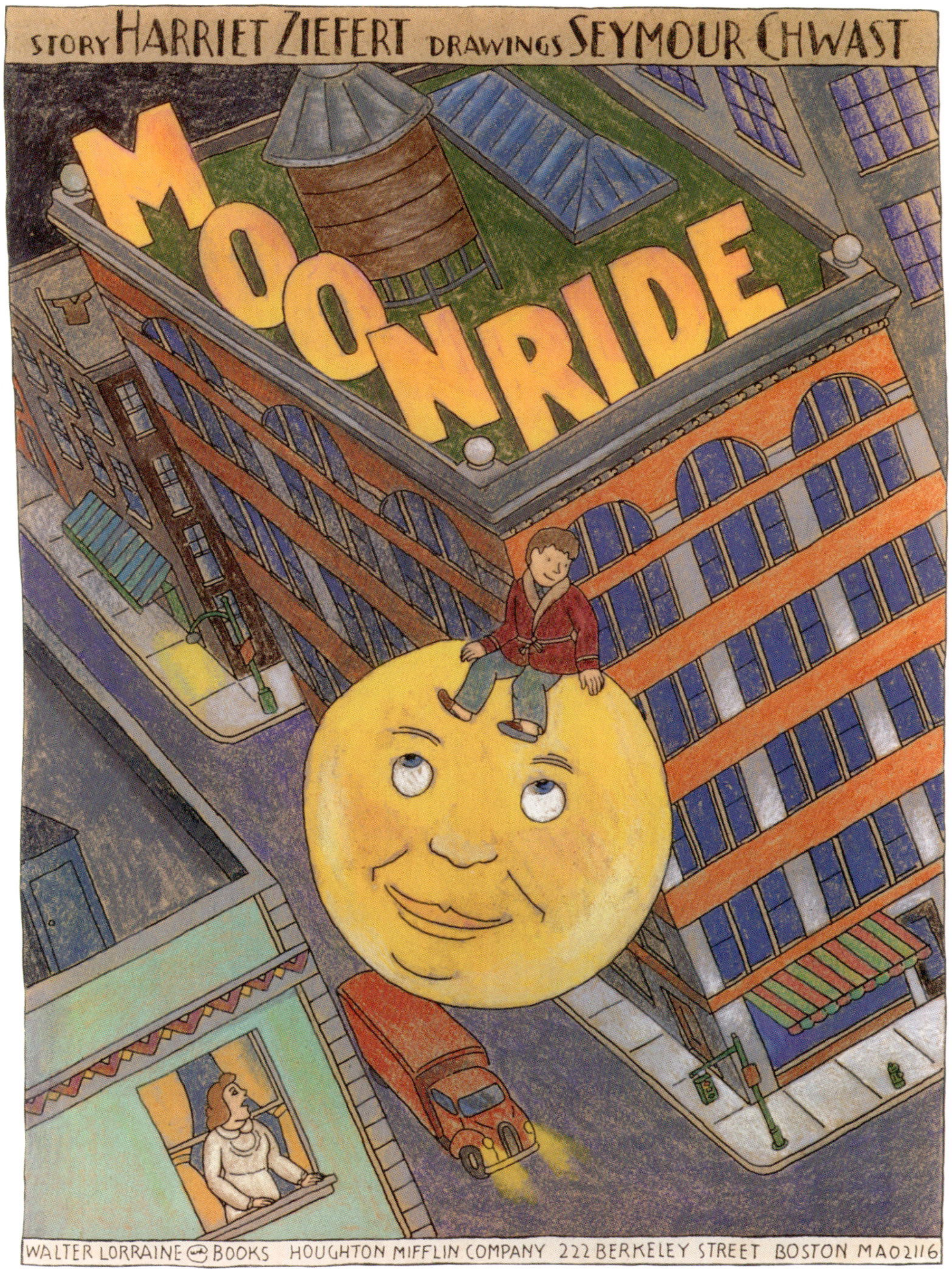

Pen and ink, acrylic and colored pencil on butcher paper, offset, 24" x 36", 2000

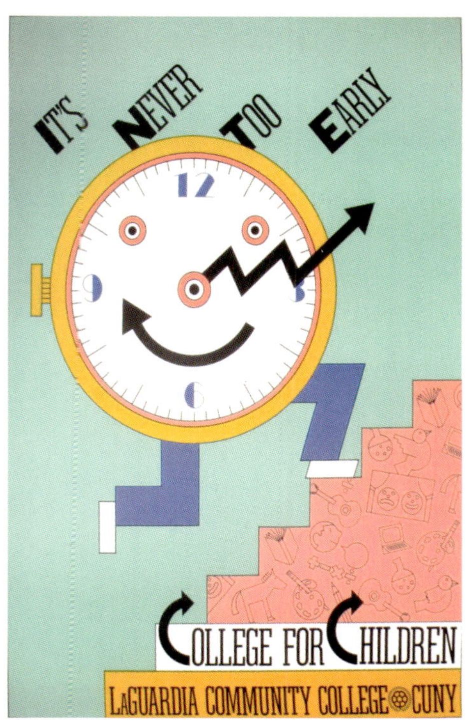

Mechanical art, separated color, offset, 23½" x 33½", ca. 1990

EXPOSICION UNIVERSAL SEVILLA.
Opposite: I've been accused of having a fetish with all of the feet I've drawn. But, I've also drawn many hands and heads. This was one of a series celebrating the famous flamenco dancer on the package of Gitanes Cigarettes.

CABRAL.
Right, top: Ernesto Garcia (the Chango) Cabral was a cartoonist, painter, and caricaturist. His work numbers almost 25,000 pieces. Xavier Bermudez, the head of the International Poster Biennal in Mexico, asked me to celebrate Cabral with a poster design.

EXPOSICION UNIVERSAL SEVILLA.
Right, below: A trade fair in Seville with a logo for the city and one for Spain, neither done by me. I drew the flying ship with a landmark building of Seville for a mast. The fair was held to celebrate Columbus discovering the New World five hundred years earlier.

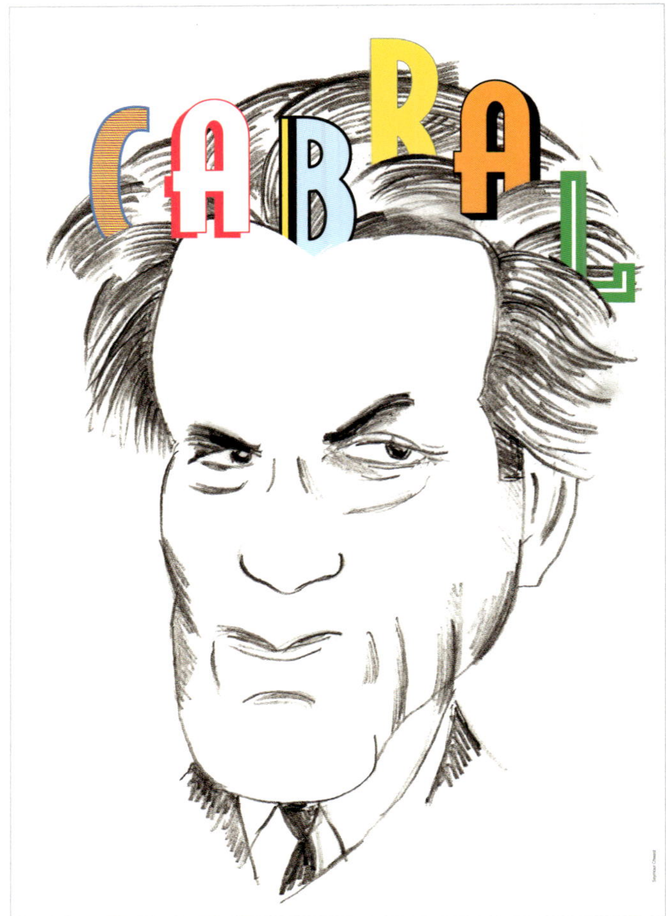

Pencil with digital typography, digital printing, 27½" x 39", 2018

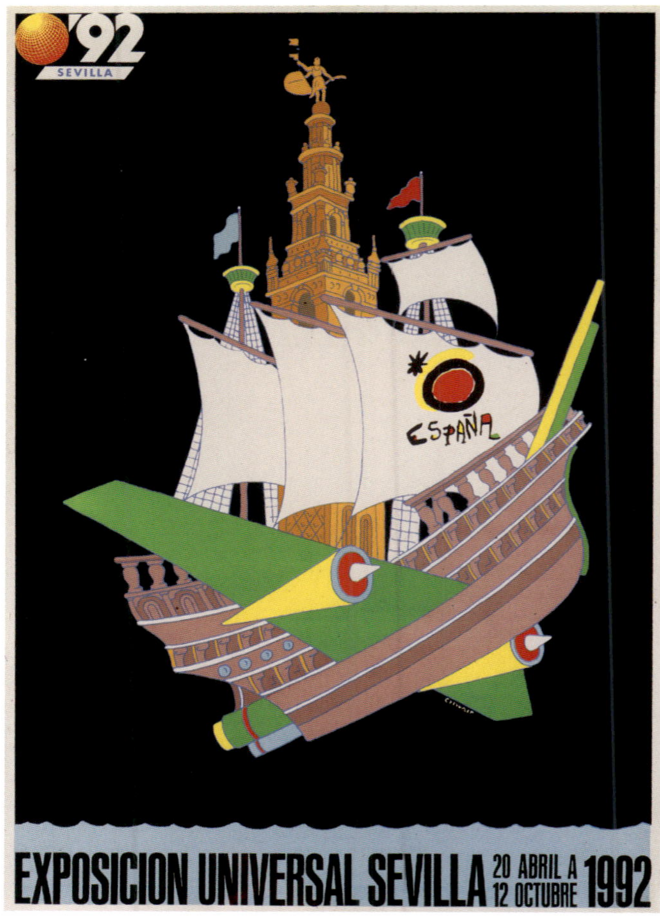

Pen and ink, color film, offset, approx. 24" x 36", 1992

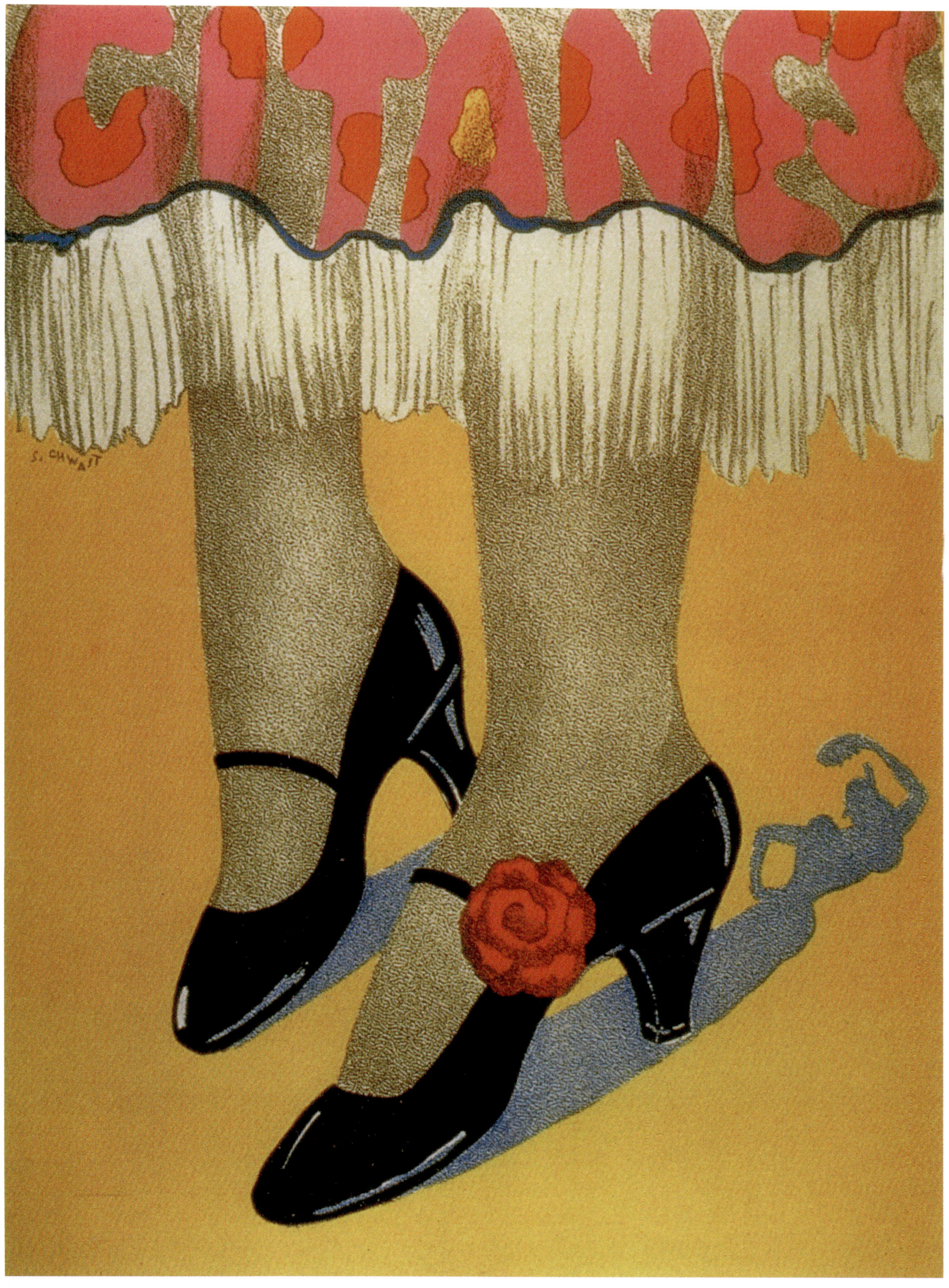

Colored pencil on textured paper, color film, offset, 24" x 36", ca. 1991

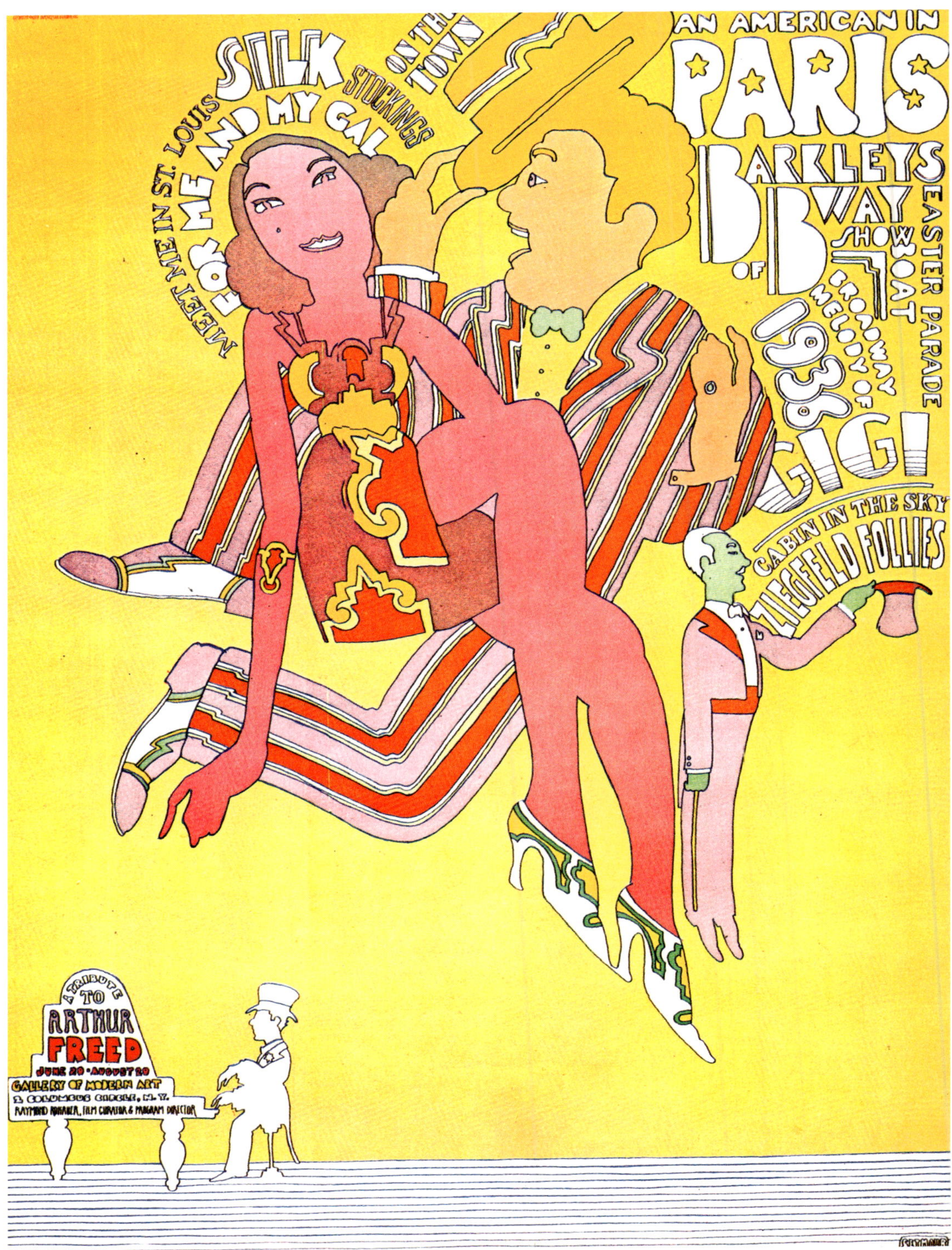

Pen and ink, hand lettered typography, color film, offset, 24" x 36", ca. 1968

Above: **A TRIBUTE TO ARTHUR FREED.** This is a celebration of the lyricist and Hollywood film producer Arthur Freed. His musical films are loved by all.

Opposite: **30s.** Visual symbols adorn this poster for a public television series on the thirties. President Roosevelt was in the front seat. Others symbols of the decade came along for the ride.

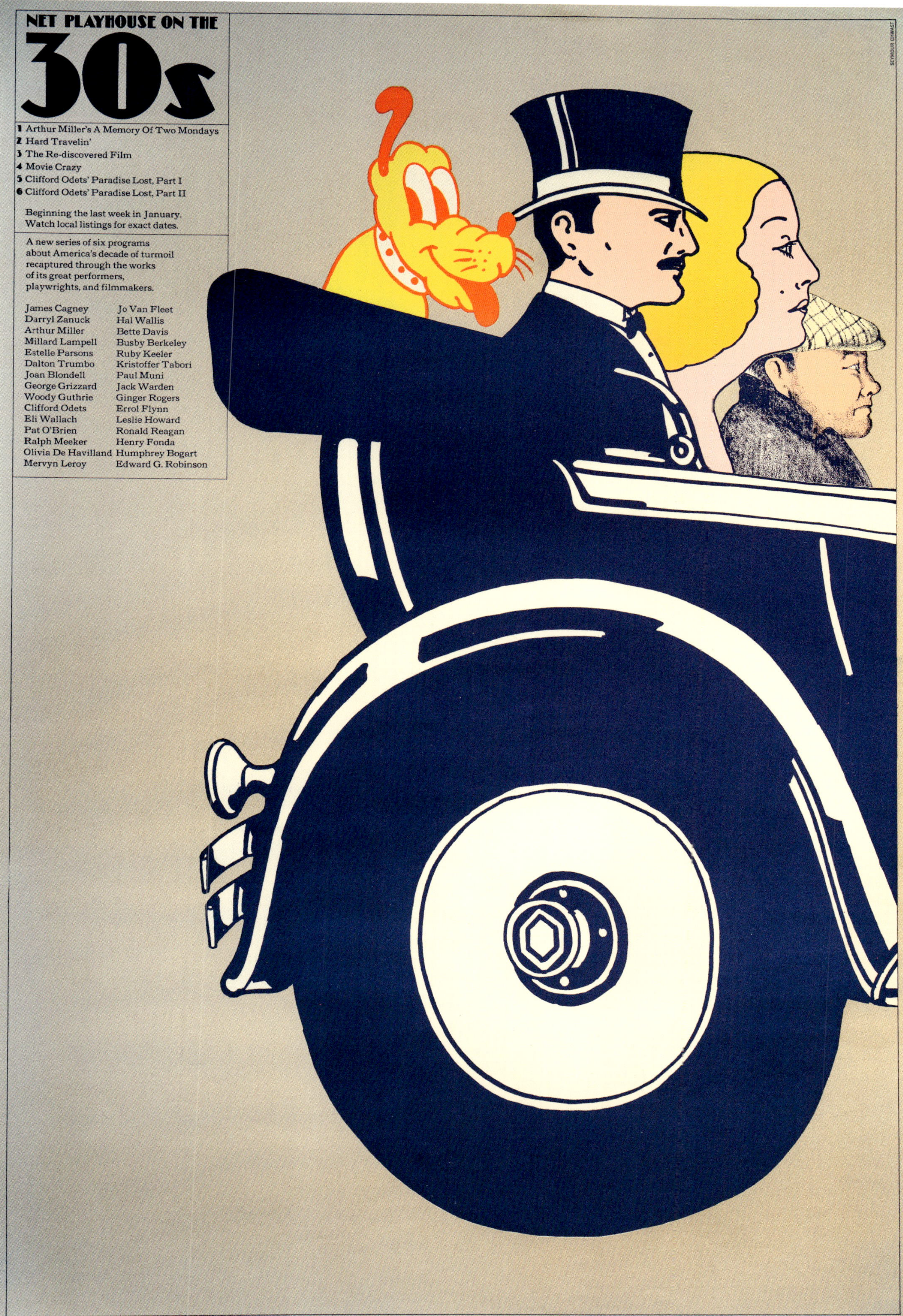

Mixed media, offset, 24" x 36", ca. 1975

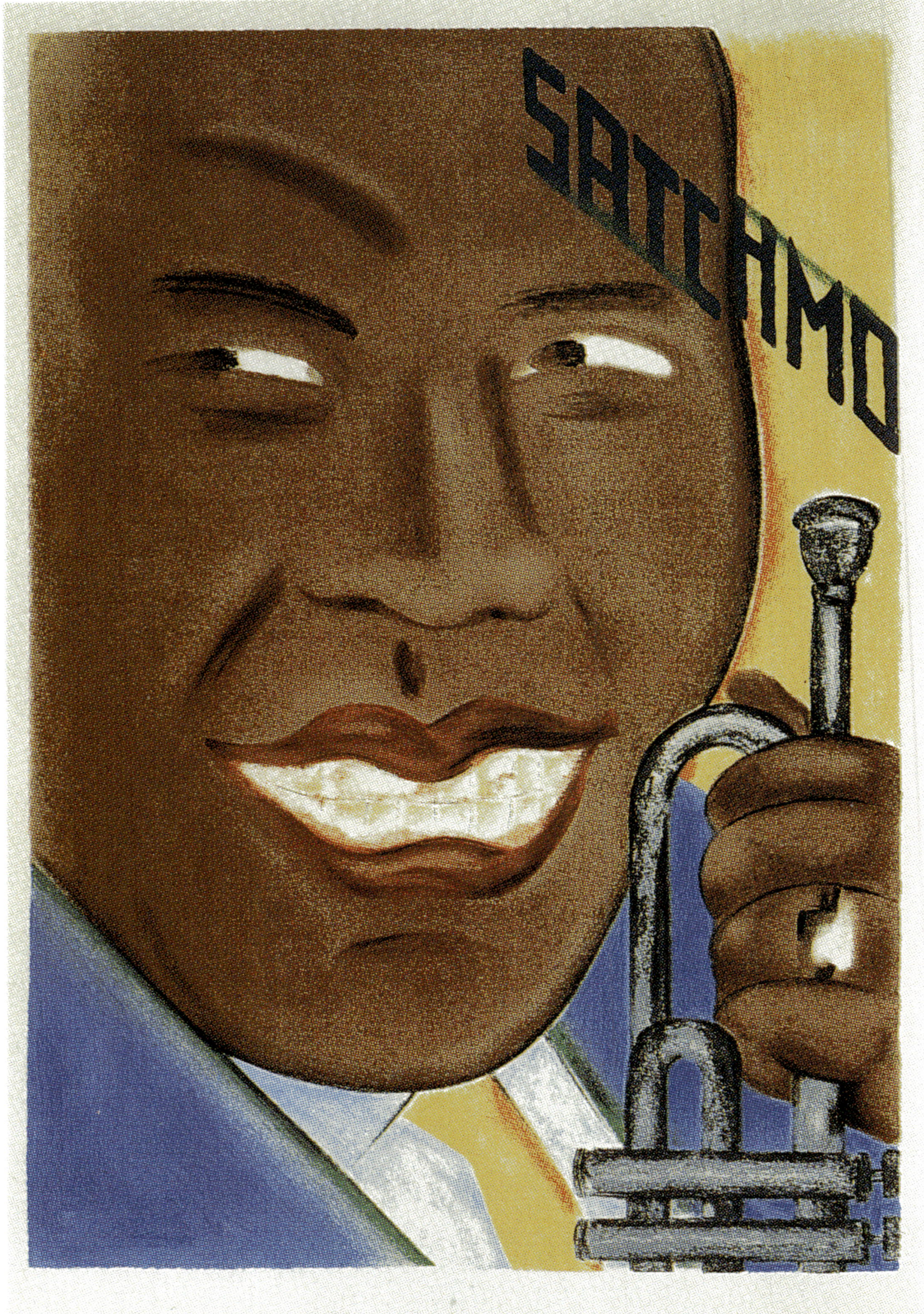

Mixed media, serigraph printing on paper, 30" x 44", 1989

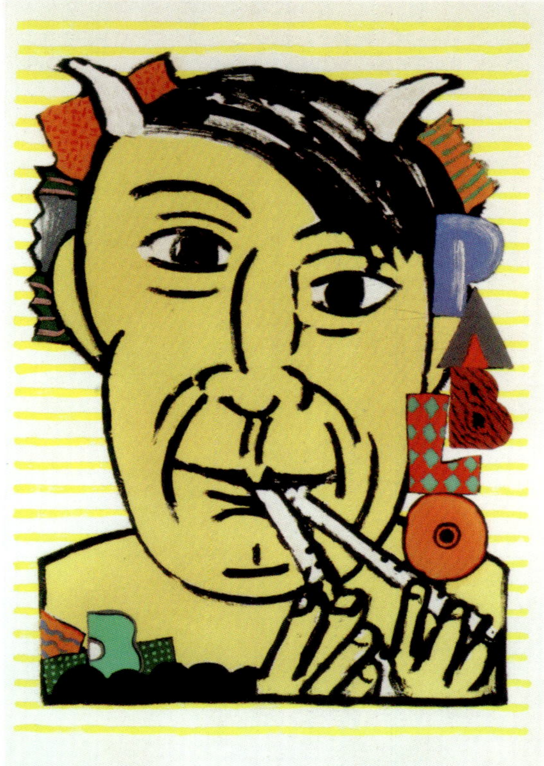

Mixed media, serigraph printing on paper, 30" x 44", 1989

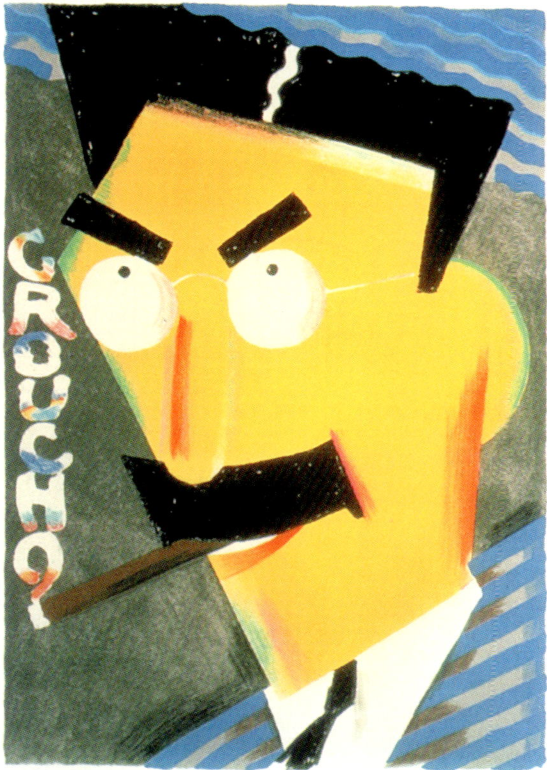

Mixed media, serigraph printing on paper, 30" x 44", 1989

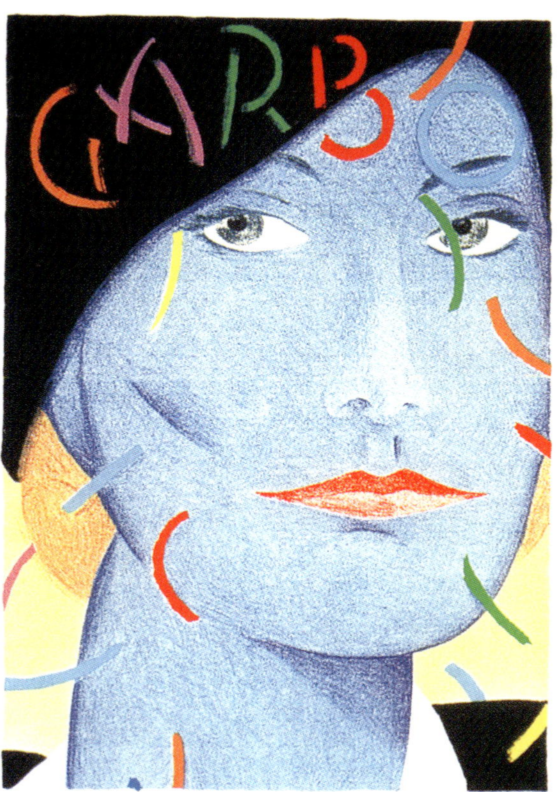

Mixed media, serigraph printing on paper, 30" x 44", 1989

THE O SERIES

SATCHMO
PABLO
GROUCHO
GARBO

Ambassador Arts produced editions of these silkscreen (serigraph) prints. I used various techniques to suit the personalities. I picked these four celebrities because their names ended in O.

Below: **ART OR PORNOGRAPHY?** New Line Cinema distributed offbeat and avant-garde films to colleges. This series, called "Art or Pornography," had my poster featuring a German decoupage that I found. I drew the outline of the torso.

Opposite: **THE END PLACE.** This was one of three mock travel posters printed in issue #52 of the *Push Pin Graphic*. James McMullan and Milton Glaser did posters for equally exotic places.

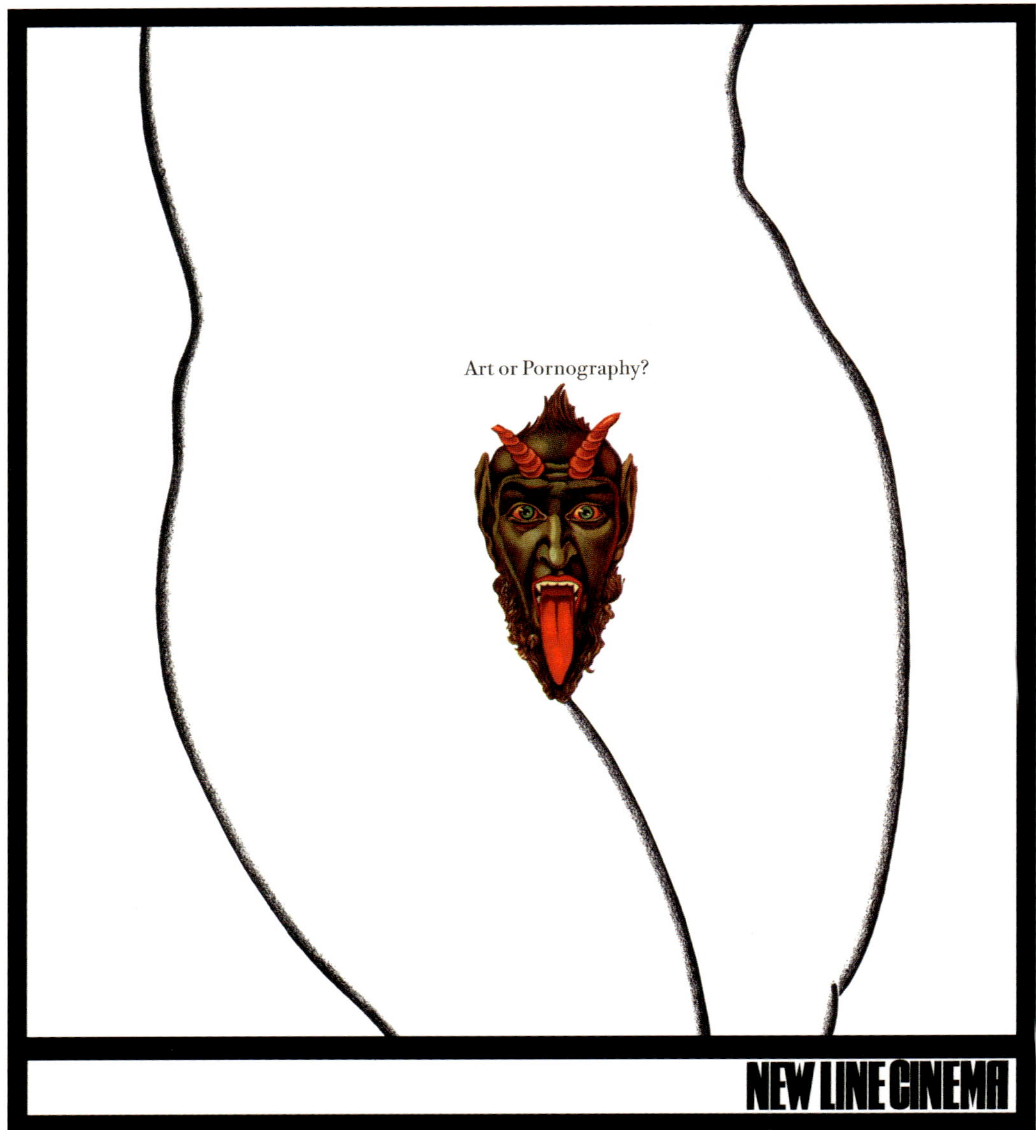

China marker, found decoupage, four color process, offset, 24" x 36", ca. 1968

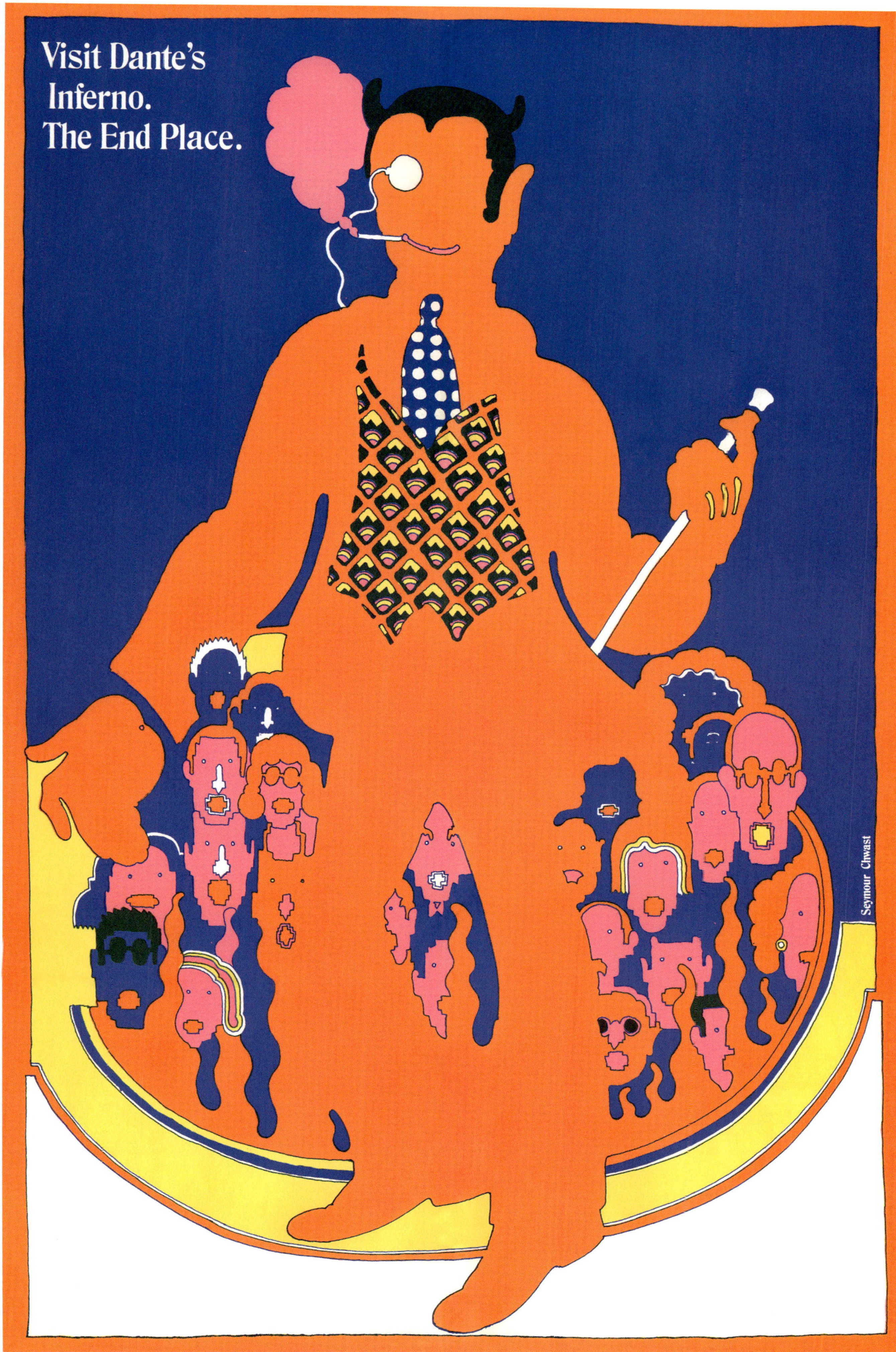

Pen and ink, color film, offset, 18" x 28", 1967

Right: **THE PANCAKE KING.** *The Pancake King* is a tale of a boy whose pancakes were good enough for a president. This book was published by Princeton Architectural Press. A musical was performed in Milwaukee for which this poster was created.

Opposite: **GROWING BY DESIGN.** The title suggested the graphic solution for this design conference in Aspen, Colorado. The theme was children.

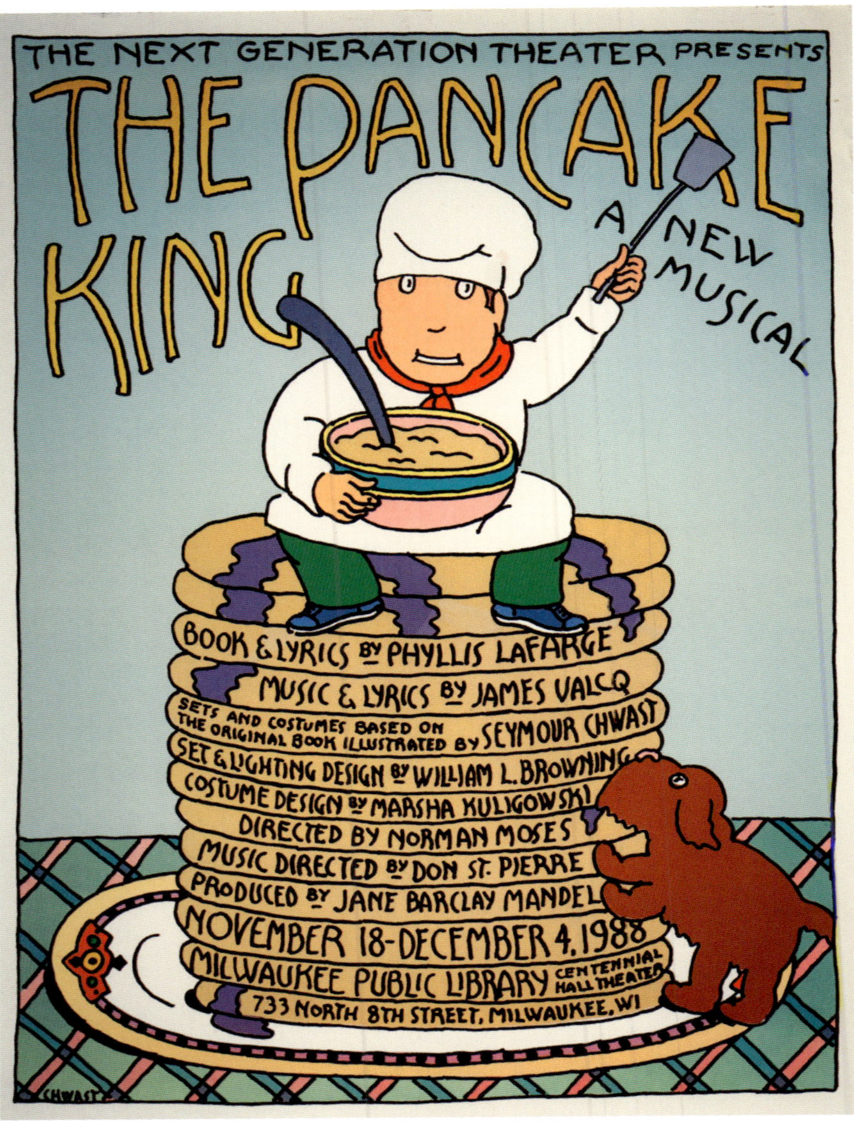

Hand lettering with marker and ink, color film, offset, 18" x 24", ca. 1988

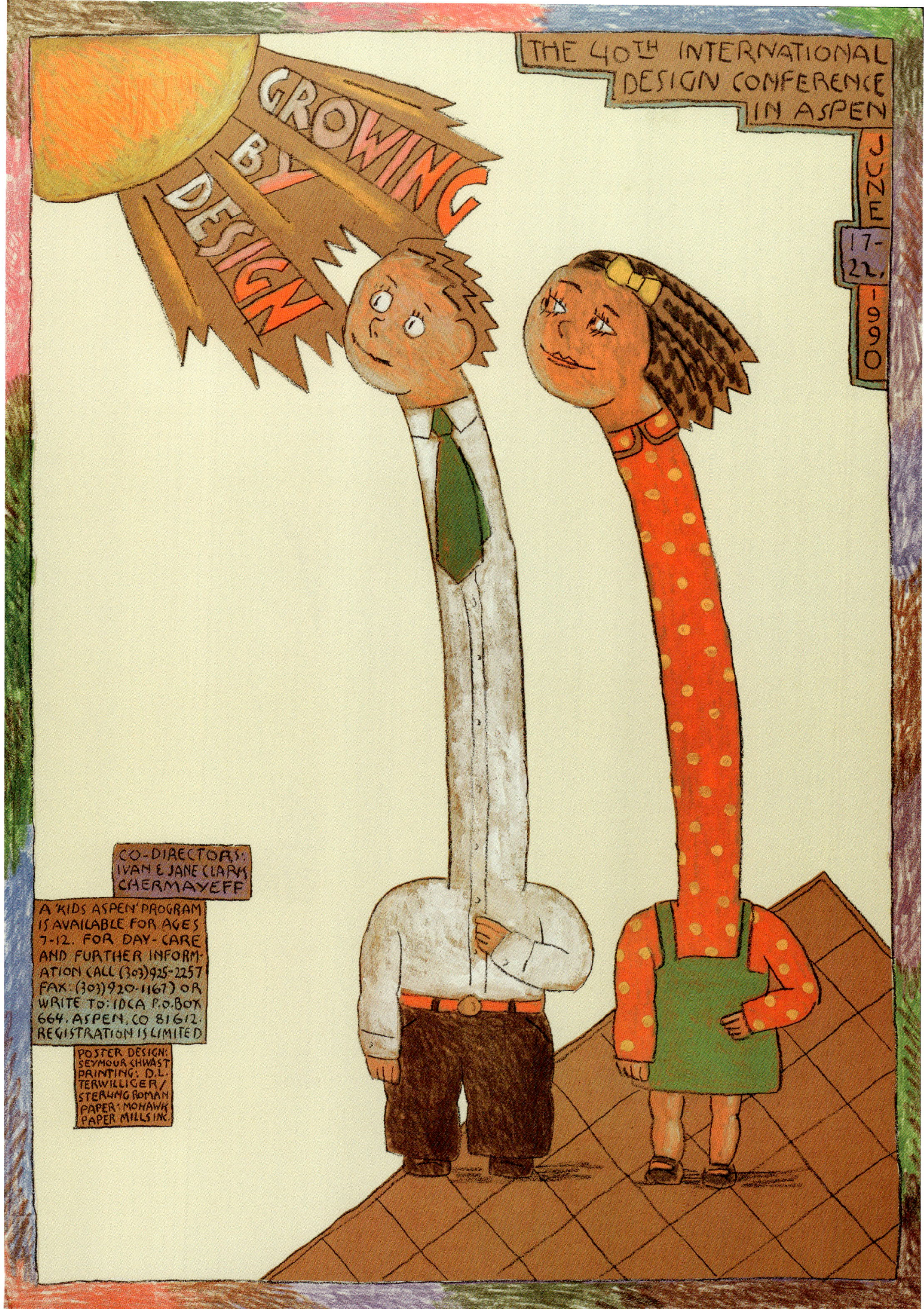

Hand lettering with marker and ink, acrylic and colored pencil, offset, 24" x 36", 1990

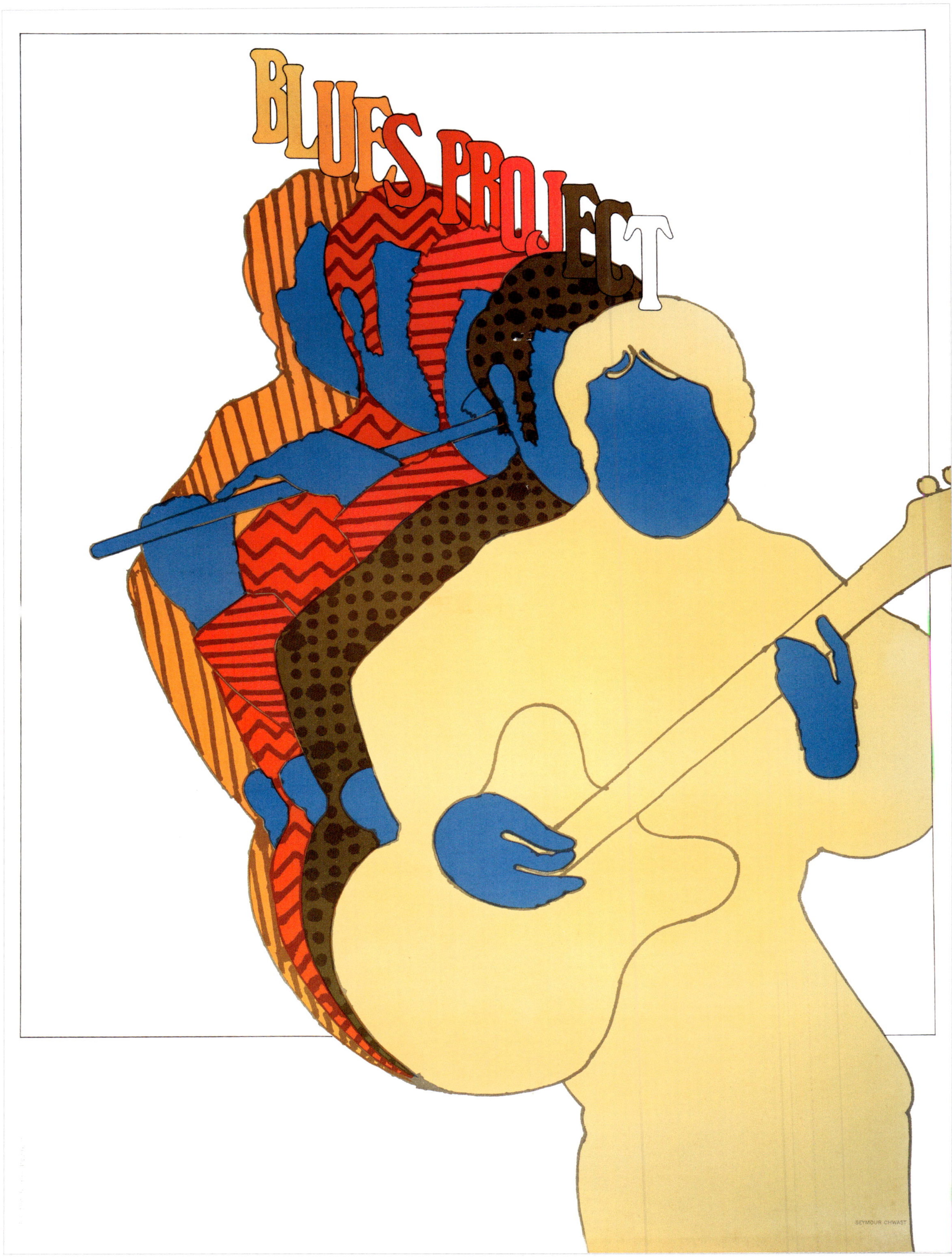

Pen and ink, color film, offset, 30" x 40", ca. 1970

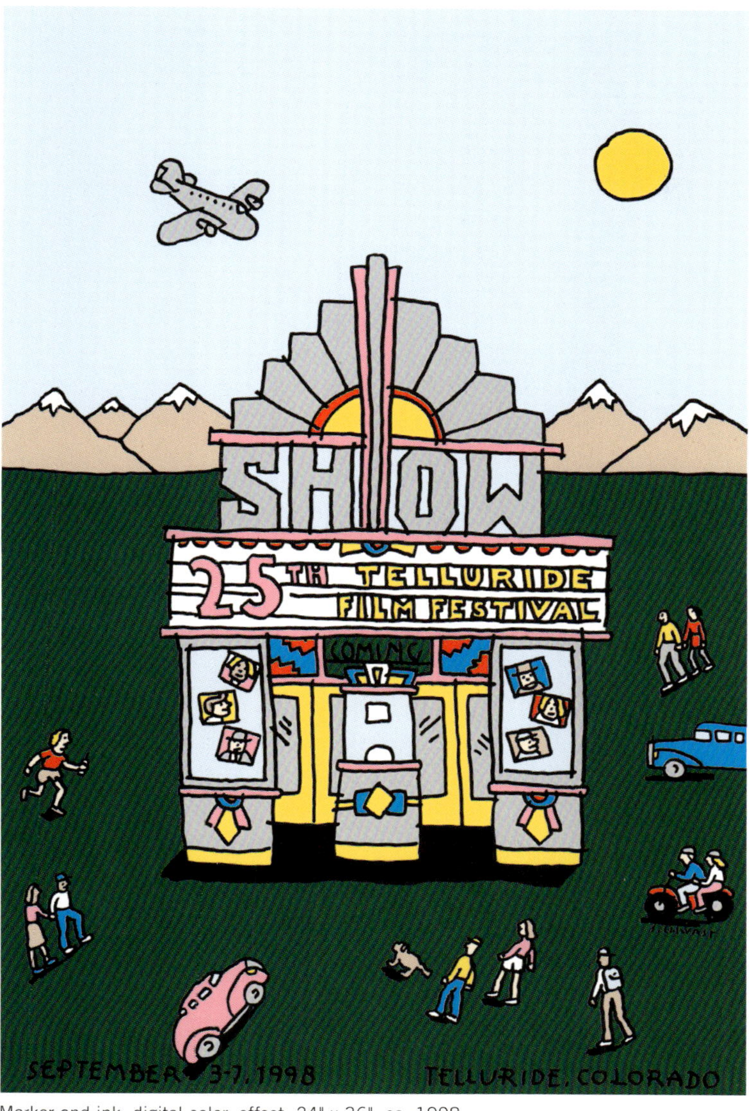

Marker and ink, digital color, offset, 24" x 36", ca. 1998

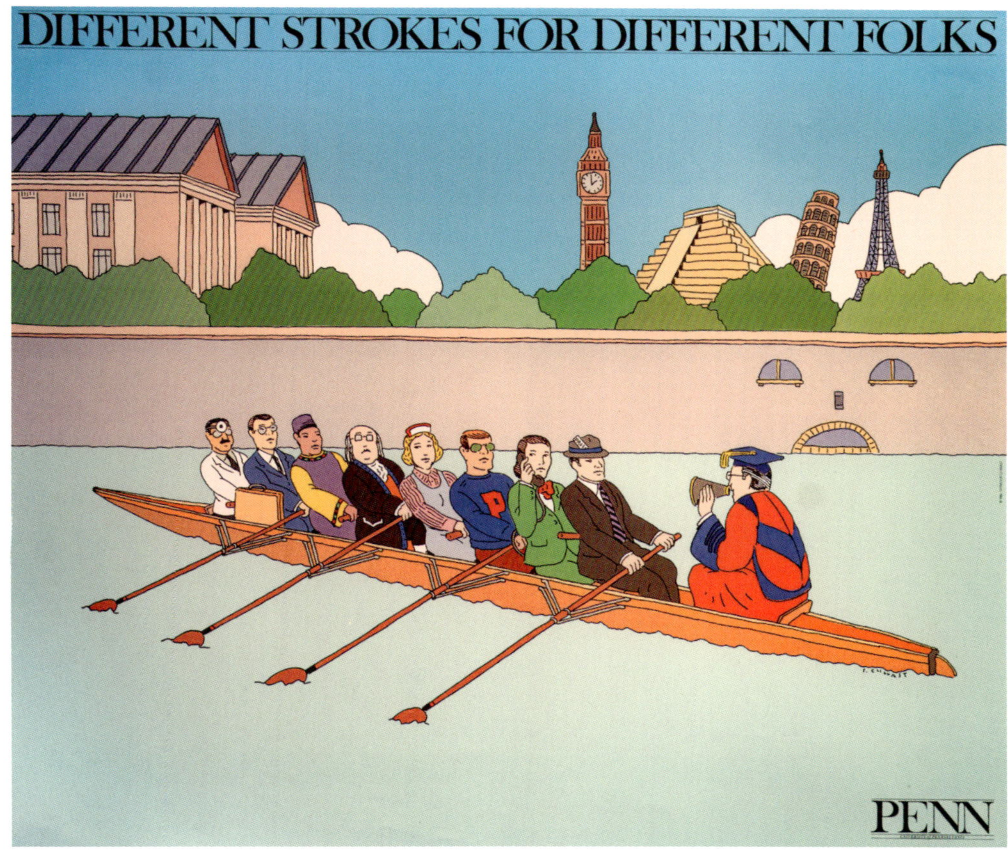

Pen and ink, color film, offset, 24" x 21", ca. 1985

Above: **25th TELLURIDE FILM FESTIVAL.** The Telluride Film Festival presents new and avant-garde films. This twenty-fifth year of the festival merited special attention.

Left: **PENN.** The diversity of the students and faculty is the theme of this University of Pennsylvania poster. The landmarks in the background promise a rich and varied life for students.

Opposite: **THE BLUES PROJECT.** The blues, psychedelic, and rock band from Greenwich Village was active between 1965 and 1967.

Below: **TYLER.** This poster promotes the Tyler School of Art in Philadelphia. Tyler would never allow a poster like this today.

Opposite: **GET STRAIGHT.** Dawn Farm is a facility for treatment of drug and alcohol addiction.

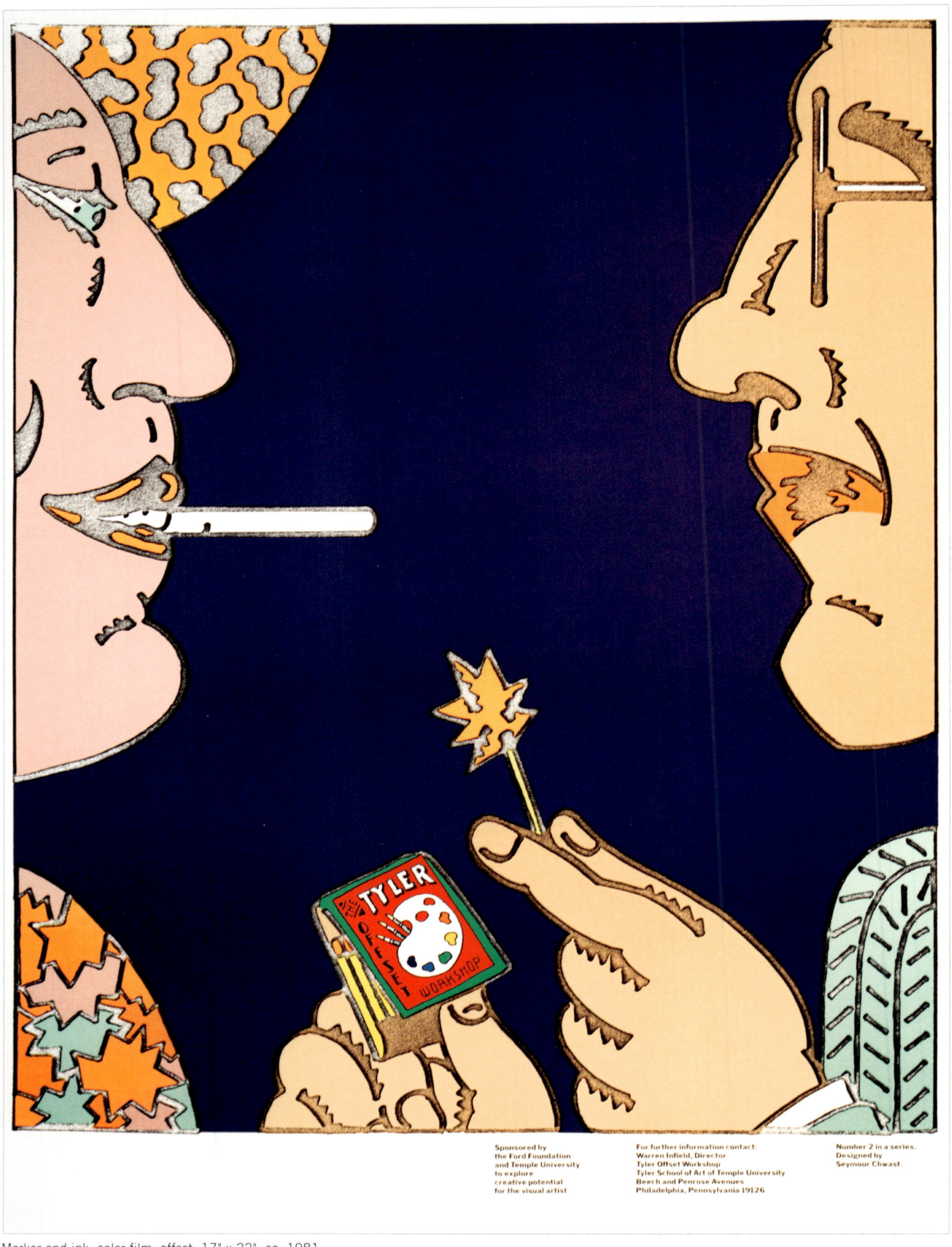

Marker and ink, color film, offset, 17" x 22", ca. 1981

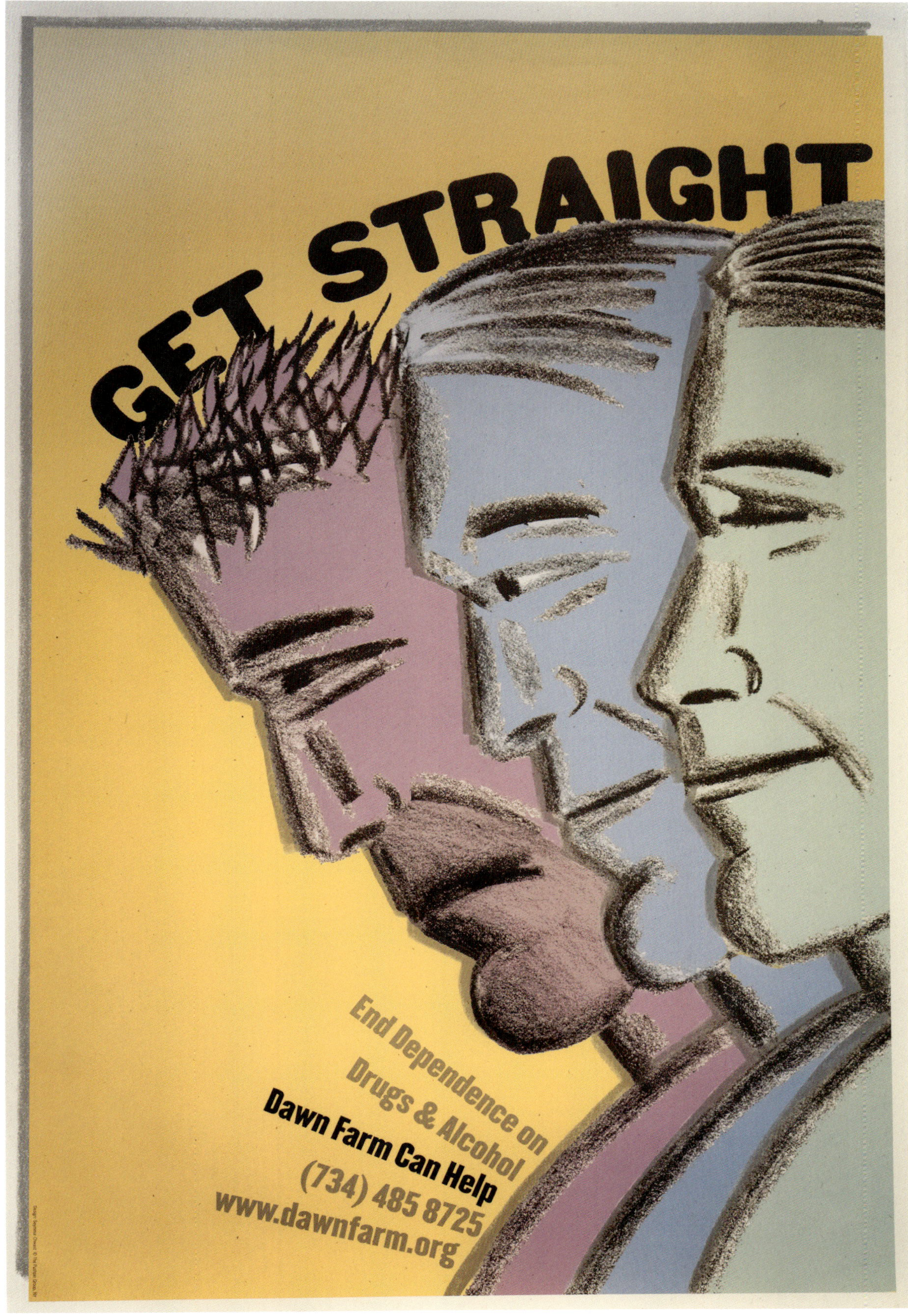

Pencil with digital color, offset, 24" x 36", ca. 2010

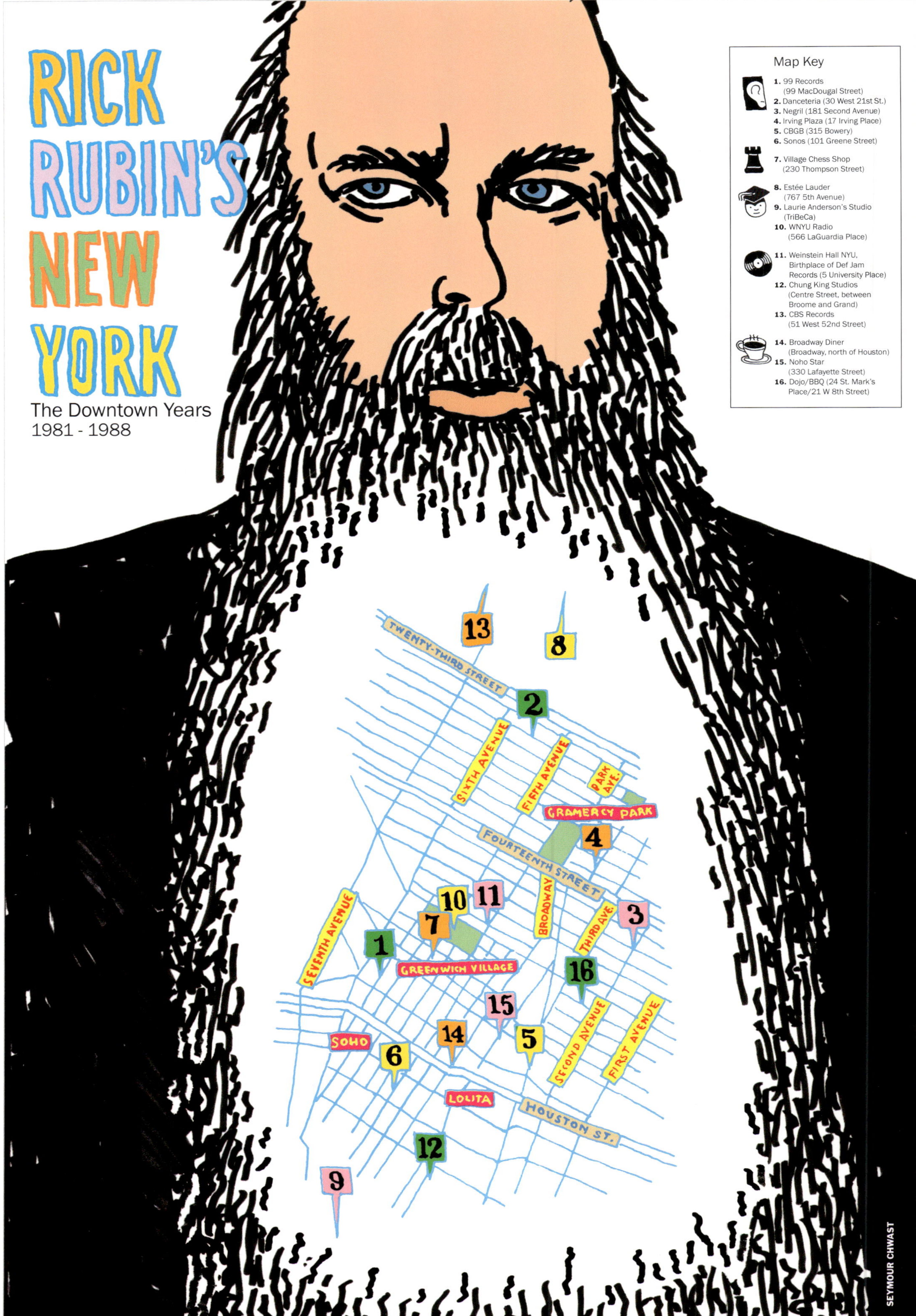

Mixed media with vector art and digital color, offset, 18" x 26½", 2016

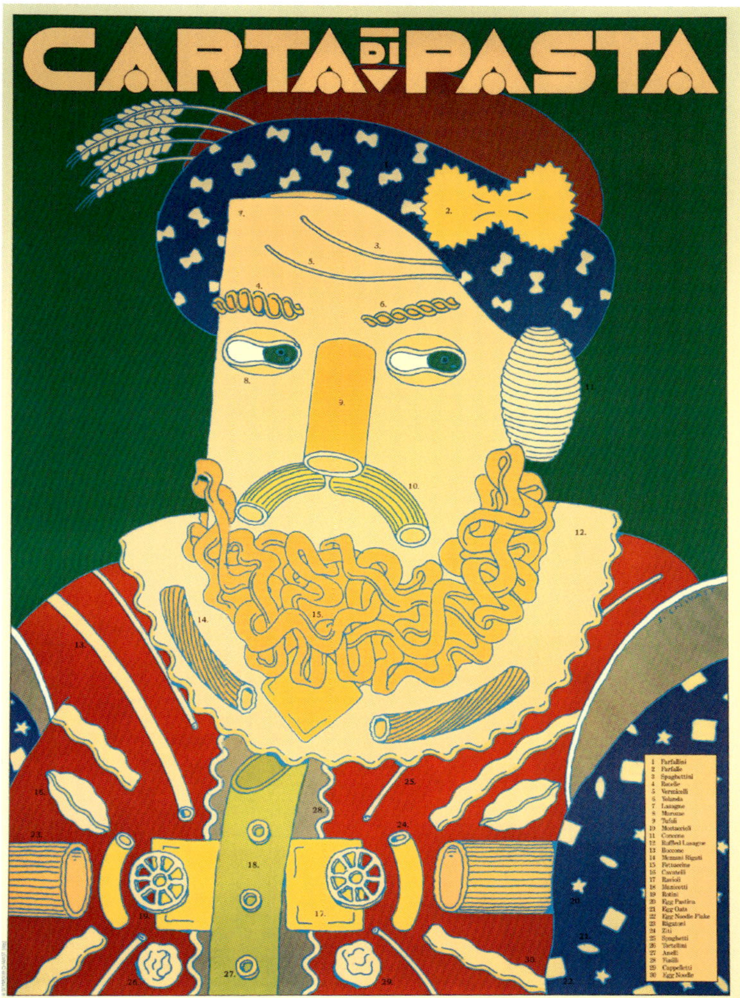

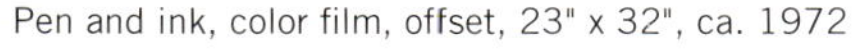
Pen and ink, color film, offset, 23" x 32", ca. 1972

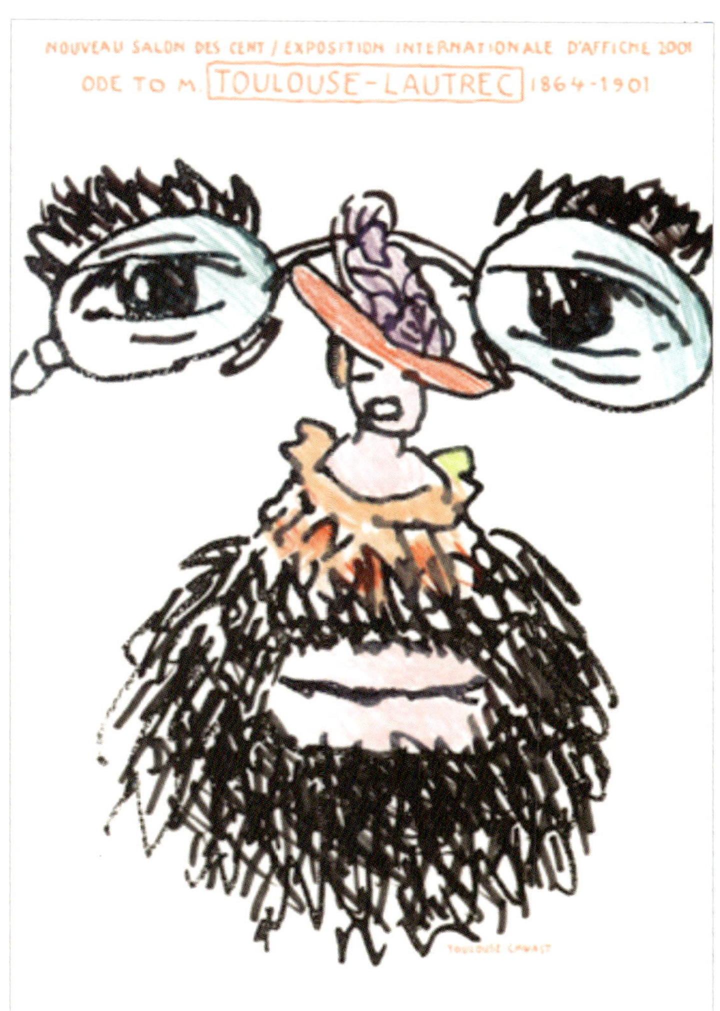

Marker, digital color, offset, 24" x 36", 2001

Left: **CARTA DI PASTA.** Giuseppe Arcimboldo was a sixteenth-century painter who created portraits with objects and food. Imitating his style, I created a poster with every variety of pasta. Hanging in an Italian restaurant in New York, it was used to point out the available pasta dishes to the customers.

Right: **TOULOUSE-LAUTREC.** For the anniversary of Henri de Toulouse-Lautrec's death in 1901, designers produced posters marking the date. My original drawing for the poster was 2 inches high.

Opposite: **RICK RUBIN'S NEW YORK.** Sonos headphones celebrated Rick Rubin, the music producer, with this map of his essential landmarks.

Below: **EXPO CAMPUS.** A promotional poster for *Madomoiselle Magazine*.

Opposite: **CÉLÉBRER.** One of many posters promoting tourism; I used a can-can figure pole-dancing with the Eiffel Tower.

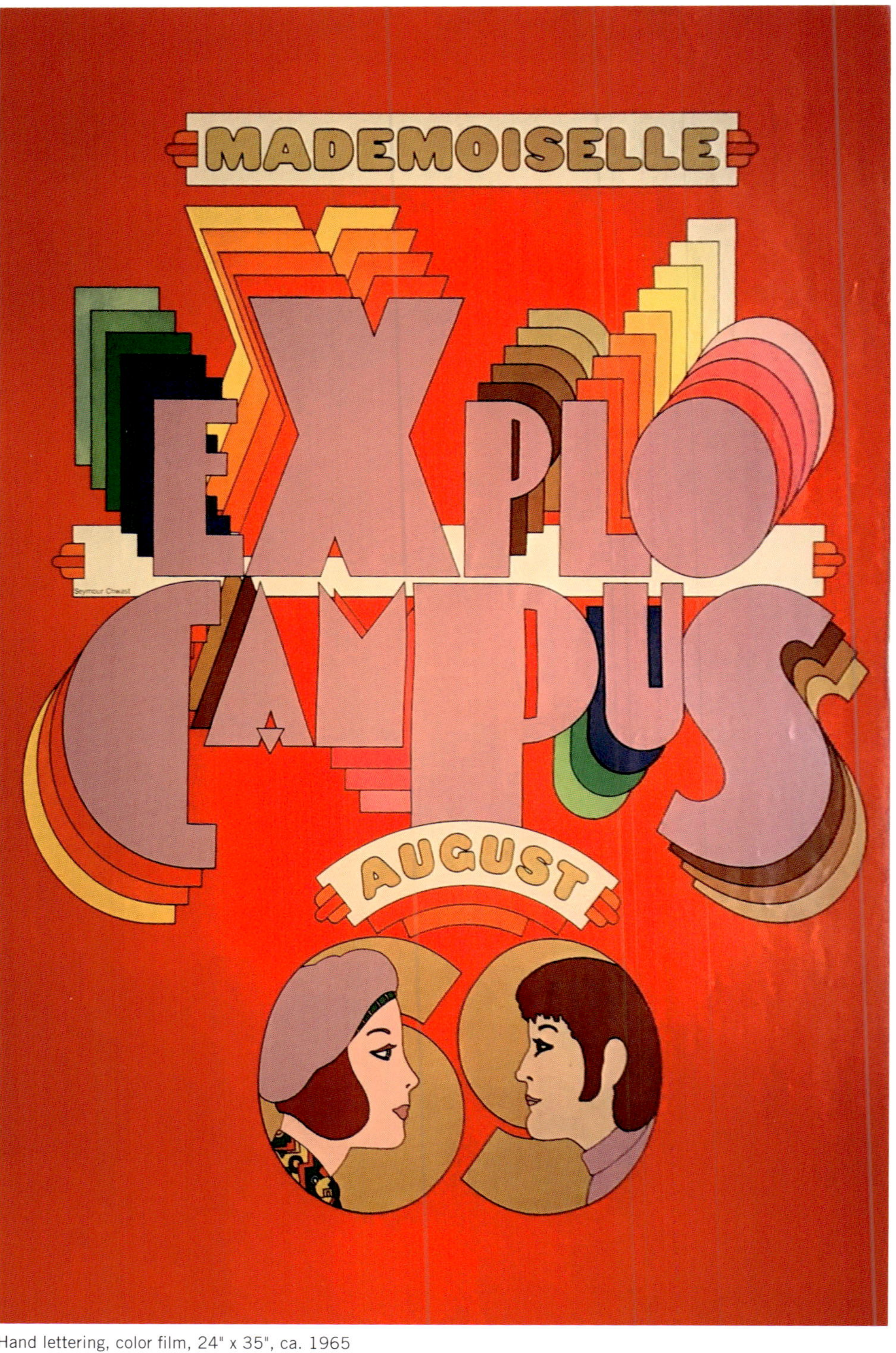

Hand lettering, color film, 24" x 35", ca. 1965

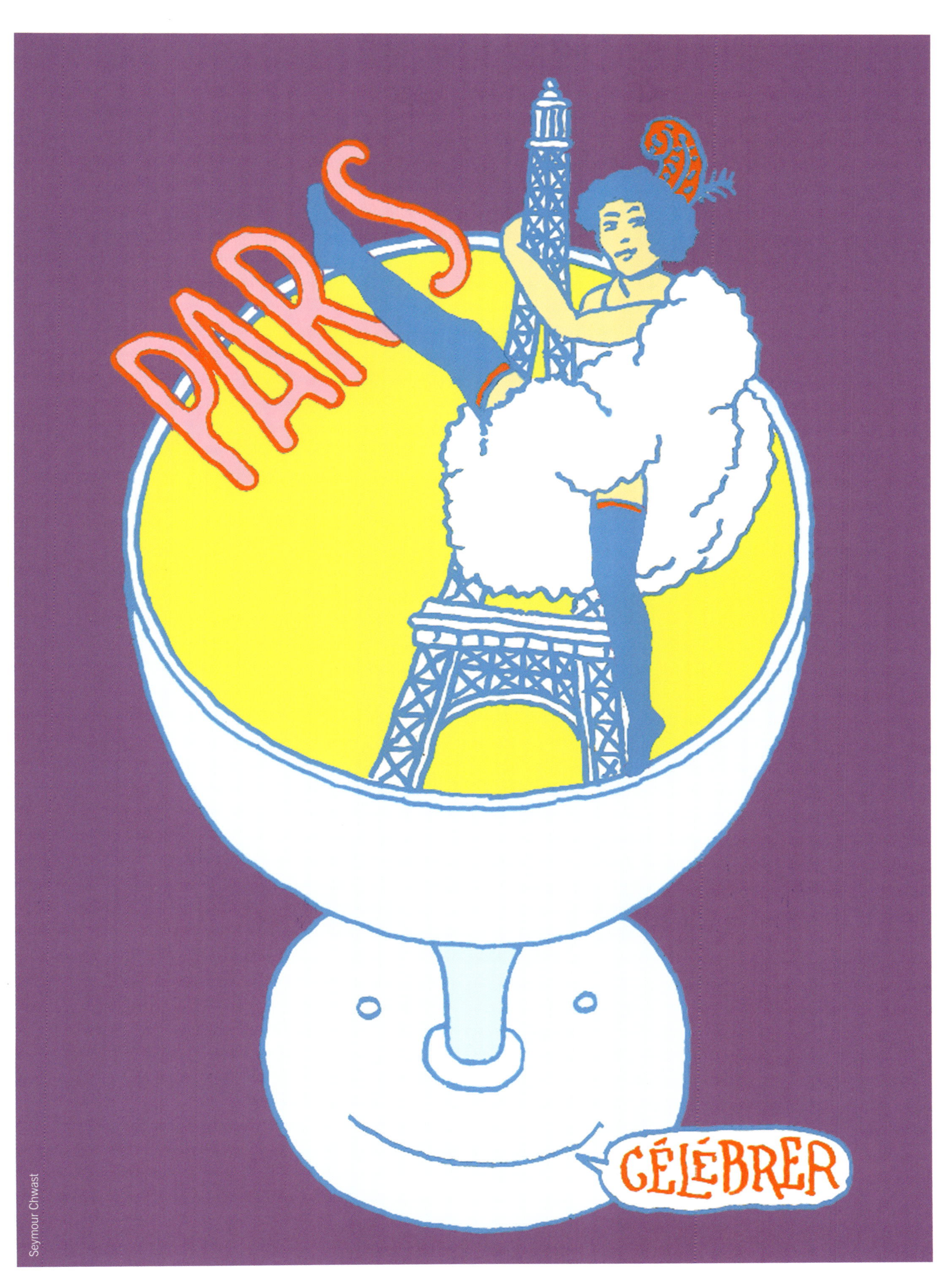

Pen and ink, digital color, 47" x 67", ca. 2013

CATCH THE RISING STARS. Arthur Ashe was the first African American athlete to win the singles title at Wimbledon, the US Open, and the Australian Open.

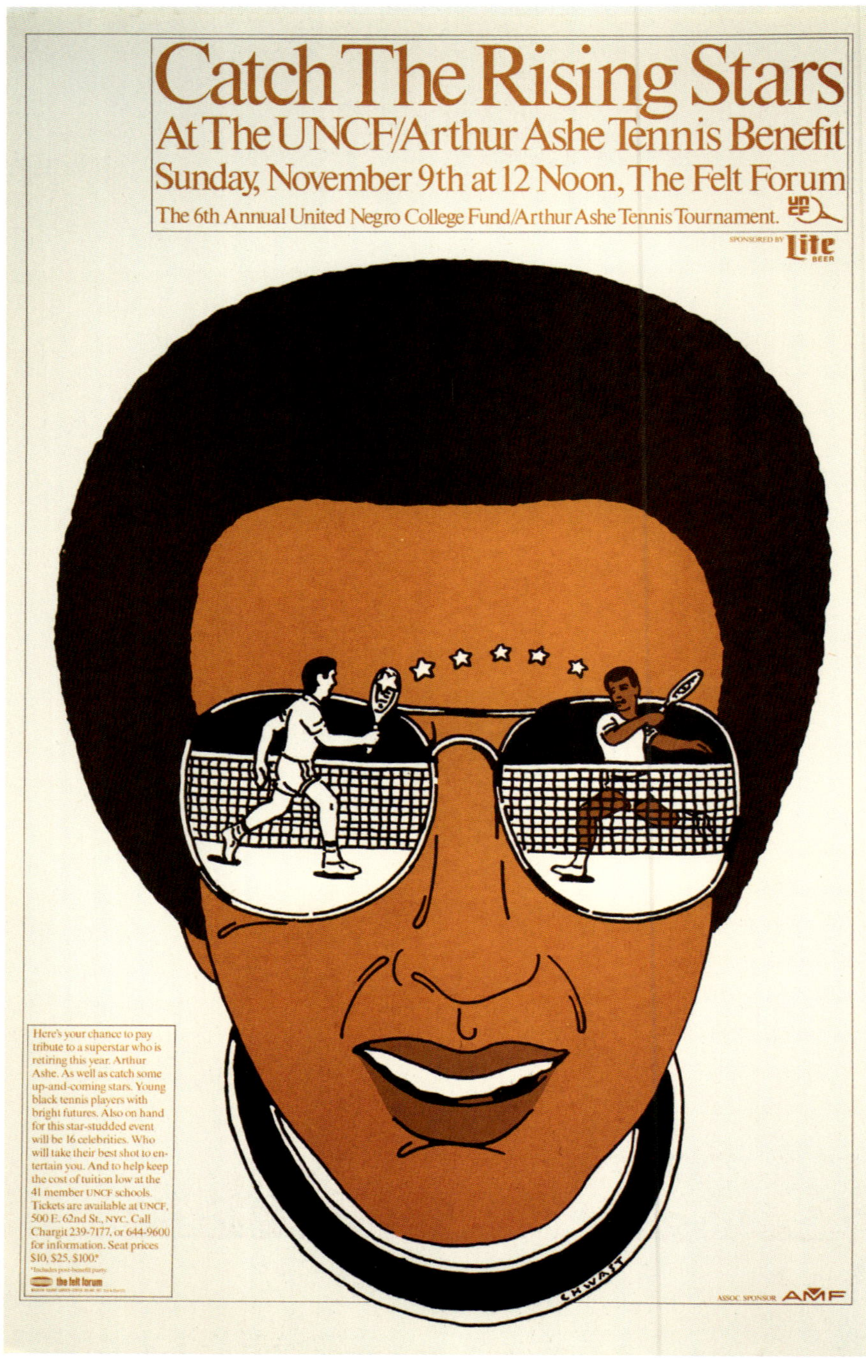

Marker and ink, filled in with color film, 14" x 22½", ca. 1978

EXHIBITS

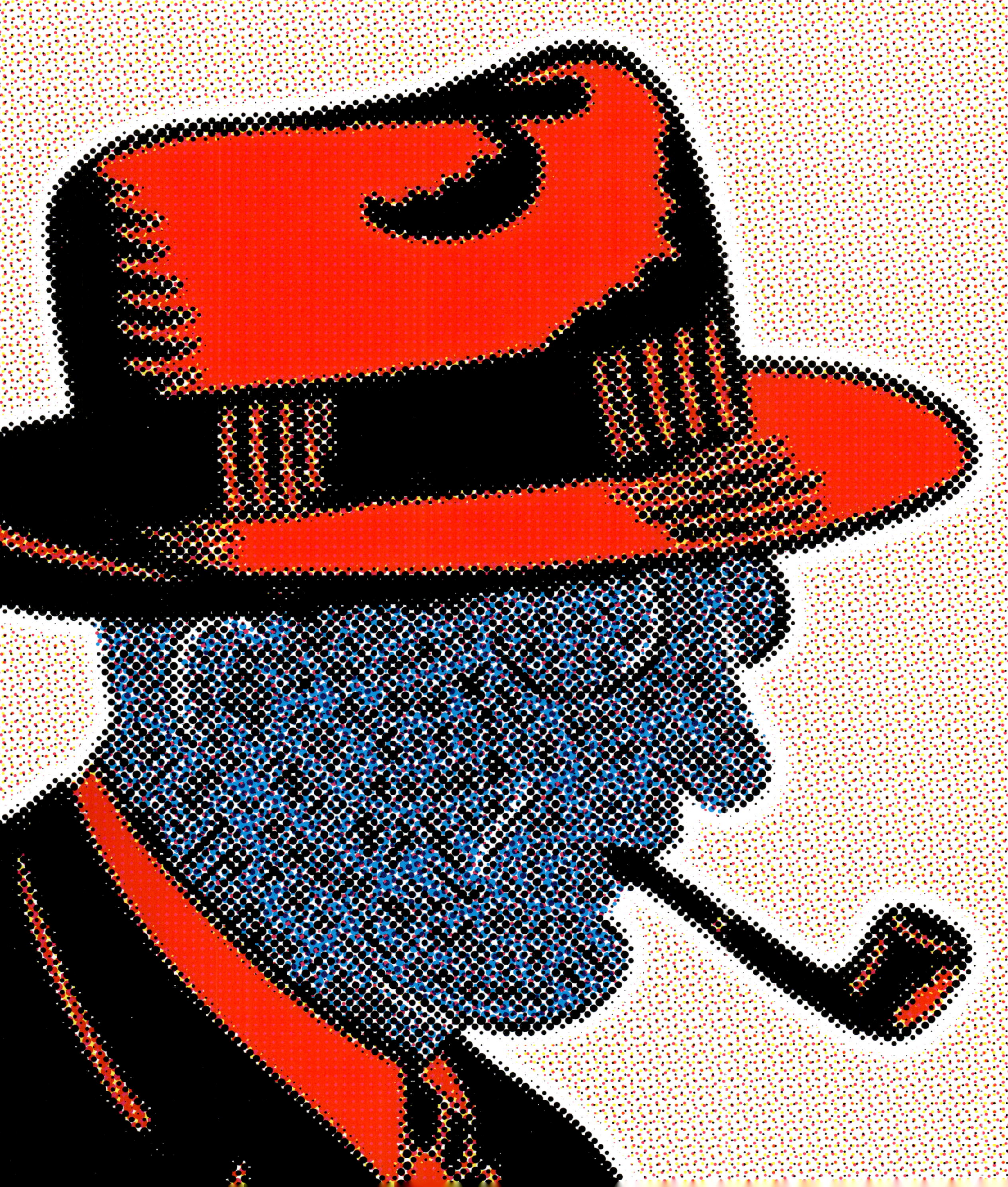

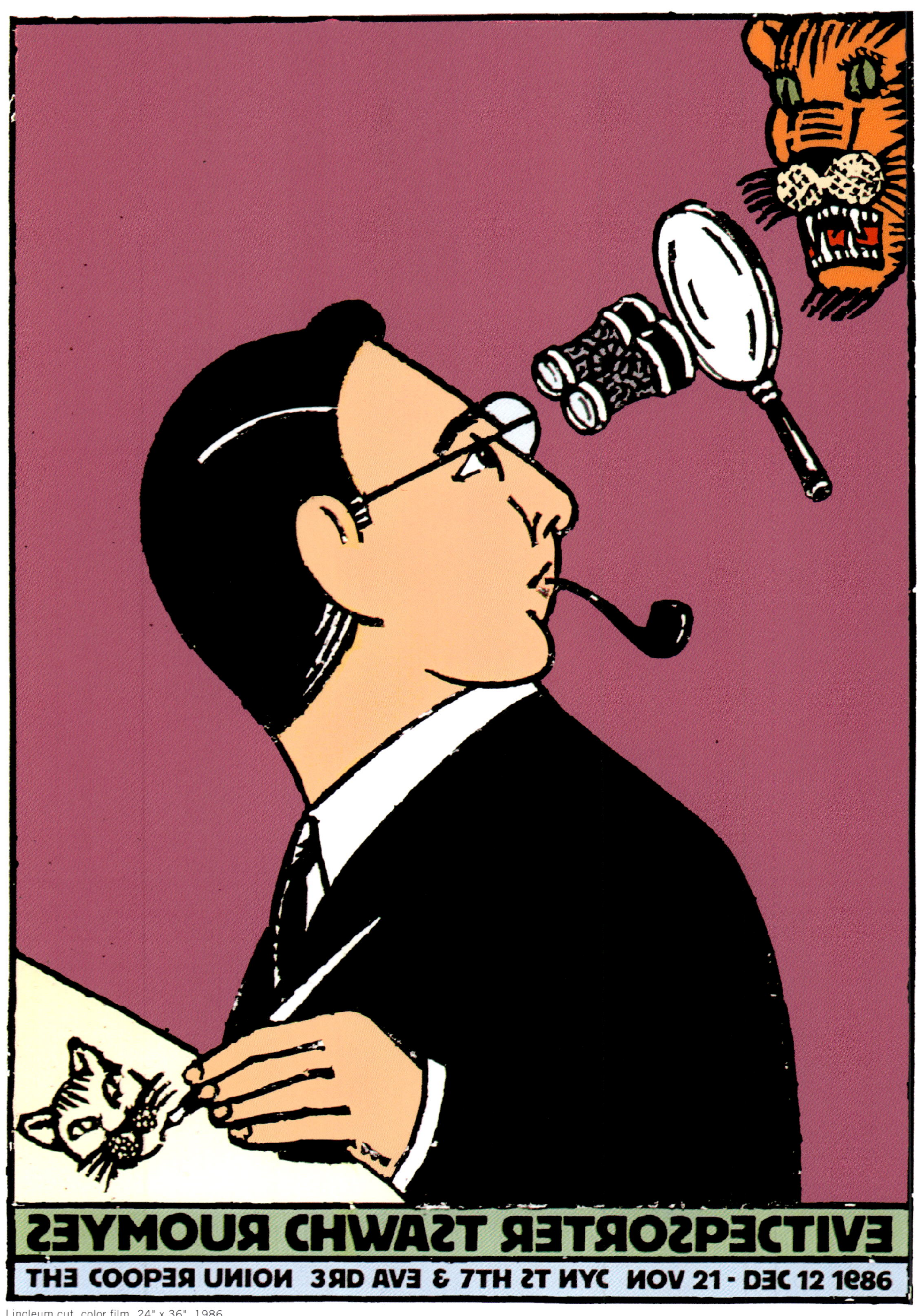

Linoleum cut, color film, 24" x 36", 1986

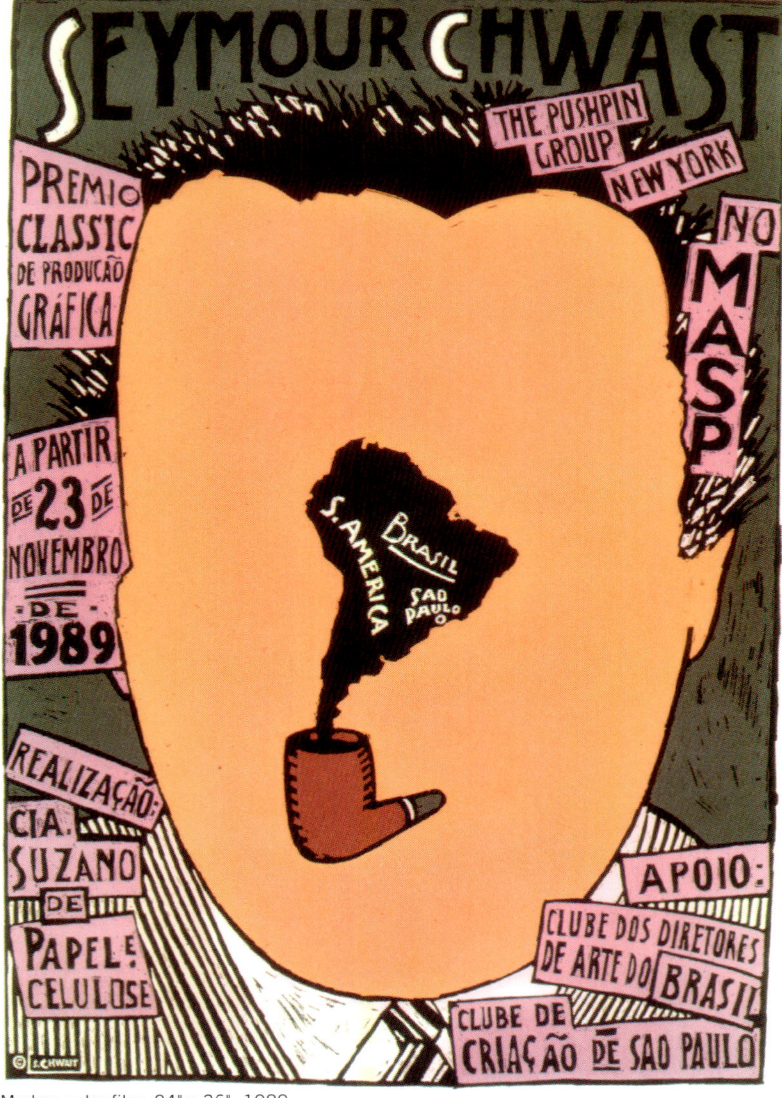

Marker, color film, 24" x 36", 1989

Opposite: **RETROSPECTIVE.** My alma mater, the Cooper Union, gave me a show of my work. The basic art was a linoleum cut. When my design was on the press, ready to print, I got a frantic call from the printer asking if the backward letters were a mistake. I assured him that they were part of the idea of a retrospective show.

Left: **SEYMOUR CHWAST IN BRASIL.** Smoke from my pipe conveniently formed the shape of Brazil, where in São Paulo I exhibited my work in their Museum of Modern Art; the woodcut style was inspired by the Mexican artist José-Guadalupe Posada.

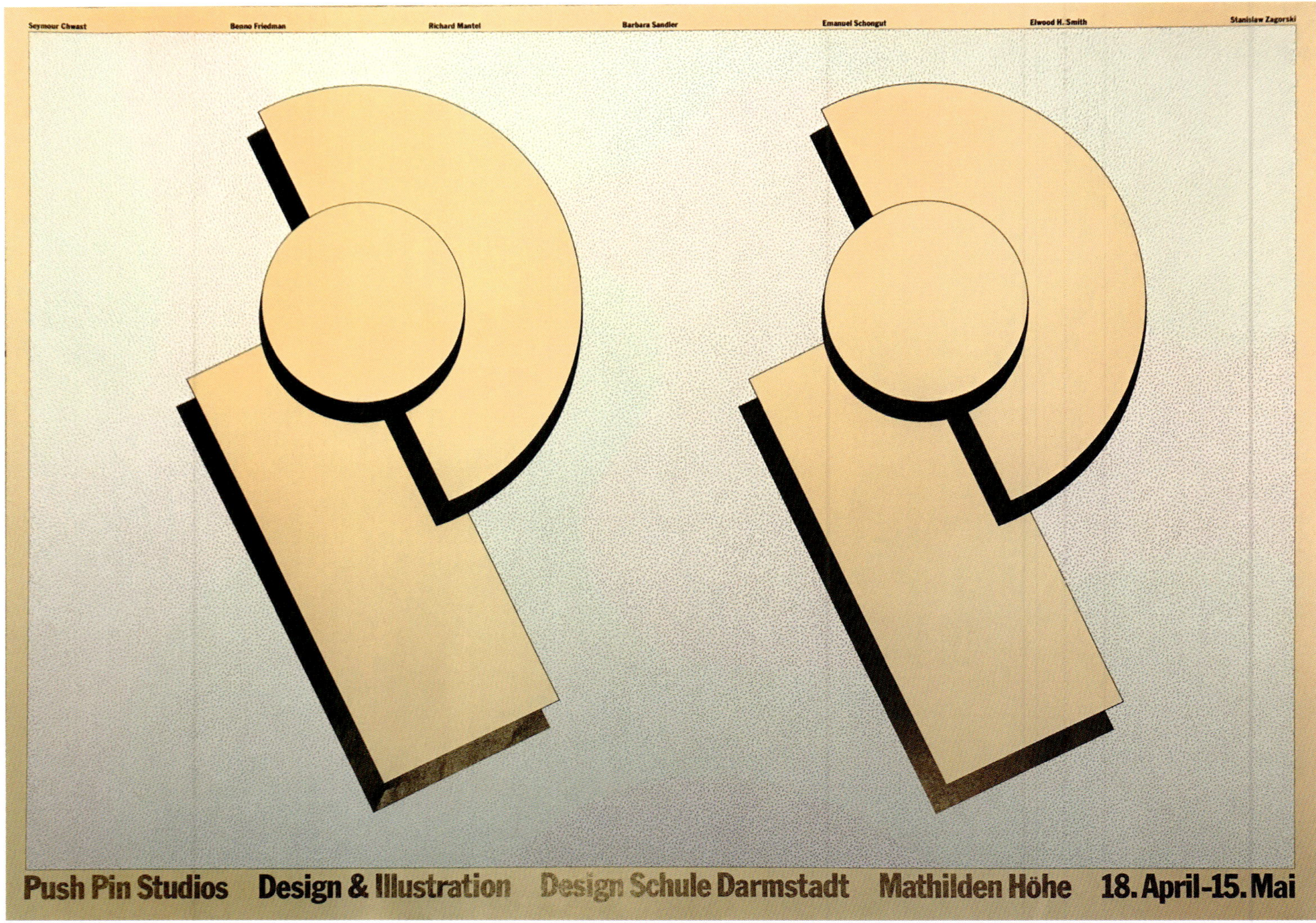

Mechanical art, offset, 27" x 19", ca. 1984

Above: **PP.** Push Pin Studios exhibited in Darmstadt, Germany. Typographic forms come in handy when no single image would work for a group show.

Opposite: **THE SHOE.** I violated my own rule that every aspect of a design must have meaning in order to communicate the message. This has none. One image is as good as another for an exhibition poster.

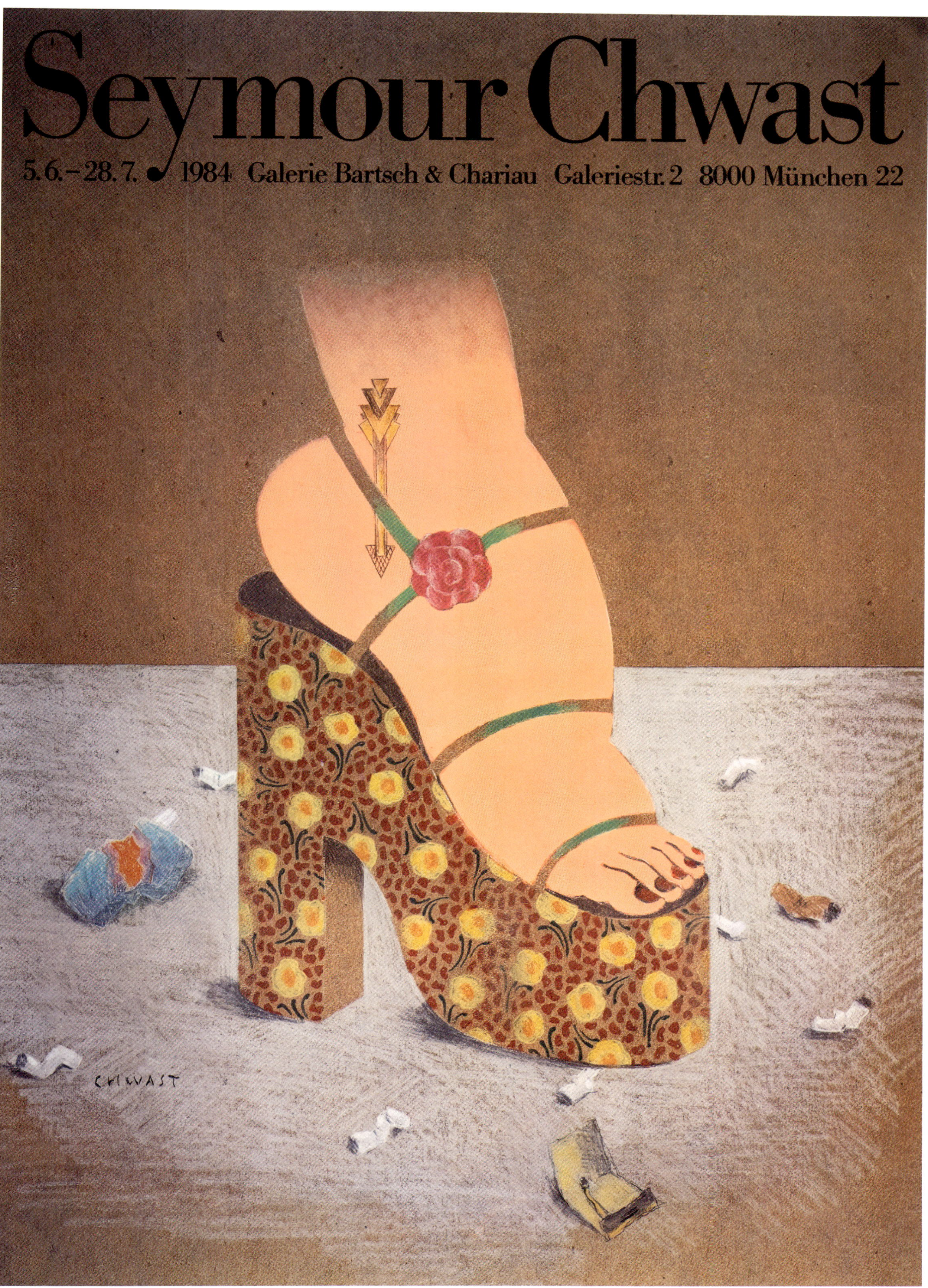

Acrylic and colored pencil on board, offset, 23.5" x 33", 1984

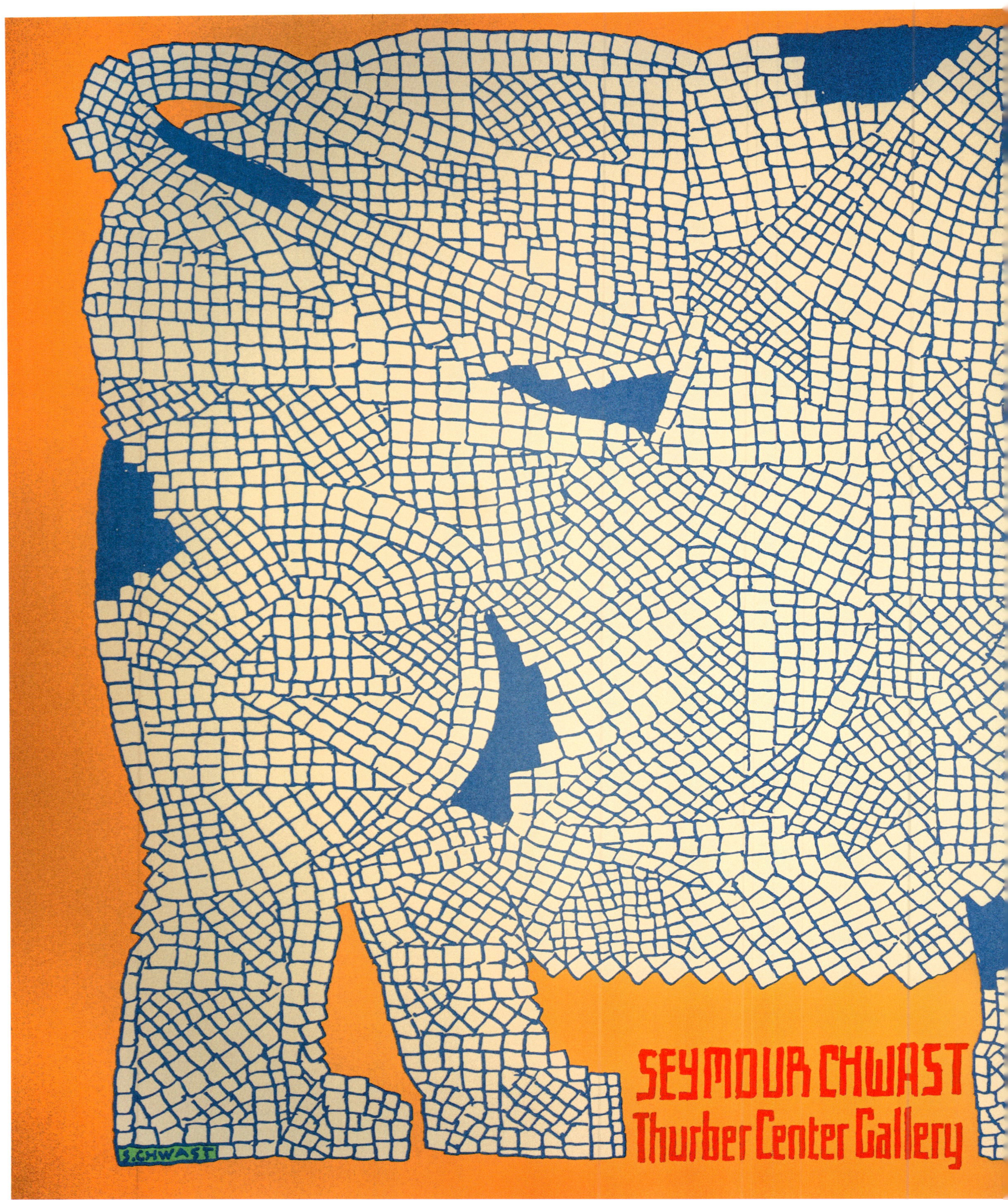

Mixed media, offset, 36" x 23", 1996

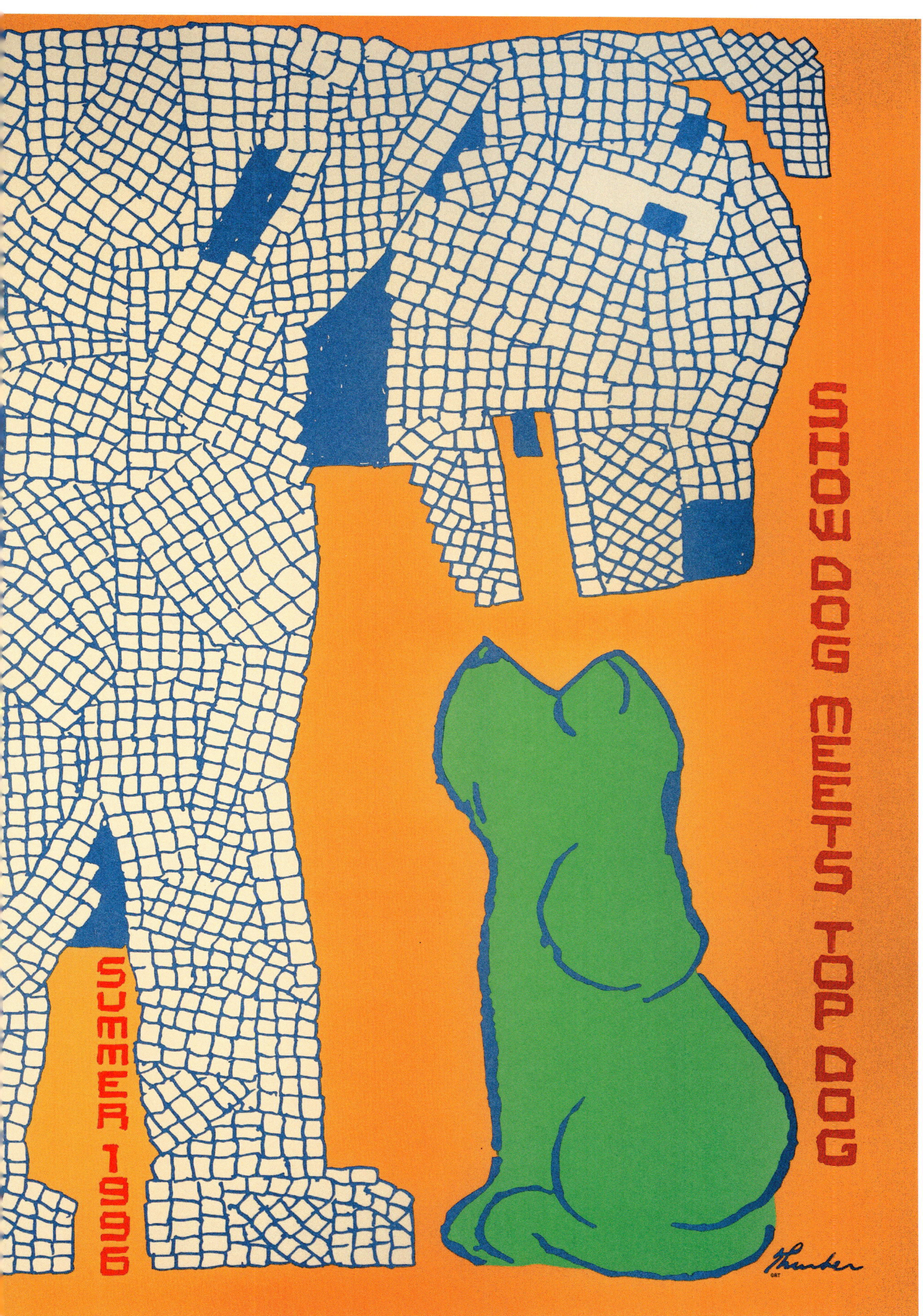

JAMES THURBER. The legacy of my favorite *New Yorker* magazine cartoonist is protected by the Thurber Center in Cleveland. For this exhibit, I used one of his iconic dog drawings to contrast in style, and size, with one of my own.

FROM BROOKLYN TO THE SEA. The posters on this and the following spread were announcements for exhibitions at the Museum of the Borough of Brooklyn.

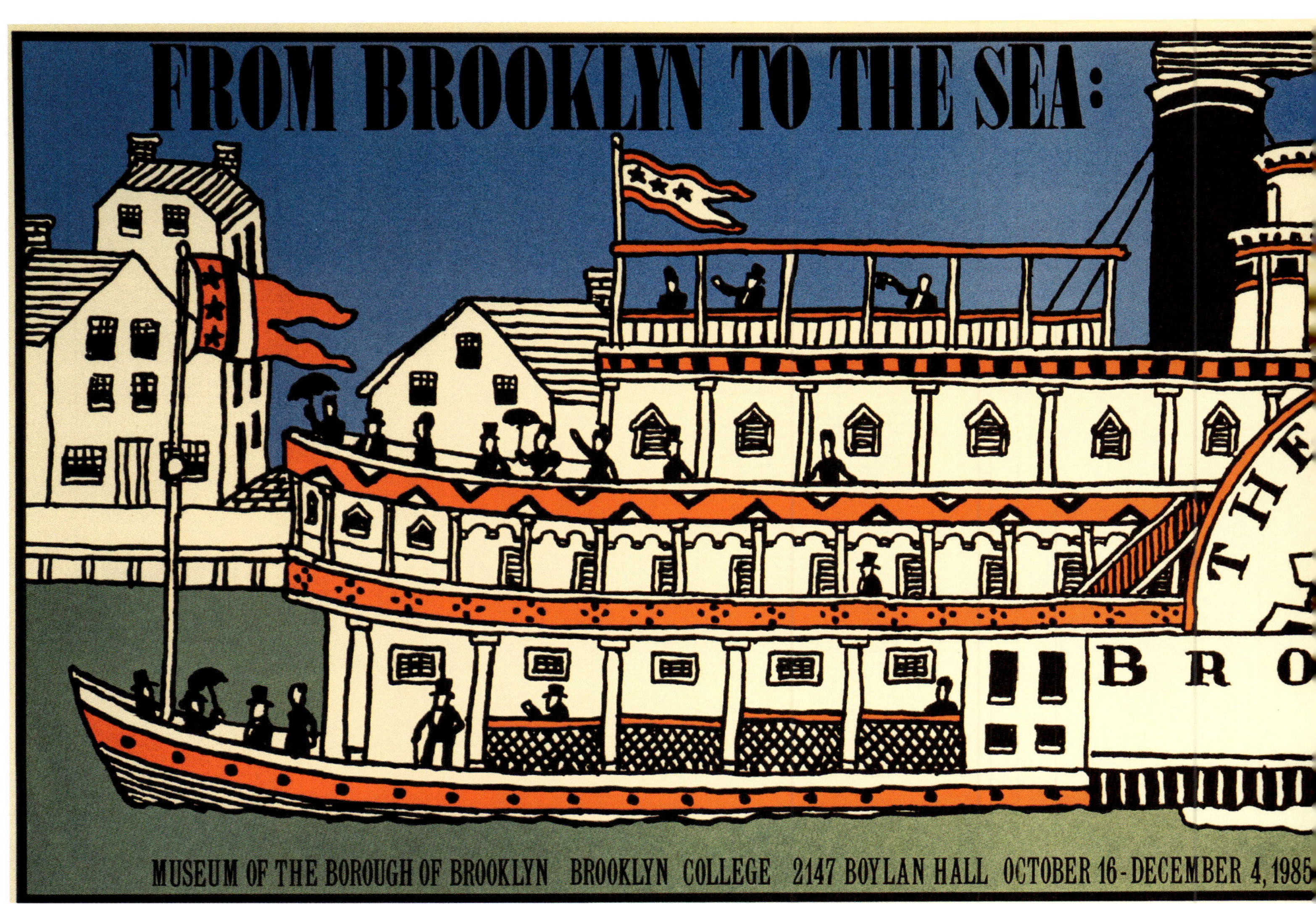

Marker, color film, offset, 23.5" x 33", 1985

THE MUSEUM OF THE BOROUGH OF BROOKLYN

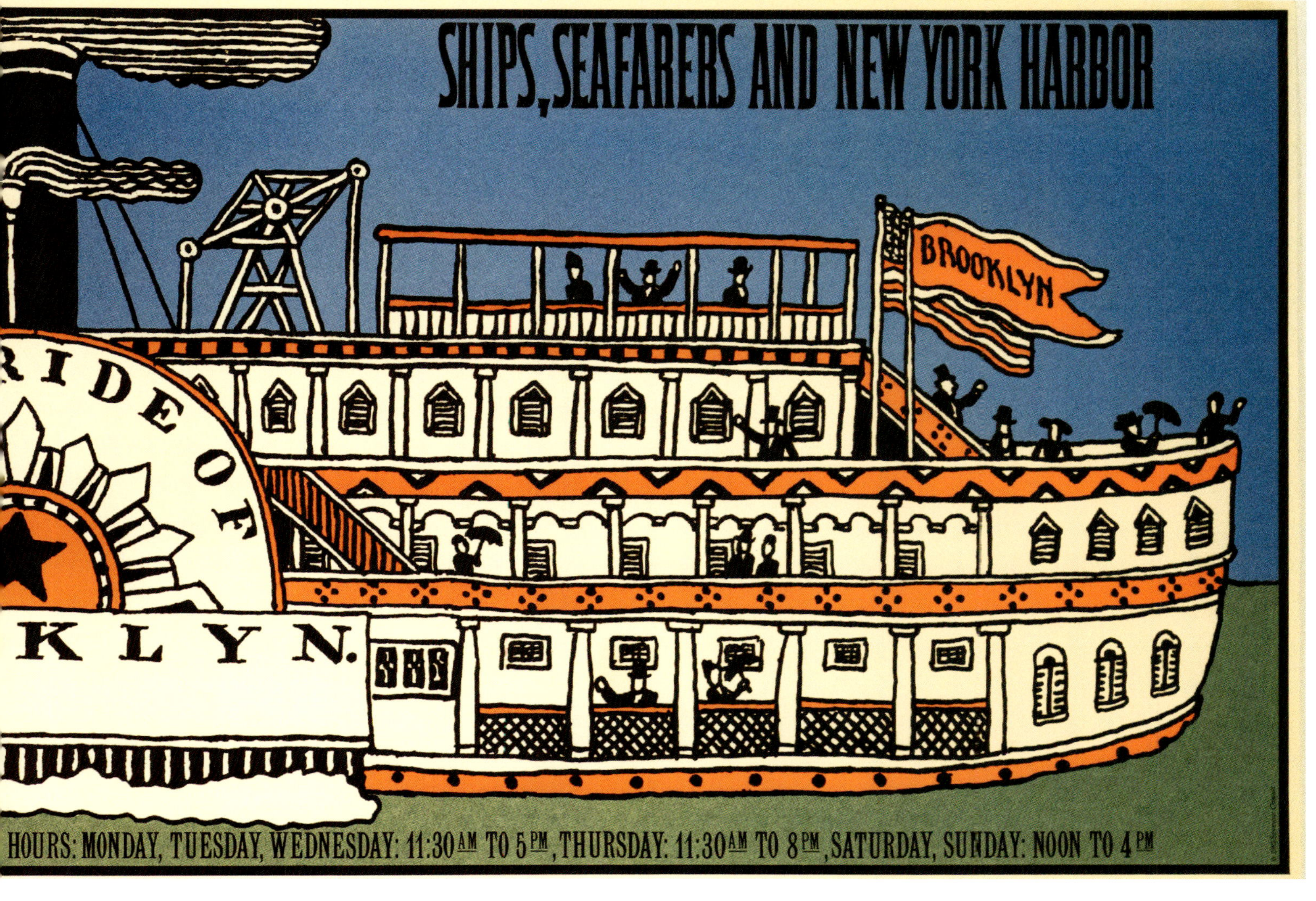

Right: **FUN AND FANTASY.** A face with an enormous grin was the mascot of the long-gone Steeplechase Park amusement center in Coney Island. This is my version with the head right side up and upside down.

Opposite: **THE GRAND GAME OF BASEBALL.** Brooklyn's favorite team, the Dodgers, is featured in an exhibit of art and artifacts.

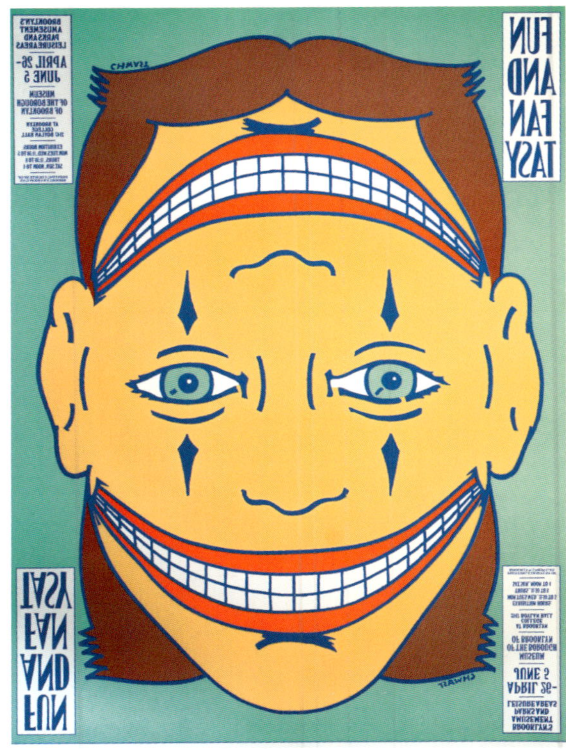

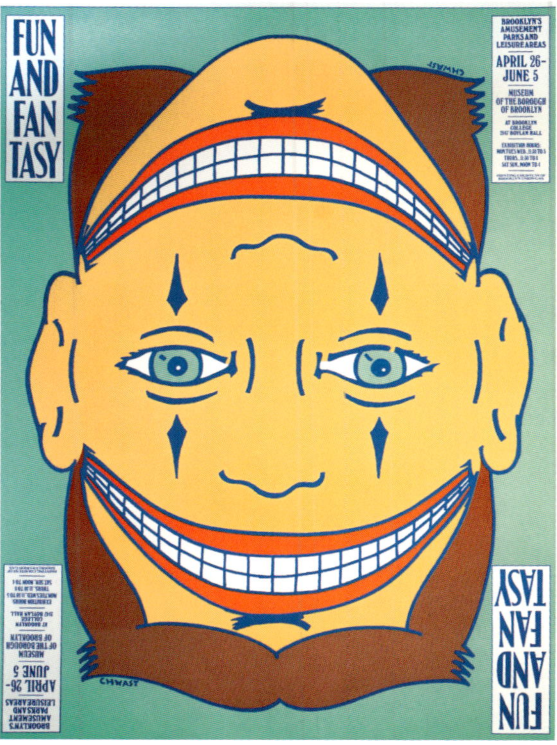

Marker, color film, offset, 24" x 36", ca. 1986

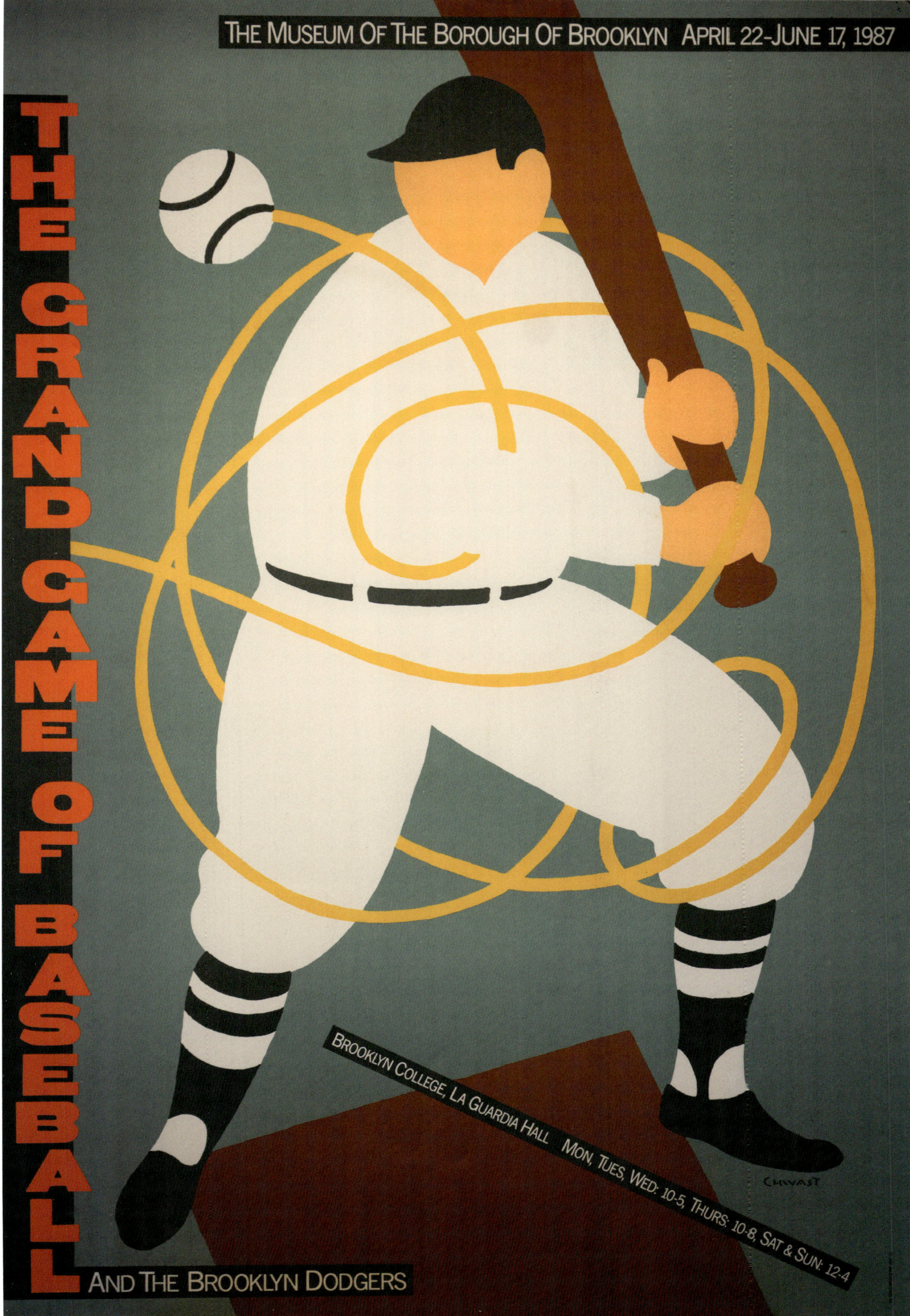

Color film, offset, 24" x 36", 1987

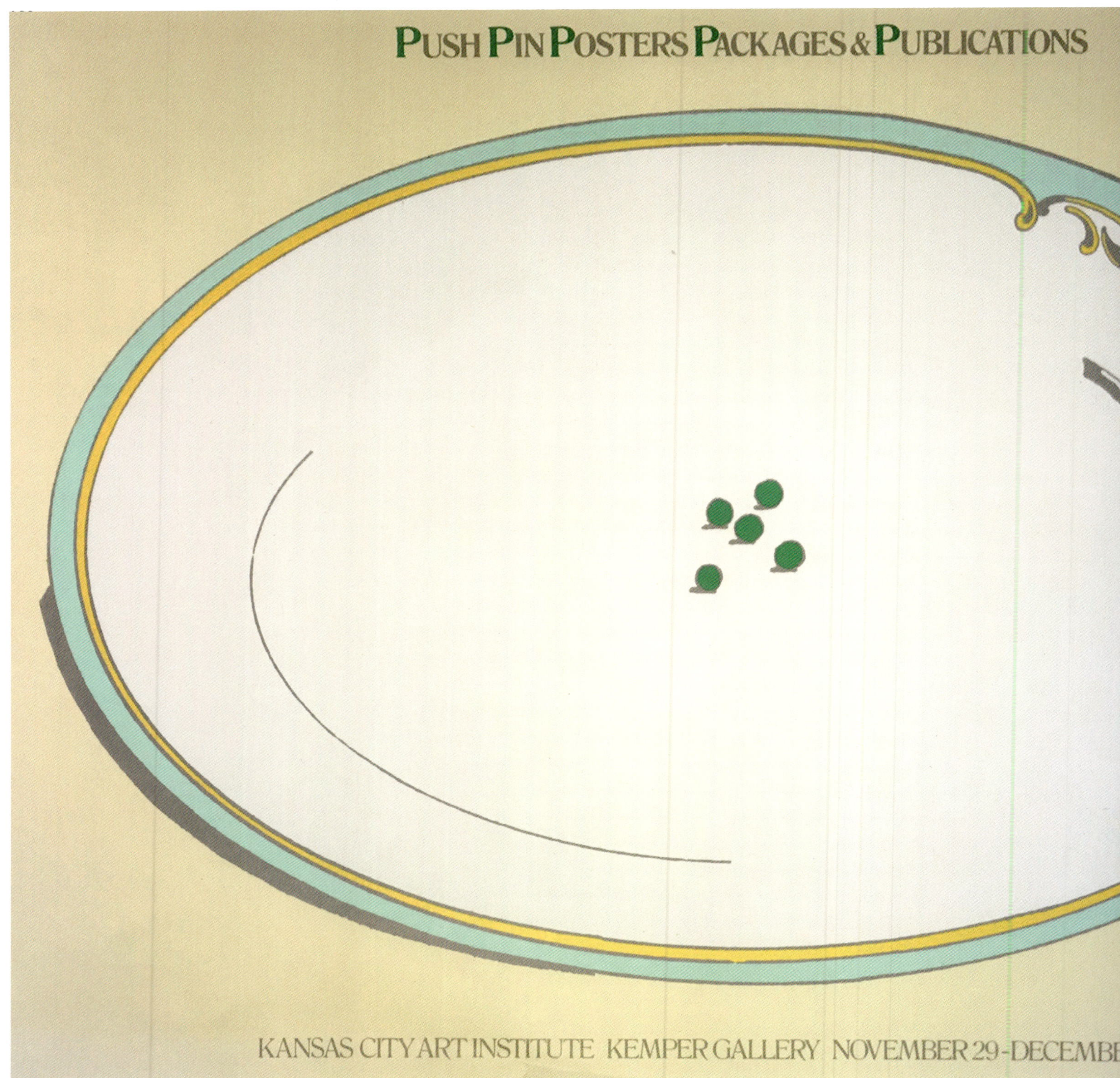

Mechanical art, color film, offset, 18" x 24", 1979

Above: **FIVE PEAS.** Five Peas was designed with Richard Mantel. Most of what we show happens to begin with a P. The charm is with the pathetically small peas in a sea of white space.

Opposite: **THE LOUVRE.** In 1970, Push Pin Studios was honored with a show of work at the Louvre's Musee des Arts Decorativs in Paris. While Glaser and I collaborated on many assignments, this design is mostly his. I include it because it was the first time an American design firm had a show at the Louvre.

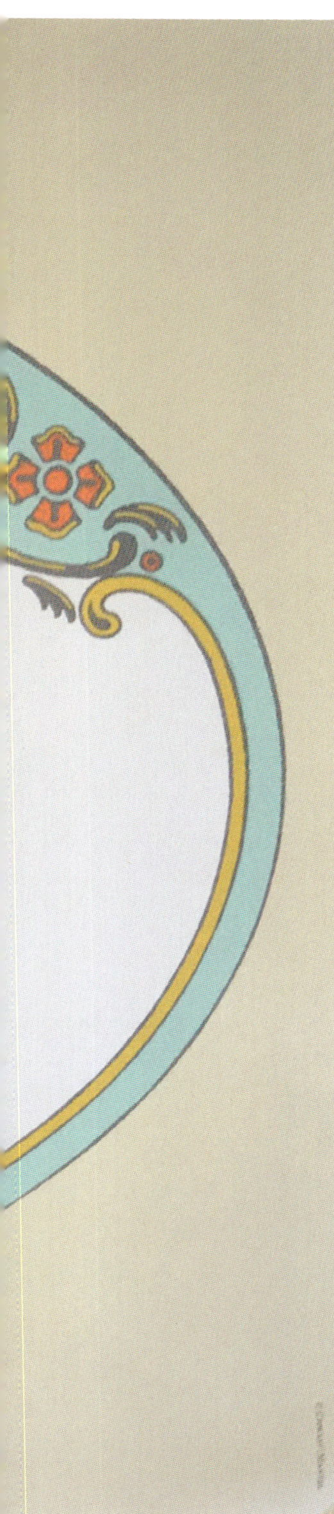

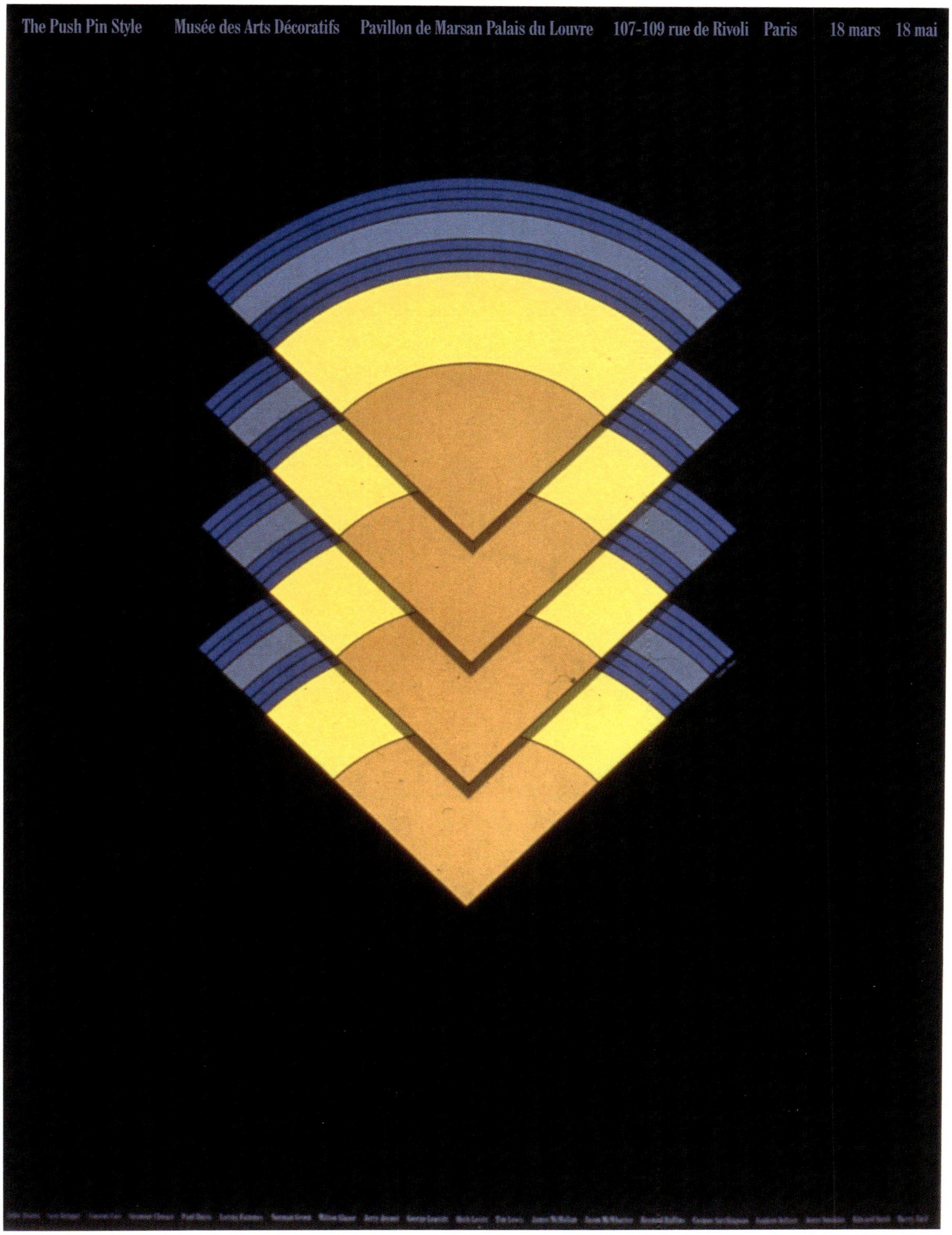

The Push Pin Style Musée des Arts Décoratifs Pavillon de Marsan Palais du Louvre 107-109 rue de Rivoli Paris 18 mars 18 mai

Mechanical art, color film, offset, 19" x 25½", 1970

"MY BEST WORK"

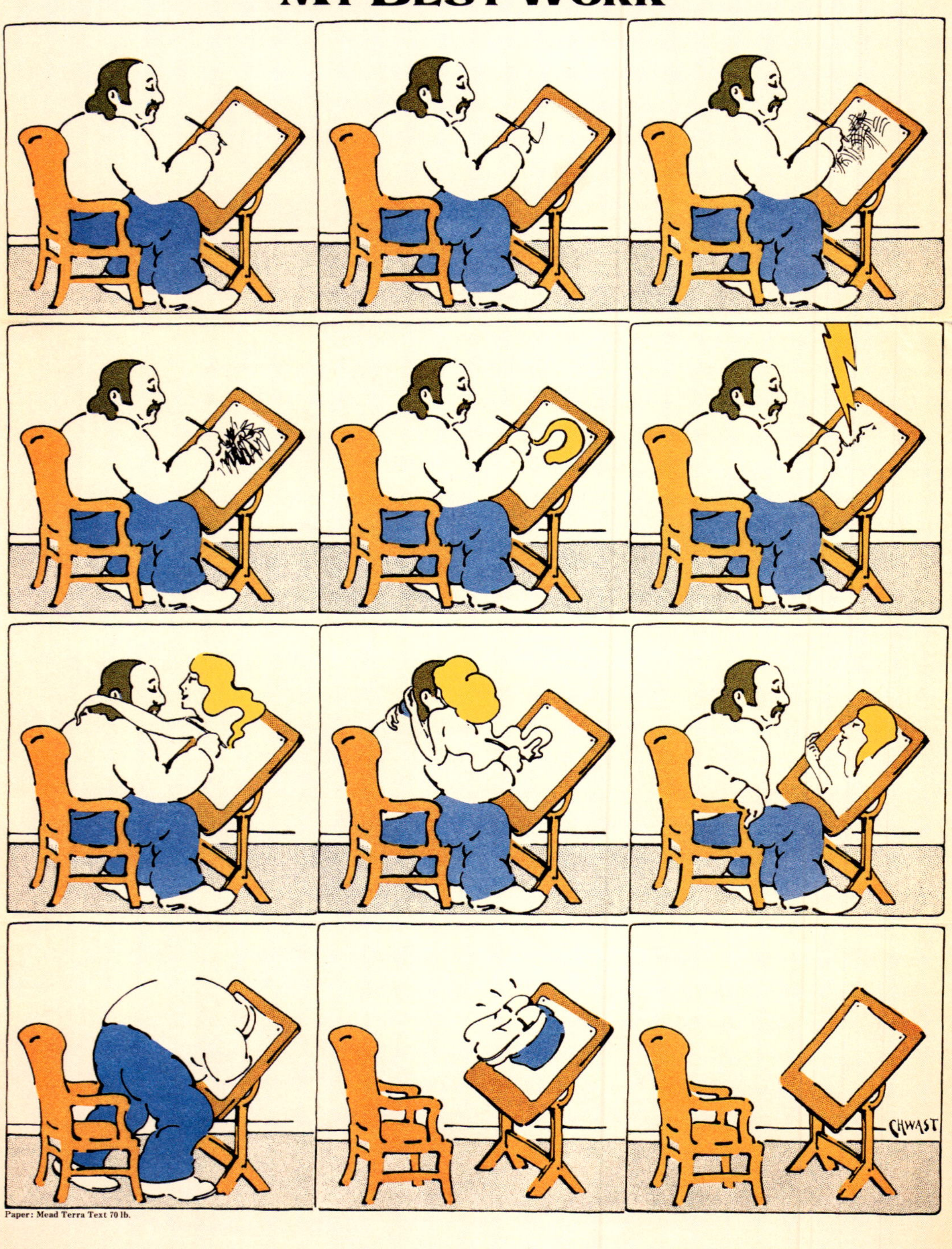

A Retrospective Exhibition of Design, Illustration and Photography Selected by the Artists

John Alcorn
Ted Andresakes
Sam Antupit
Emil Antonucci
Dominic Arbitrio
Herman Aronson
R. O. Blechman
Bruce Blackburn
Arthur Boden
Ewald Breuer
Bruno Brugnatelli
Will Burtin
Jesse Califano
Vincent Ceci
Ivan Chermayeff
Roger Cook
Al Corchia
Seymour Chwast
Richard Danne
Paul Davis
Rudolph de Harak
Joseph del Gaudio
Joseph Bourke Del Valle
Seldon Dix
Lou Dorfsman
Bill Duevell
David Enock
Sandy Erickson
Ed Fitt
Beau Gardner
Thomas Geismar
John Gilbert
Milton Glaser
Diana Graham
Norman Green
Norman Griner
Robert Grossman
Richard Henderson
Dick Hess
Clyde Hogg
Harry Jacobs
Hedda Johnson
Art Kane
Mo Lebowitz
George Lois
Herb Lubalin
Giuseppe Lucci
Jay Maisel
Mary Matthews
Peter Max
James Mc Mullan
James Miho
Tomoko Miho
John Milligan
Ron Morgan
Luanne Mount
Jon Naar
David November
Robert Paganucci
Don Page
Tony Palladino
Jim Pringle
Paul Rand
Jack Reich
Kenneth Resen
Doyle Robinson
Arnold Saks
Robert Salpeter
Cosmos Sarchiapone
Sheldon Seidler
Isadore Seltzer
Gene Sercander
Don Shanosky
Amasa G. Smith, Jr.
Edward Sorel
William Tobias
Don Trousdell
George Tscherny
Massimo Vignelli
Barry Zaid
Roger Zimmerman

March 17 to April 30, 1971
Monday through Friday
9 am to 5 pm

Mead Library of Ideas
Pan Am Building
200 Park Avenue,
New York, N.Y.
(212) 972-2347

Marker, color film, offset, 12½" x 24", 1971

Opposite: **MY BEST WORK.** This cartoon, announcing a show of illustrators, was influenced by work in *Jugend*, a popular German magazine. It was published between 1880 and 1920. The work was unusual because his lines were disconnected, giving it a unique quality. I followed this style for years and was copied by others.

Below: **GREENGRASS GALLERY.** A woodcut monkey announced a show of artists who designed record covers.

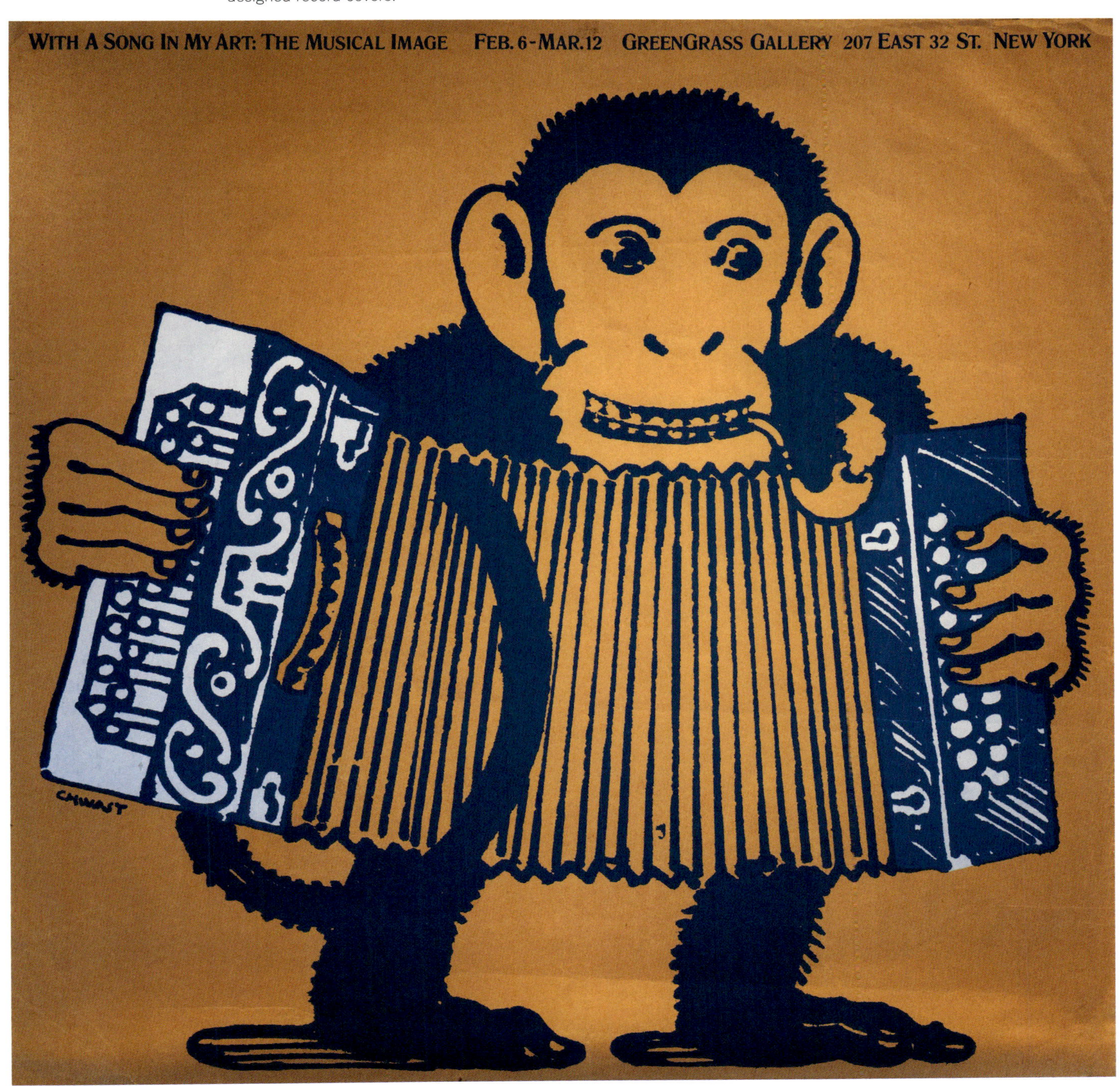

Marker, silkscreen, 36" x 36", ca. 1976

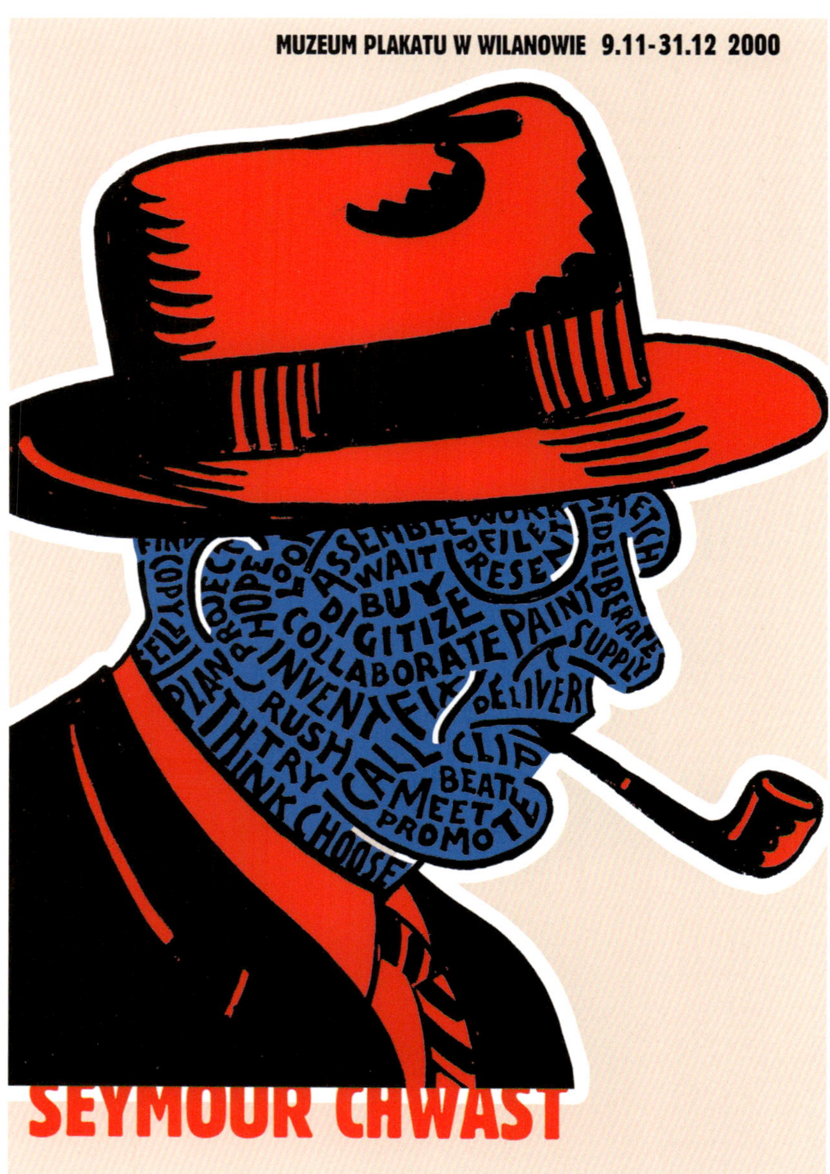

Marker and ink, color film, offset, 23½" x 36", 2000

Left: **POLISH POSTER MUSEUM.** This was a major exhibit of my work in the Muzeum Plakatu Wilanowie, the poster museum outside Warsaw.

Below: **IN AMBROSIANA.** I was judge in a poster biennial in Brno in the Czech Republic. A local gallery presented my work. Do not look for meaning in my broken cup.

Opposite: **AMERICAN HEAD.** This map shows the route from my apartment to the School of Visual Art, where my exhibit was held. It was one of the Master Series shows of designers and illustrators.

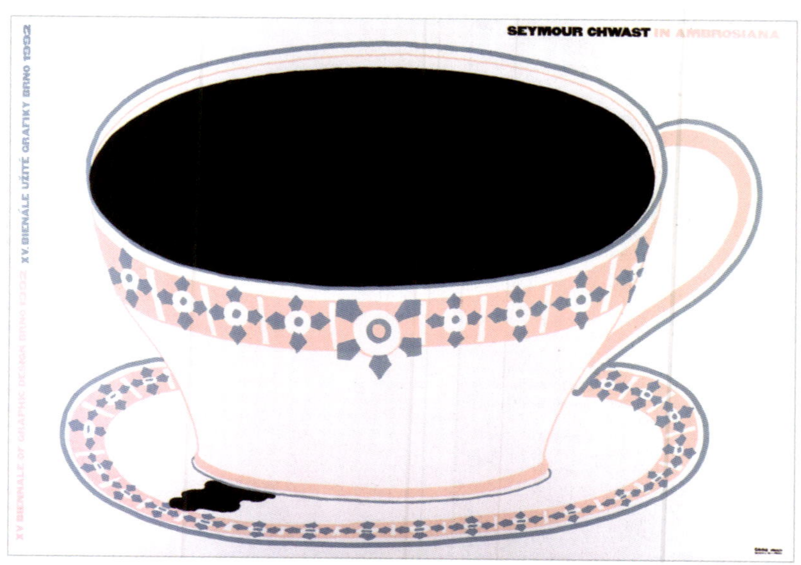

Marker and ink, color film, offset, 33" x 23½", 1992

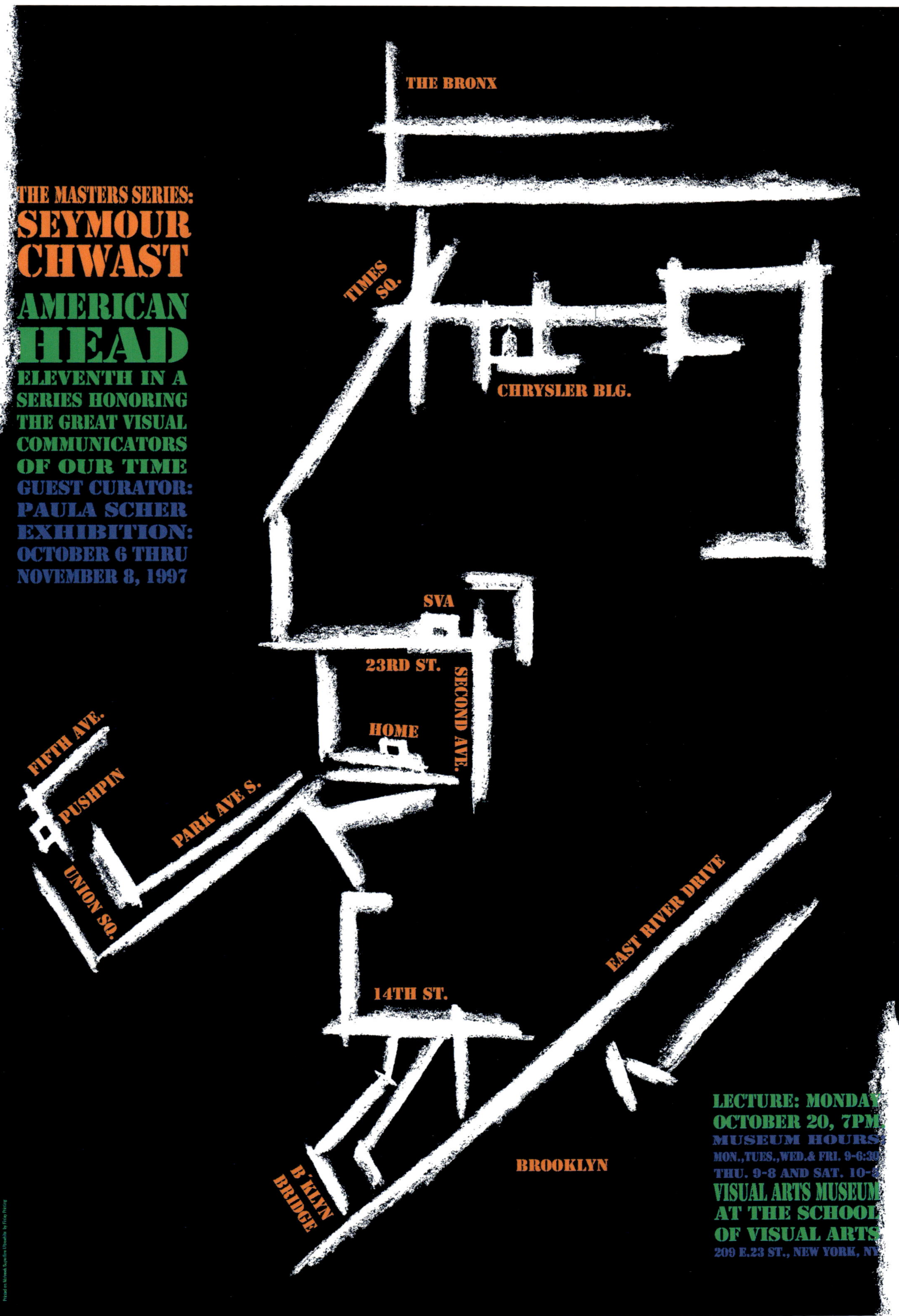

Brush and ink, offset, 24" x 36", 1997

Below: **PUSH PIN BUTCHER.** For a Push Pin exhibit in Paris, the butcher's apron offered me a white space to announce other shows. Alas, it was used only once. I gave the butcher sunglasses to add character, but some viewers thought him a blind butcher who would not last on the job.

Opposite: **PUSHPIN AND BEYOND.** Glaser, along with Jim McMullen, Paul Davis, and I, had a show at the Suntory Poster Museum in Osaka, Japan. To promote the show, each of us rendered his own idea of a robot for a poster. This was mine.

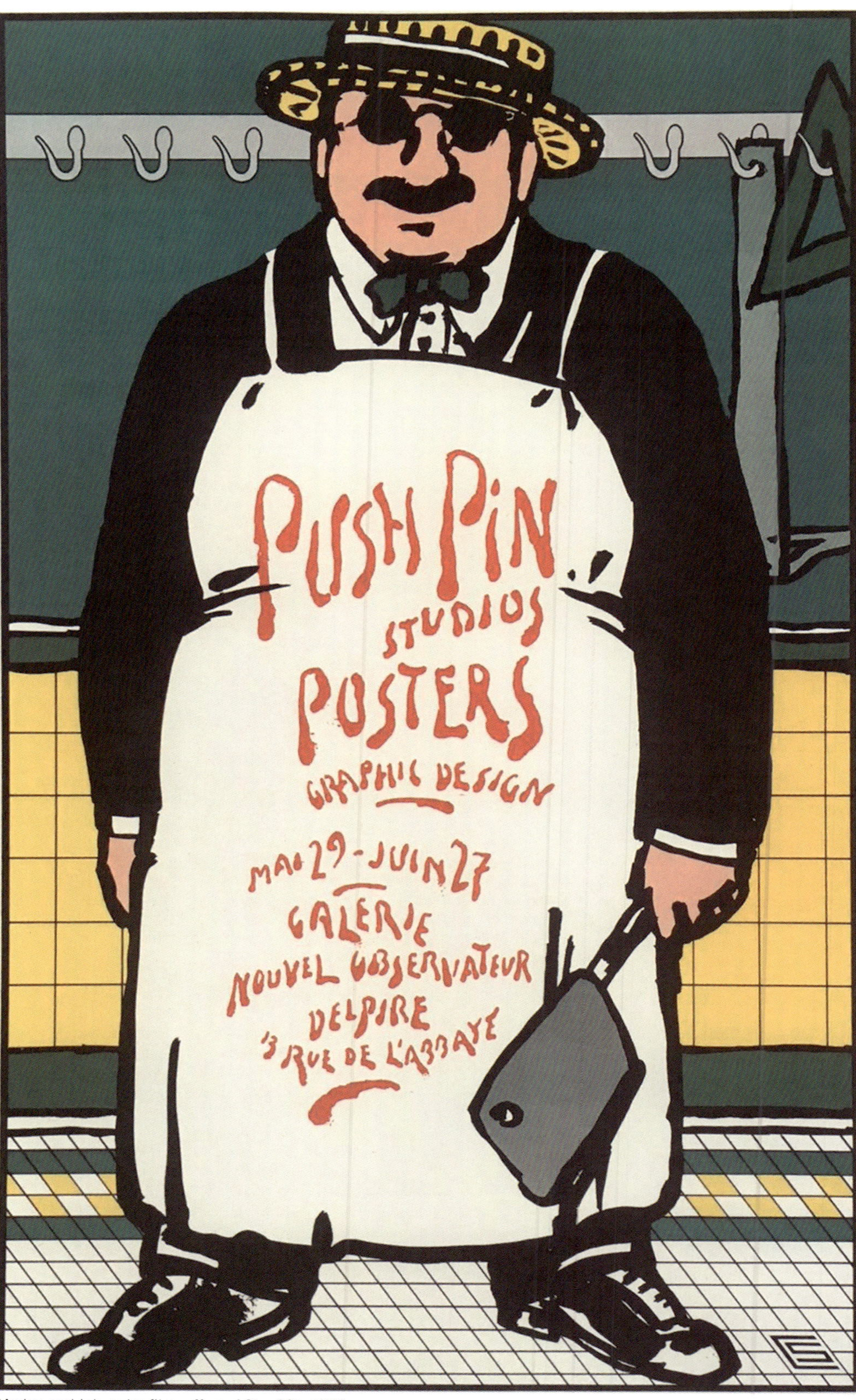

Marker and ink, color film, offset, 18" x 29", 1981

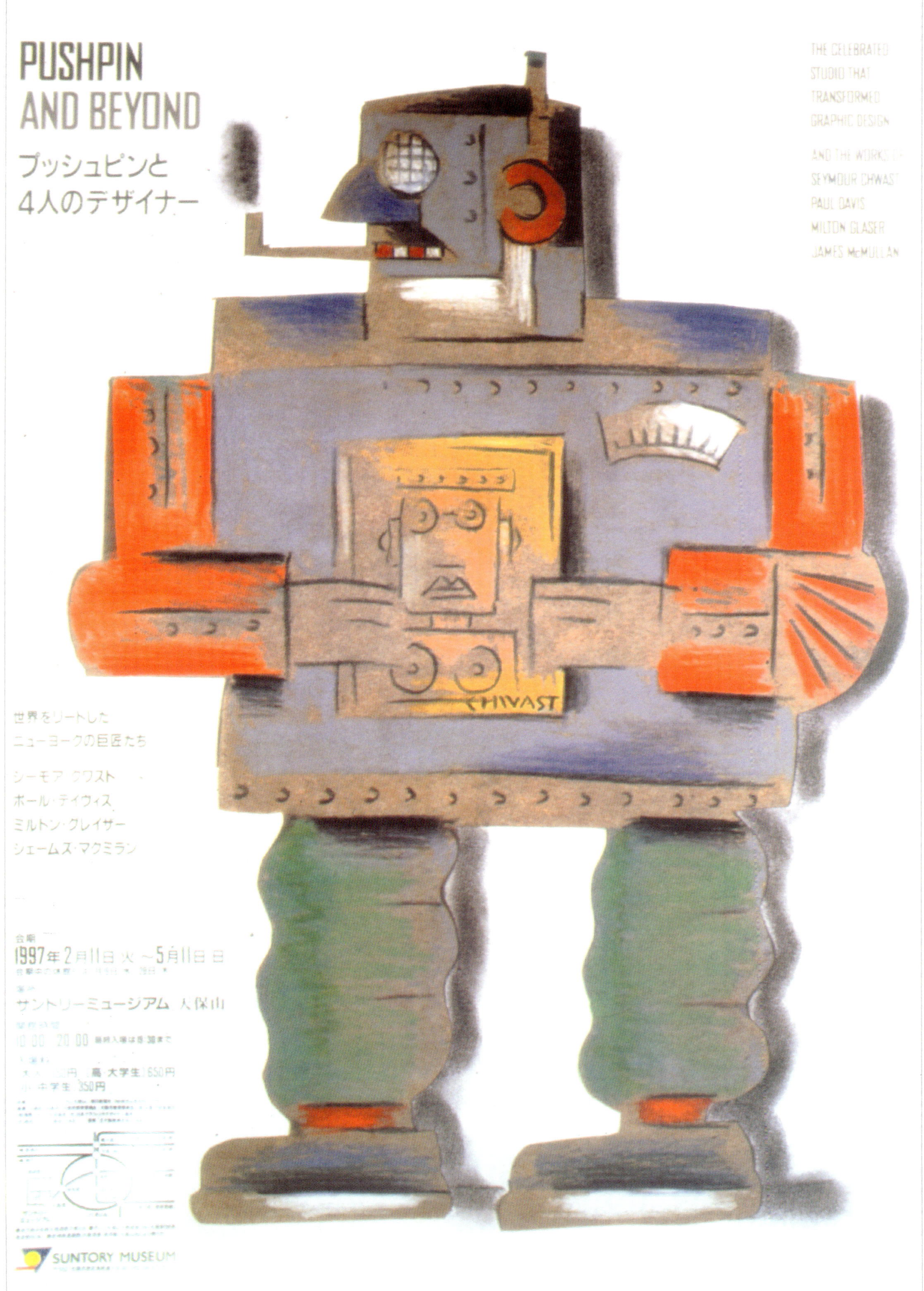

Colored pencil and acrylic on wrapping paper, offset, 29" x 40.5", 1997

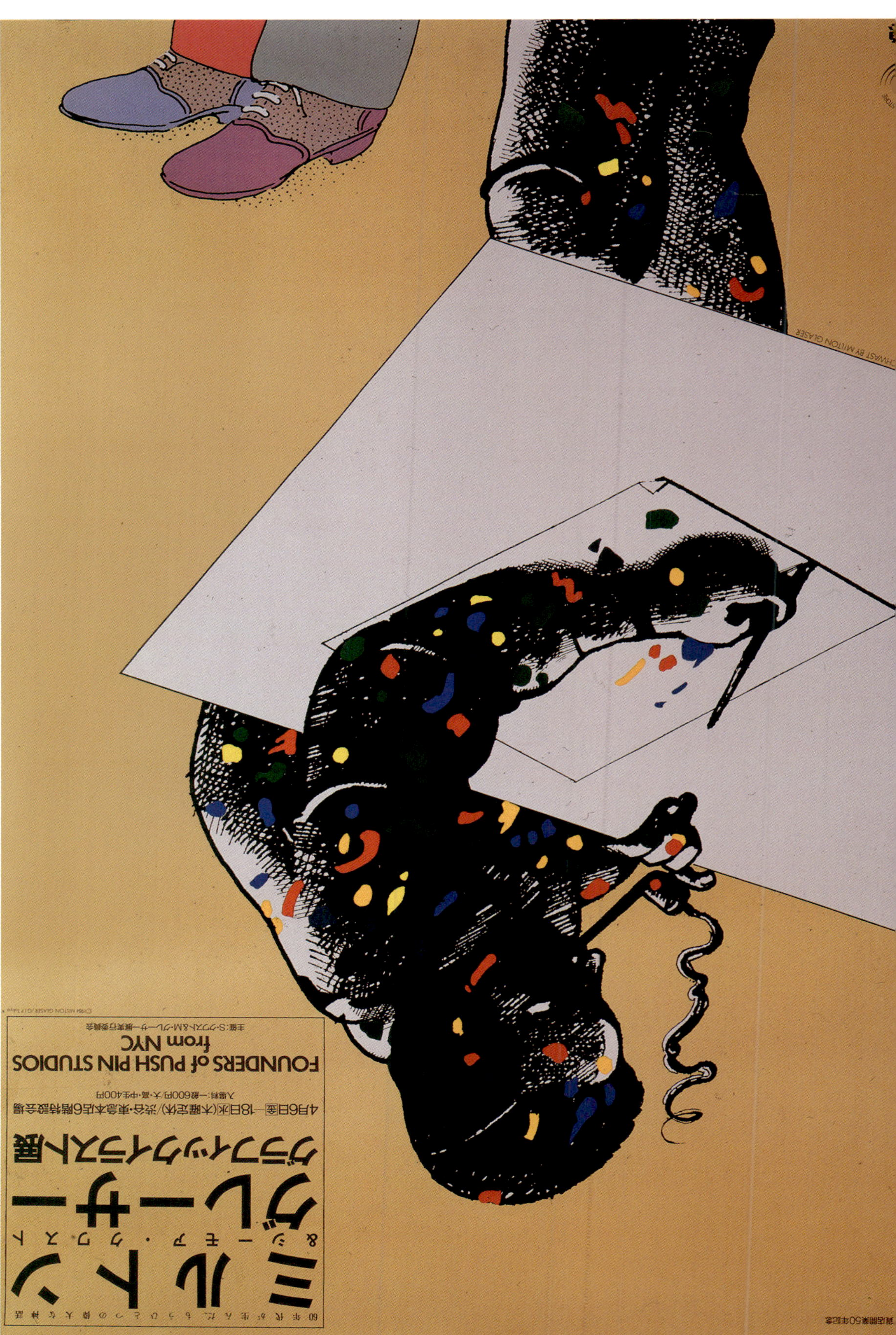

Mixed media, offset, size N/A, ca. 1983

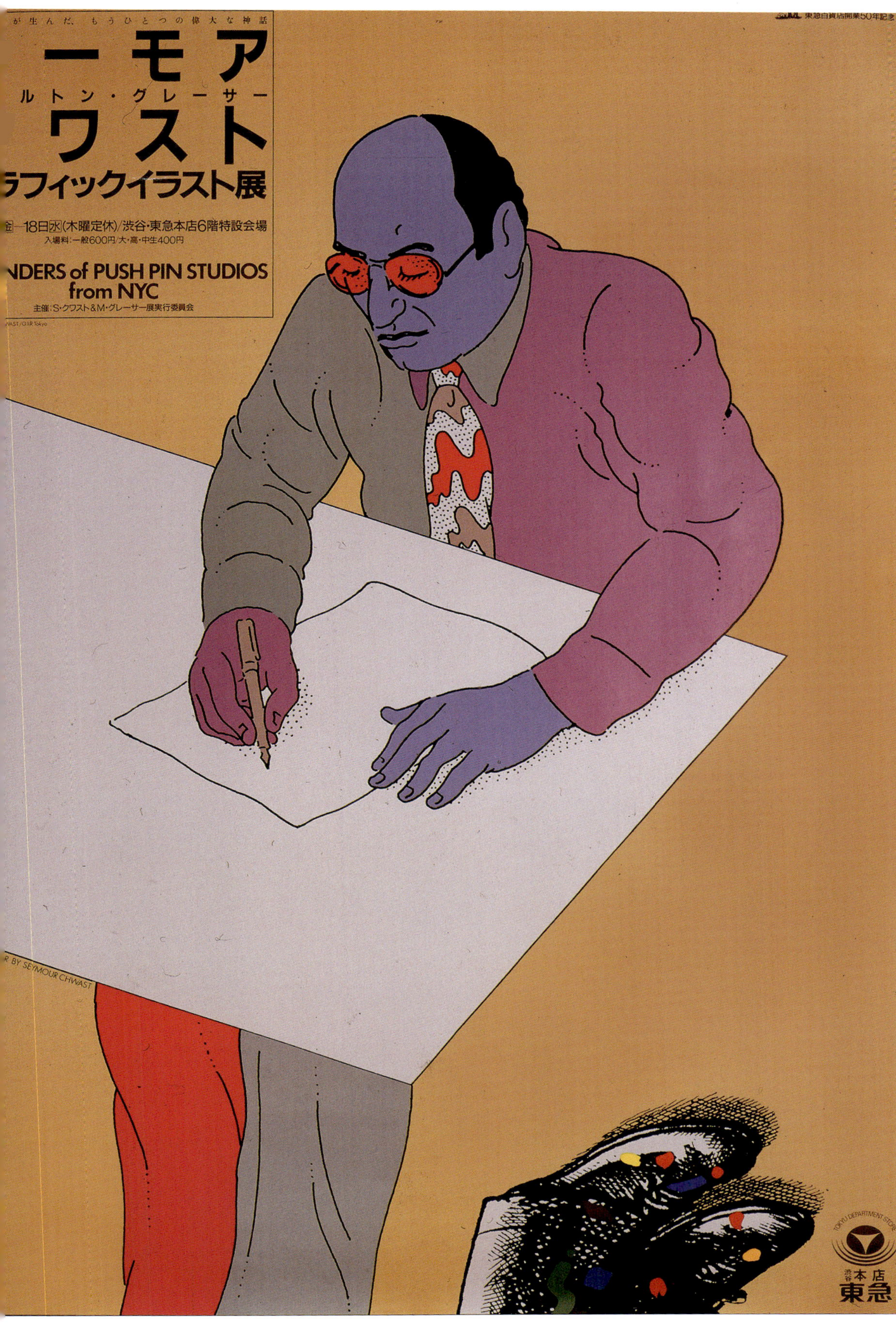

TOKYO EXHIBIT. In Tokyo, department stores have substantial art galleries. Glaser and I had a show in one of them. When combined as shown here, these posters become an all-over pattern of him drawing me and of me drawing him. They covered a wall at the gallery. This is an homage to Shigeo Fukuda.

GUTENBERG MUSEUM. The Gutenberg Museum gave me my first one-man museum show. My hand lettering is somewhat art nouveau. Since I was given text to be in three languages, I had no choice but to give in with a uncharacteristically crowded design.

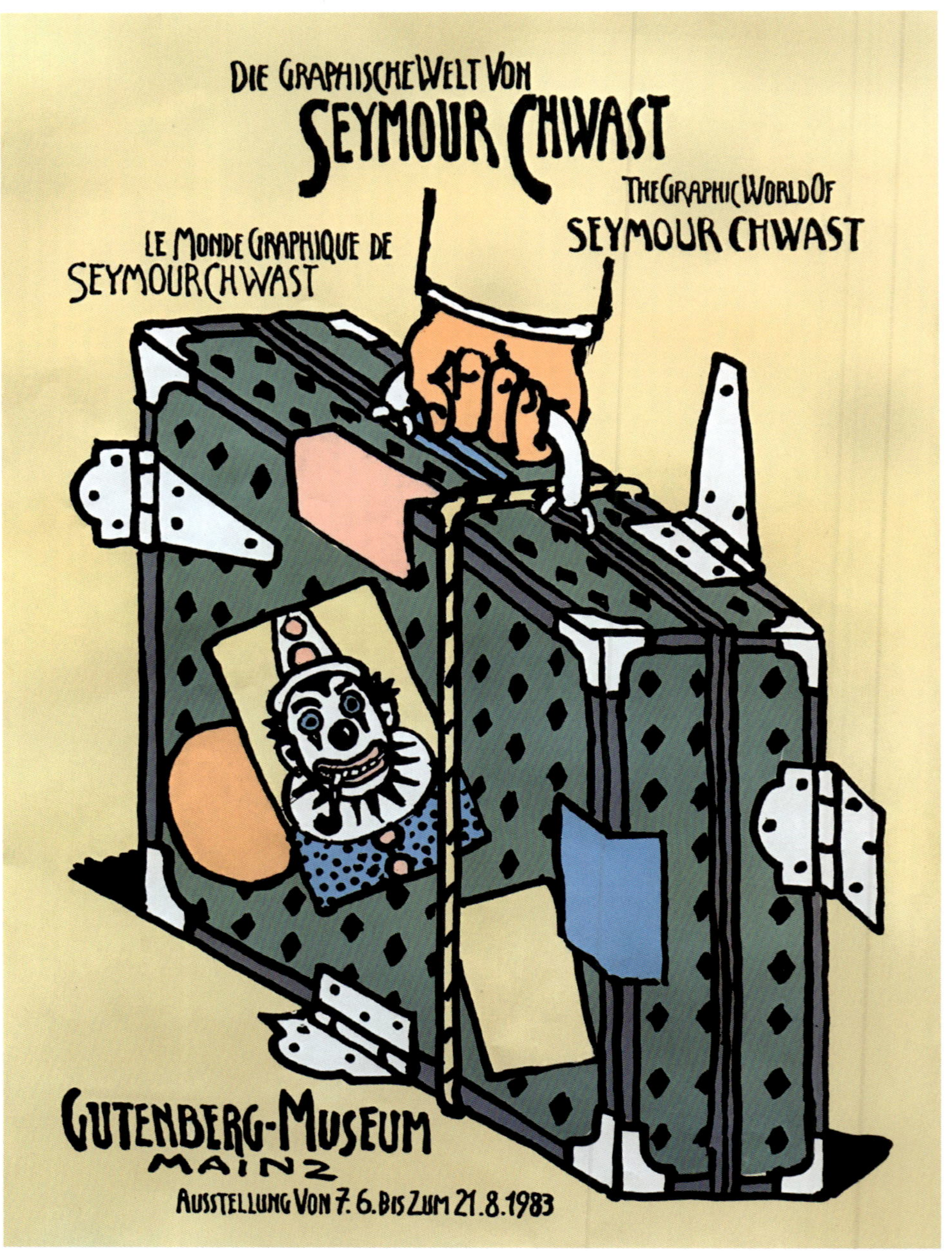

Marker and hand lettering with color film, offset, 12½" x 17", 1983

LECTURES

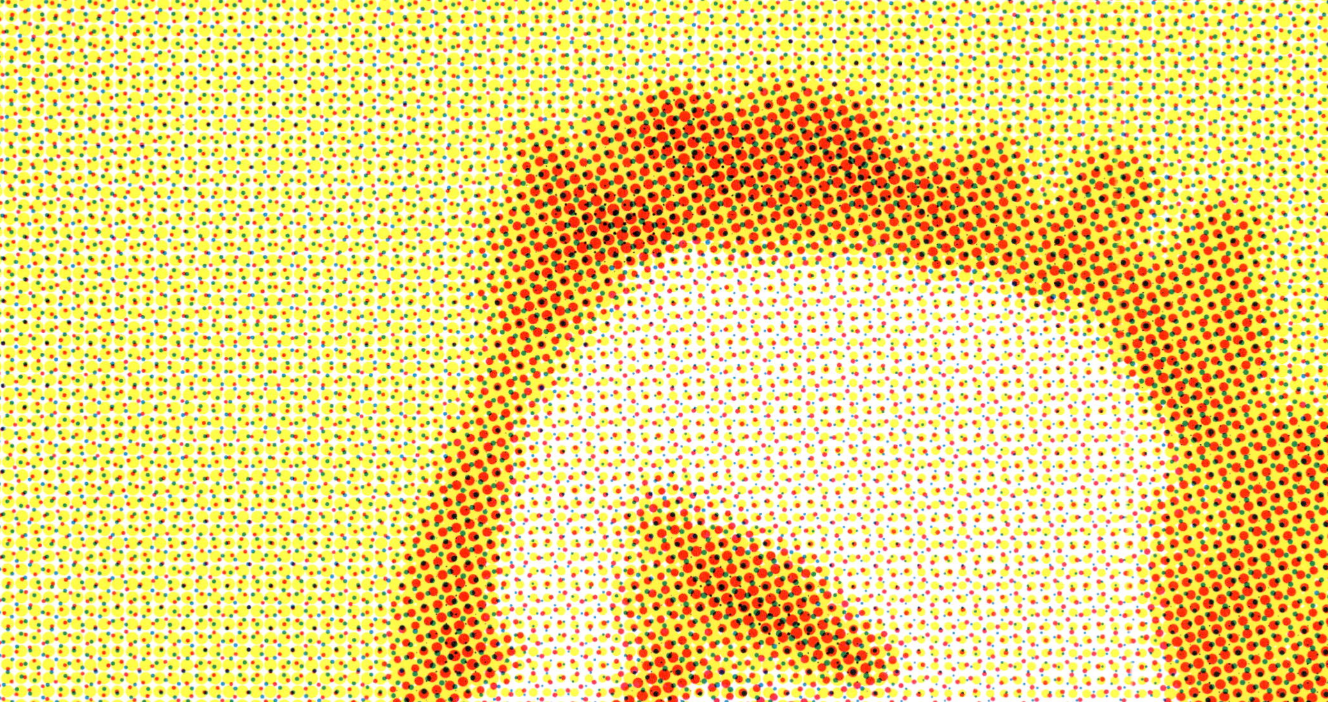

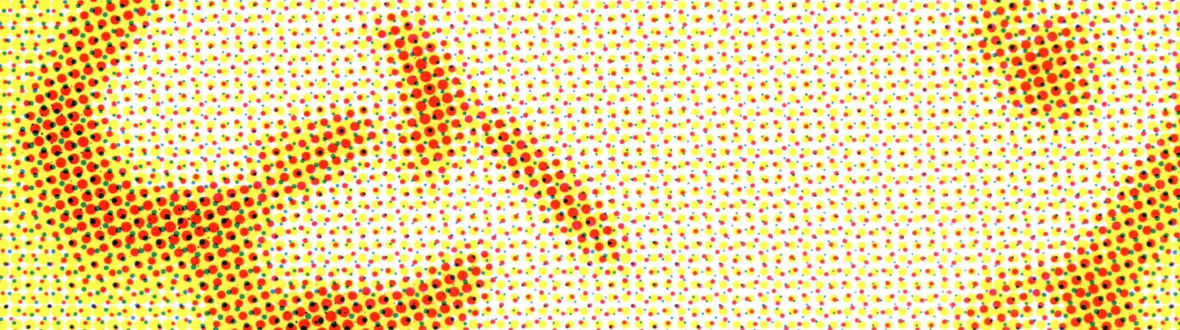

Below: **CLEVELAND.** I lectured in many cities for the American Institute of Graphic Art and other design organizations. I used the pun "exposing" myself in more than one poster announcing a lecture. The predigital 35 mm slide is now obsolete. Slides were loaded in a tray called a "carousel" and attached to a projector that would display my work on a screen.

Opposite: **OKLAHOMA CITY.** The Oklahoma Panhandle provided me with a self-deprecating idea. The problem for me was the lack of cities, rivers, or anything that would make the pan more like a map.

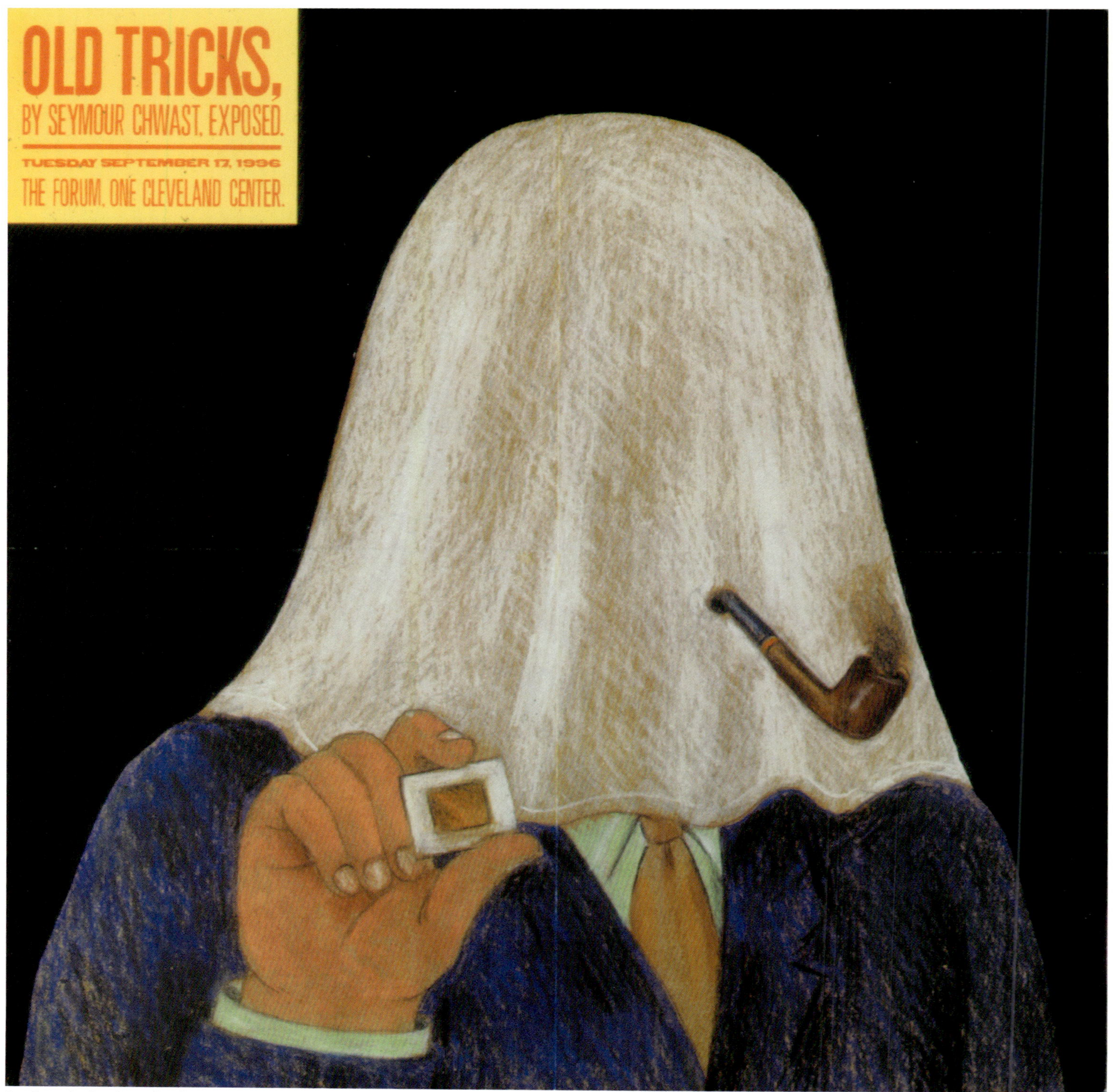

Acrylic and colored pencil, offset, approx. 10" x 10", ca. 1996

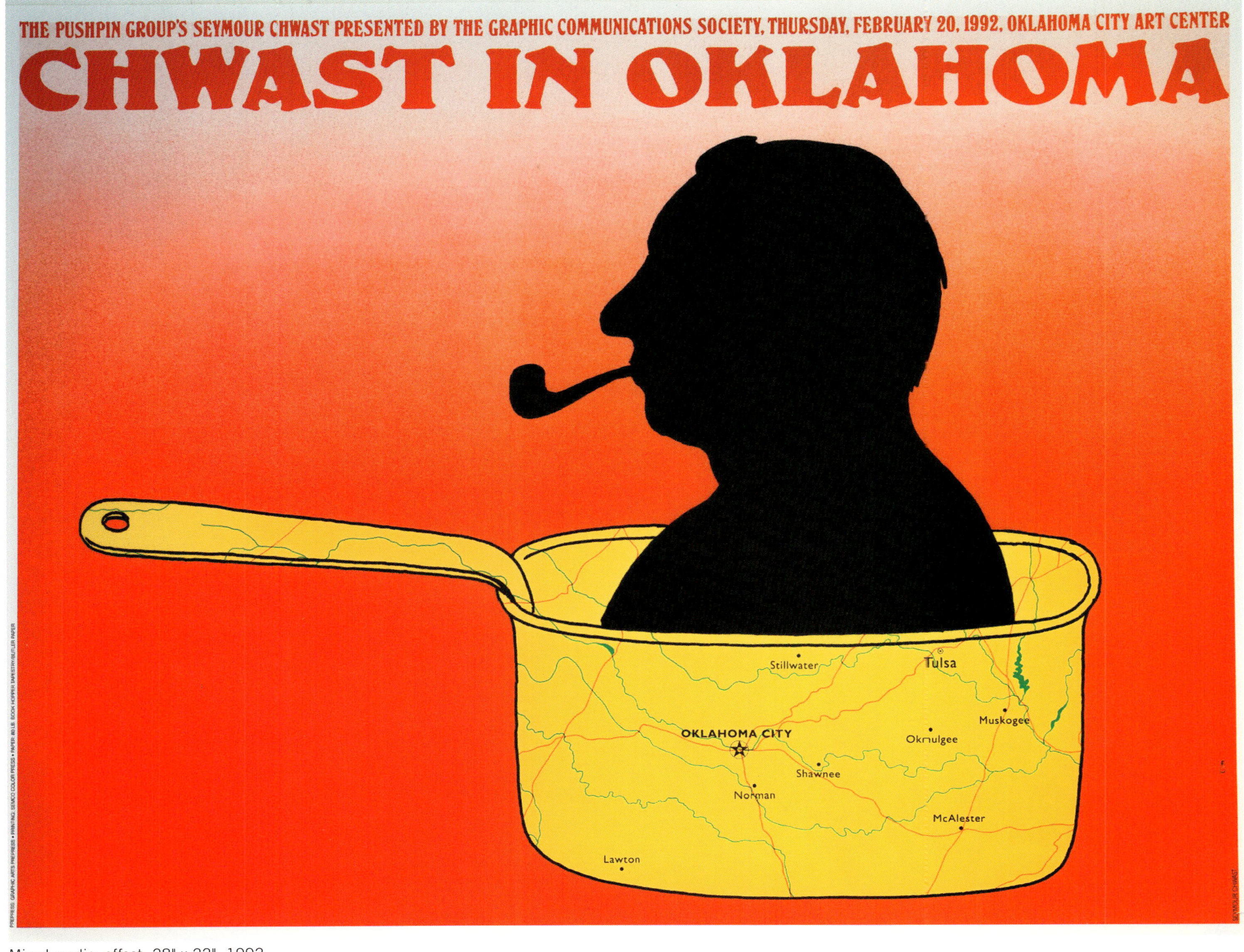

Mixed media, offset, 28" x 22", 1992

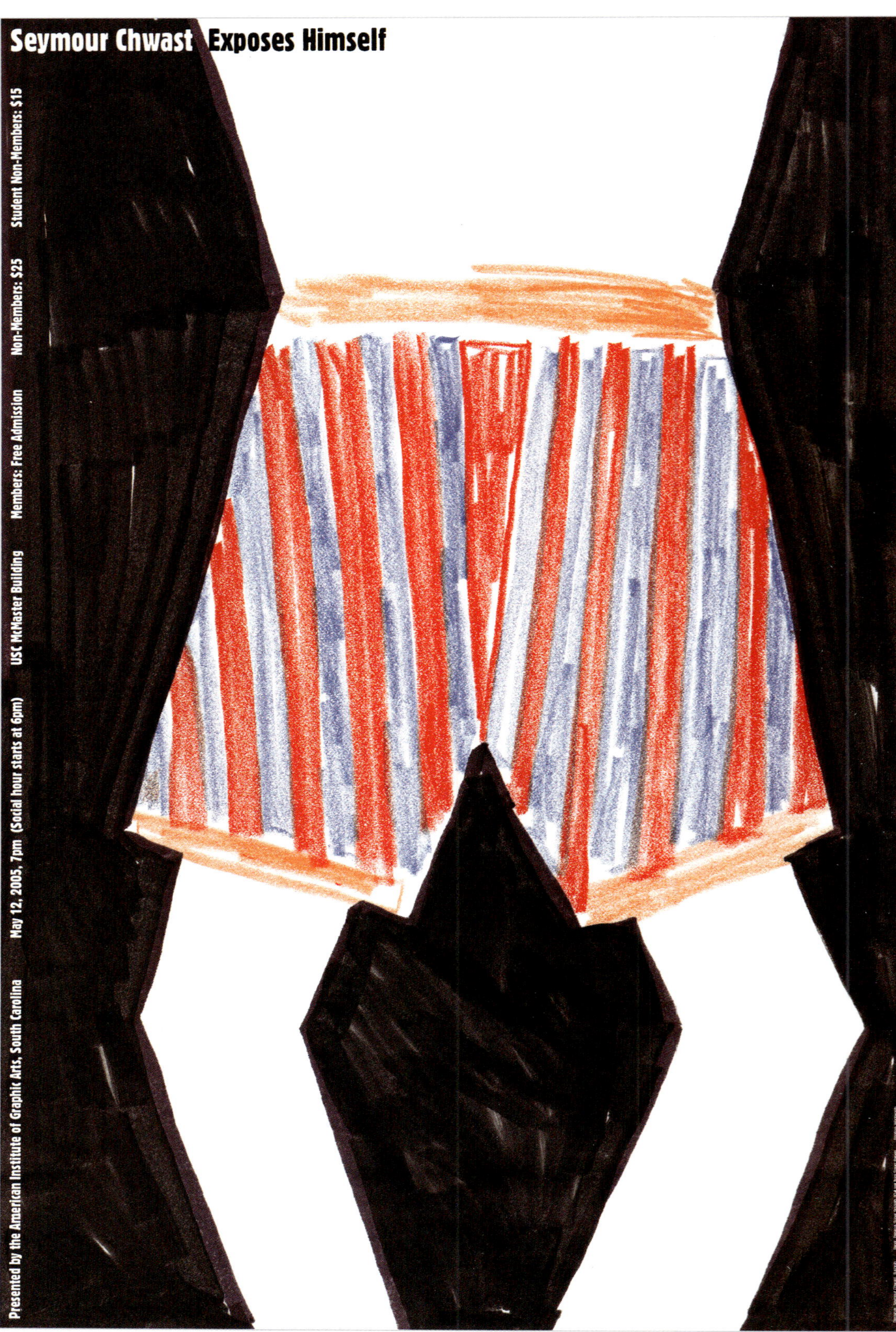

Marker and ink, colored pencil, offset, 24" x 36", 2005

Below: **HILLSIDE, NEW JERSEY.** I cut up, resized, and repositioned this Dapper Dan from an old department store catalog.

Opposite: **COLUMBIA, SOUTH CAROLINA.** Here is another "Chwast Exposes Himself" poster. I thought that by being slightly naughty I might get better attendance to my lecture.

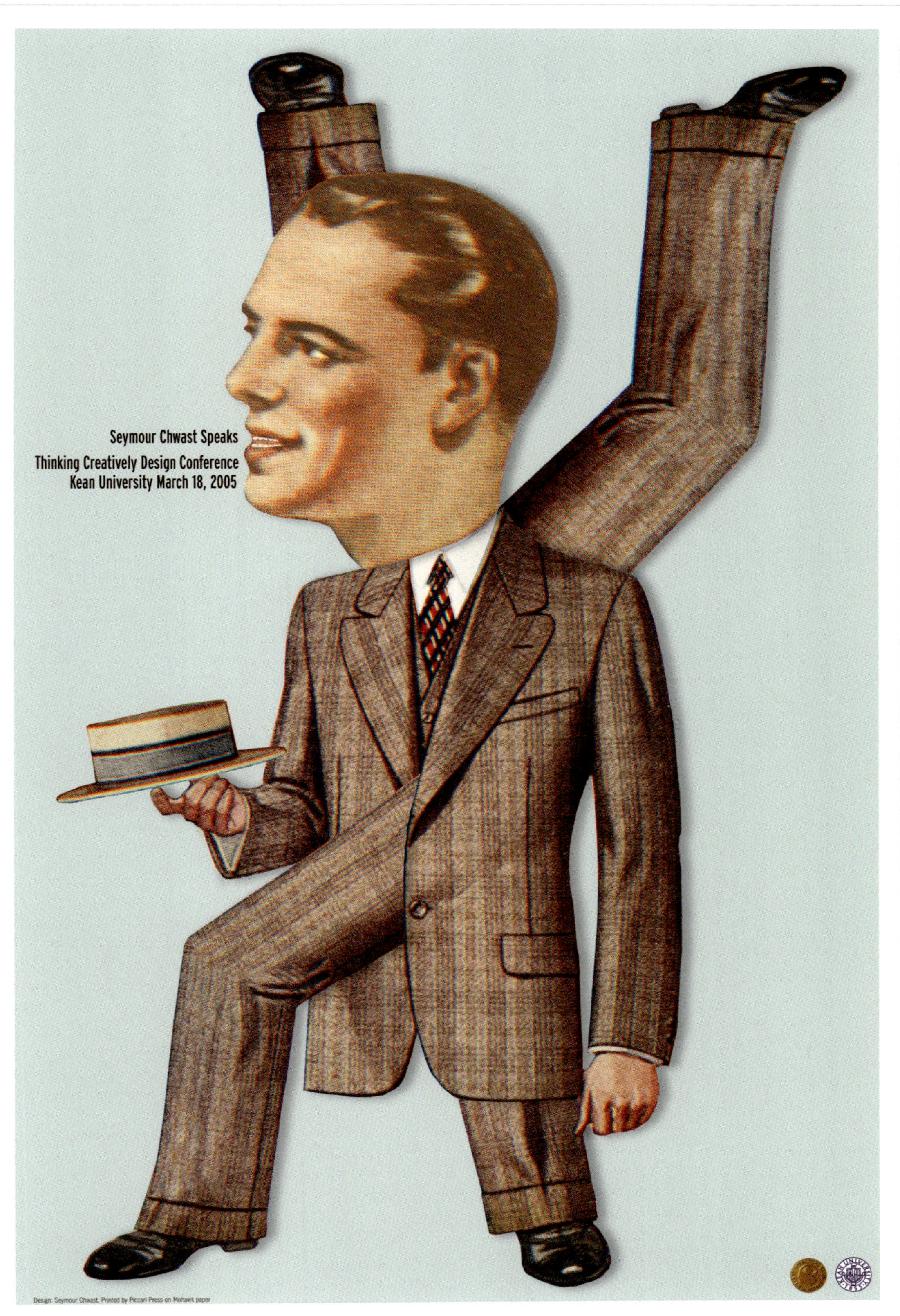

Collage, offset, 20" x 30", 2005

Below, left: **NEW YORK.** This poster announced a series of talks by internationally known designers. This may be the closest I ever came to doing a poster or illustration with no image. I fail at trying to do work that is pure design.

Below, right: **MINNEAPOLIS.** My hosts came up with the title of my lecture. Credit is due to the designer, who used this image from my six-sided jacket for my monograph *The Left Handed Designer, Harry N. Abrams, 1985.*

Opposite: **DALLAS.** Texans are proud. In an effort to elevate my importance, I tried to identify myself as one of them. But the joke is on me, since, with a face like mine, I couldn't fool anyone.

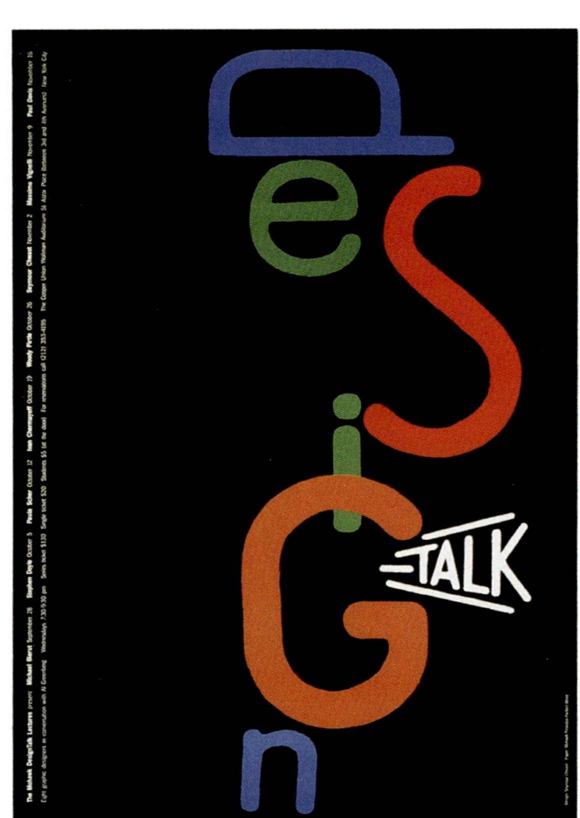

Hand lettering, color film, offset, 24" x 35", 1996

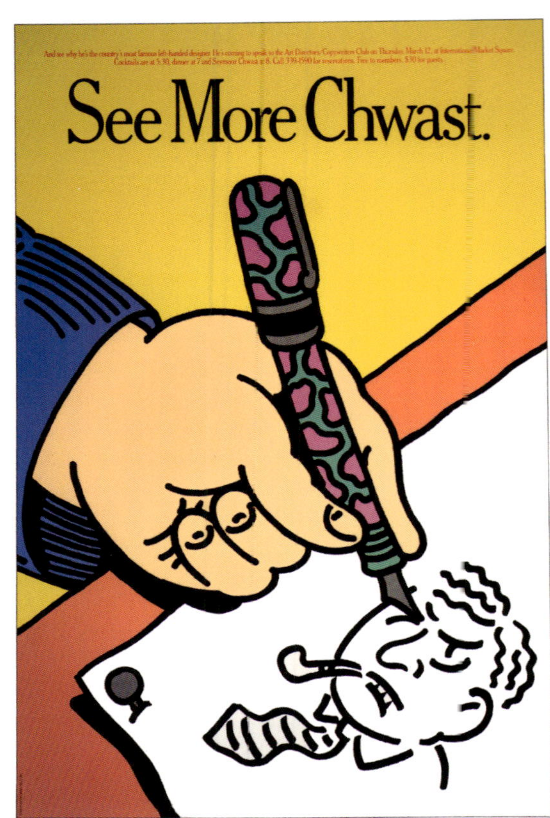

Marker and ink, color film, offset, 24" x 36", ca. 1993

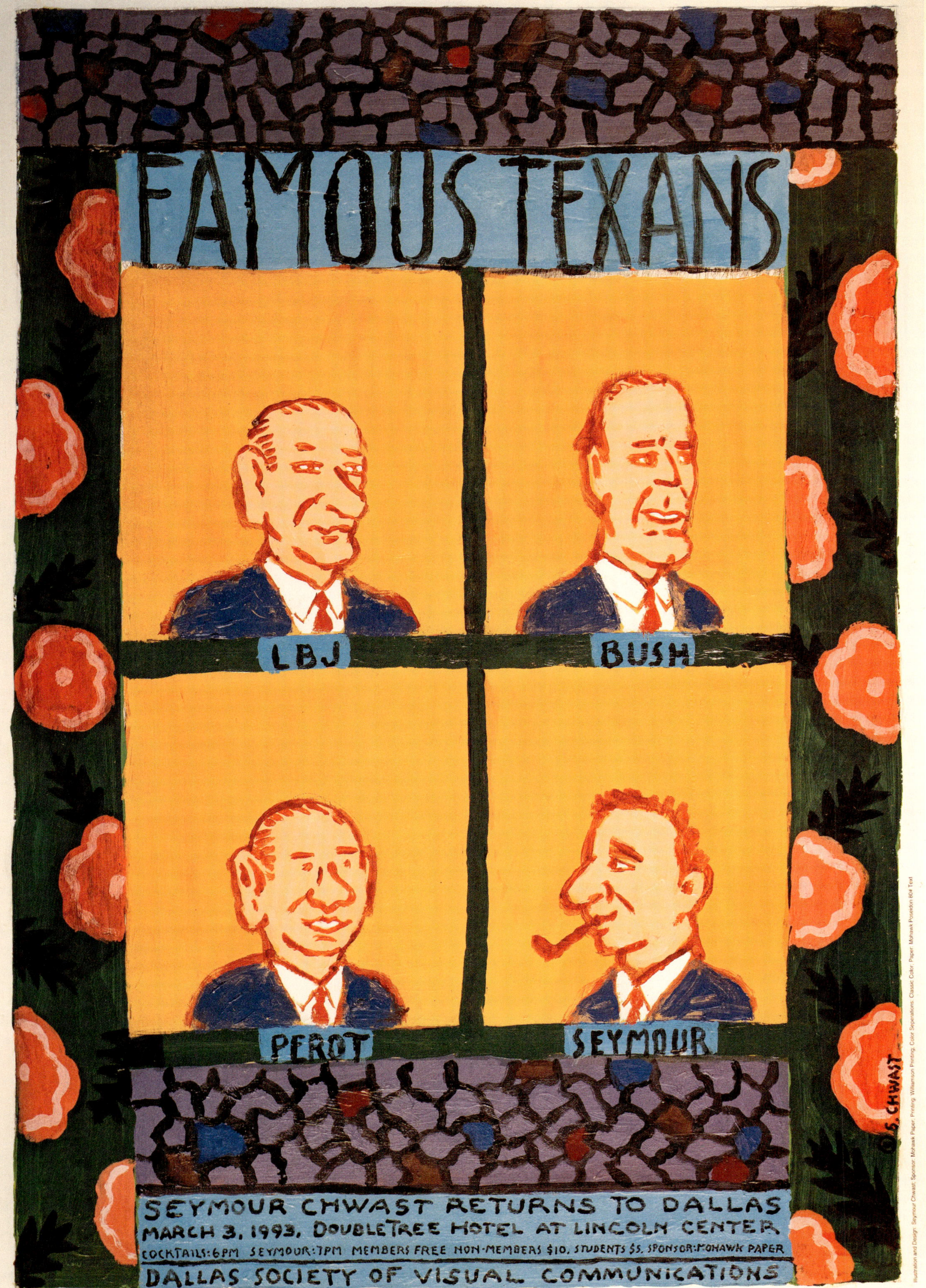

Brush and acrylic on paper with hand lettering, offset, 24" x 36", 1993

Below: **MILLERSVILLE.** I hadn't heard of Millersville University when they asked me to exhibit and talk to the students. It's in the middle of Pennsylvania. I feel lucky that as a New Yorker, I had an advantage with my education and career, and yet digital communication has made proximity to major markets less critical.

Opposite: **BRNO, CZECH REPUBLIC.** The Statue of Liberty was employed this time as a symbol of American democracy. She is carrying a sign on a motorcycle to suggest urgency. The exhibit originated in New York and traveled to the Czech Republic.

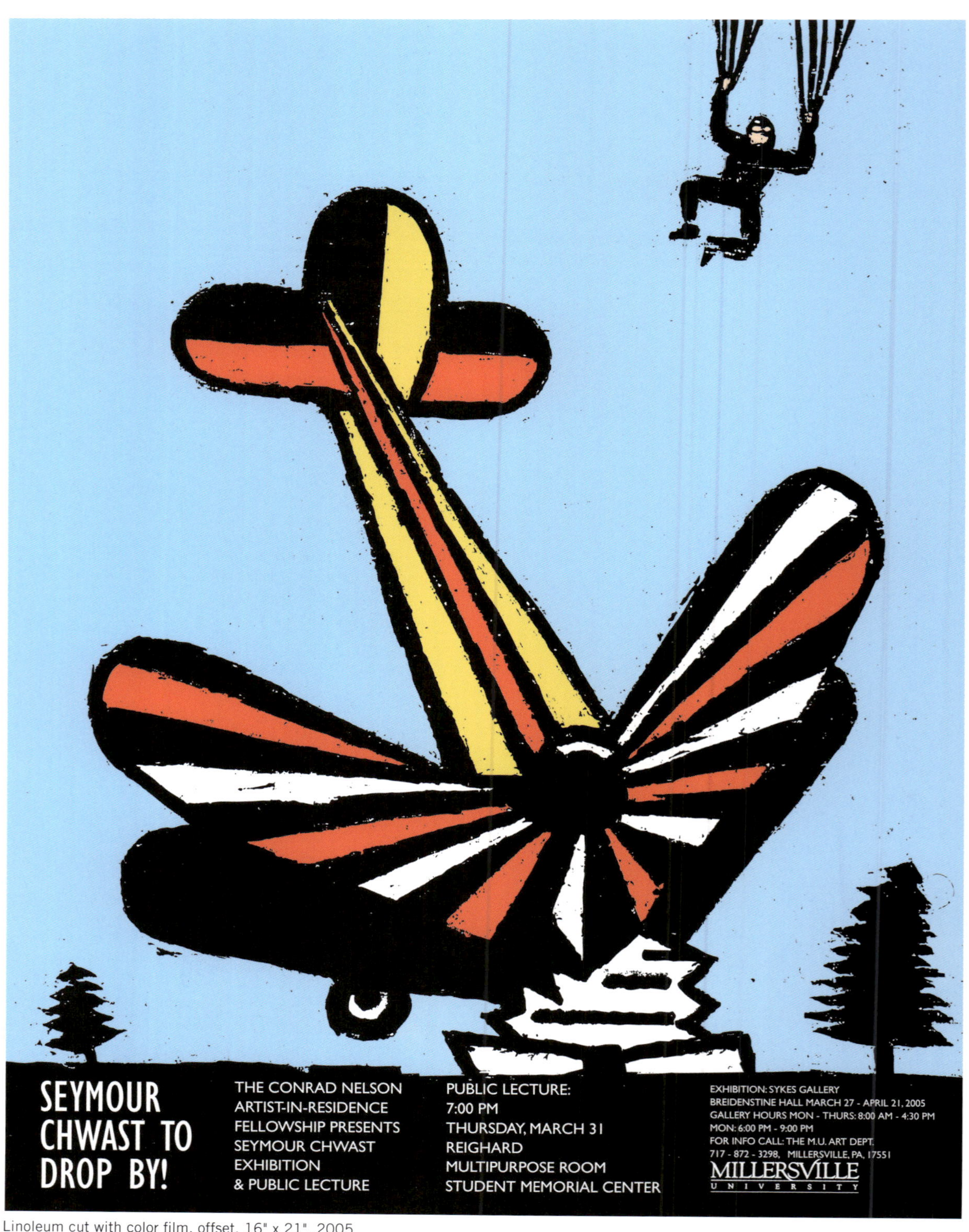

Linoleum cut with color film, offset, 16" x 21", 2005

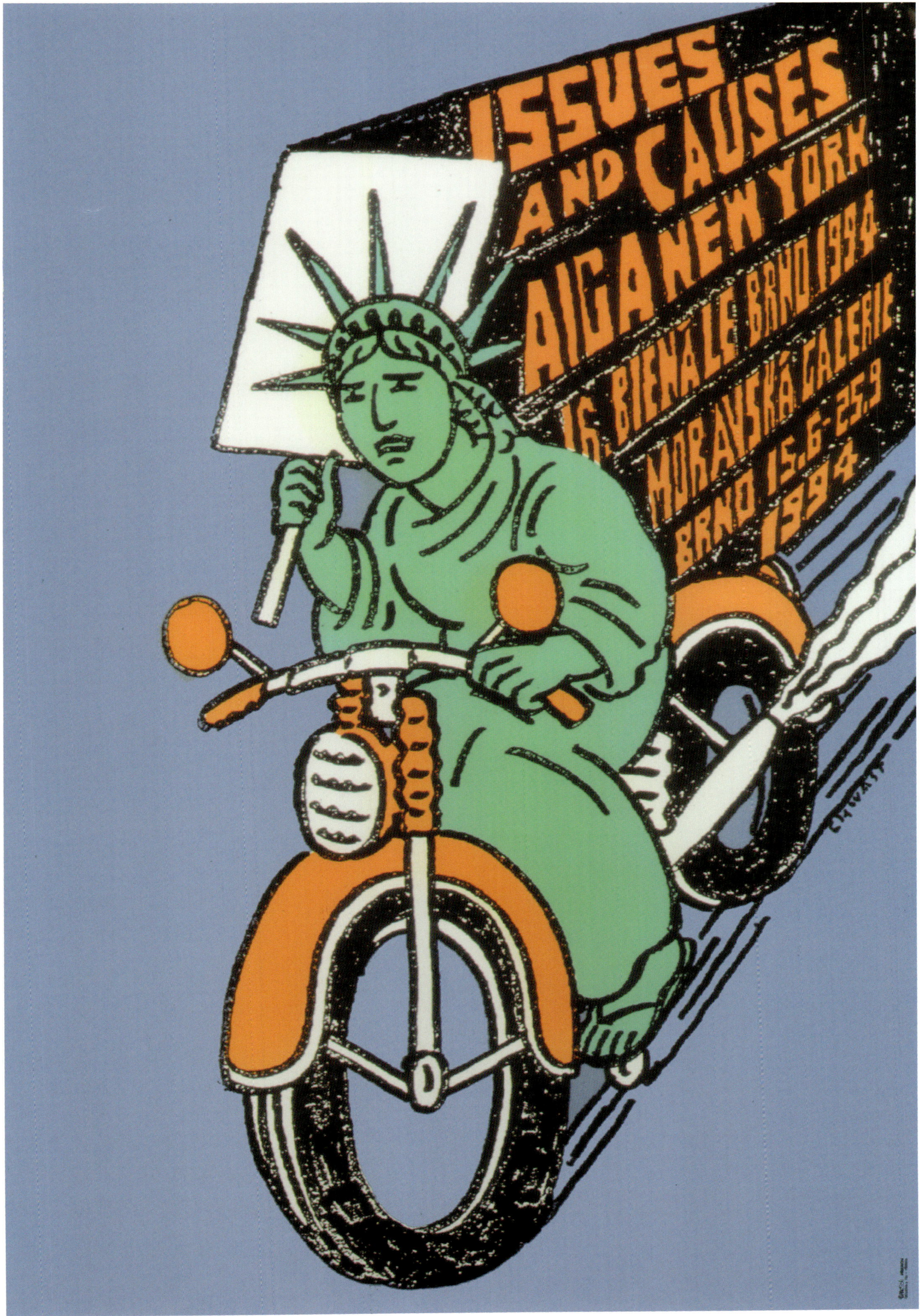

Hand lettering, marker and ink, color film, offset, 24" x 36", 1994

NEW YORK. For a talk promoting my book *Seymour: The Obsessive Images of Seymour Chwast*. This image appears on the cover.

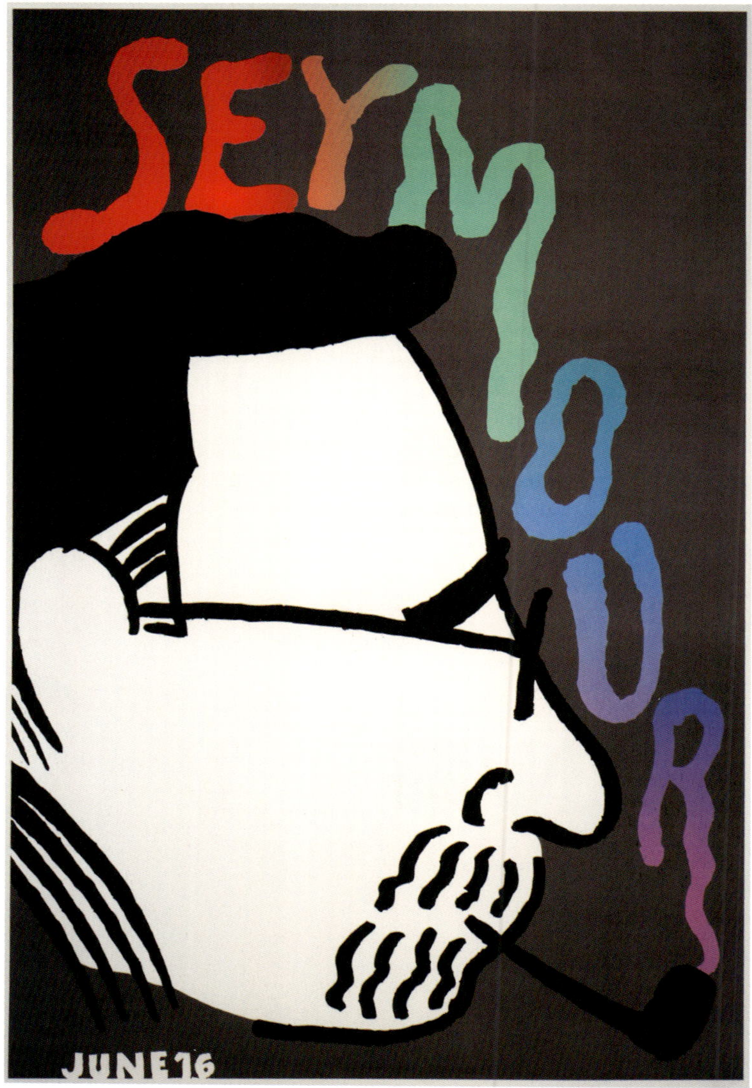

Hand lettering, marker and ink, digital color, offset, 23" x 34", 2005

Epilogue

This is a short review of a long career in posters. While I loved to draw anything, especially comic strips, I had no interest in posters before 1945. That was when my parents and I moved to Coney Island, Brooklyn. I went to Abraham Lincoln High School, where my teacher, Leon Friend, who had come from Germany, taught something called Graphic Design. In his class I learned about the great poster designers of the past, including A. M. Cassandre, Lucian Bernhard, and Ludwig Hohlwein. We entered every poster competition meant for high school students. He held us to high standards, with his arrival at school at 6:30 in the morning and his tough criticism. The only design magazine, now called *Novum*, was around his office for us to peruse. I belonged to an elite group called the Art Squad, where we produced posters for the school bulletin boards.

After high school, I entered Cooper Union in New York City, where I studied drawing, painting, and advertising art. In my favorite class I learned the basics of typography and how to apply them to projects. Three classmates and I banded together to get freelance work before graduation and jobs after. They were Milton Glaser, Edward Sorel, and Reynold Ruffins. After three years of dead-end jobs, Milton, Ed, and I established Push Pin Studios. Reynold joined us two or three years later. Getting work was slow at first, but with promoting ourselves with the Push Pin Graphic, we gained work and reputation with art for advertising, book publishing, and magazines. Milton's breakthrough came with doing posters for the School of Visual Art and for popular music concerts. Mine came with my antiwar posters.

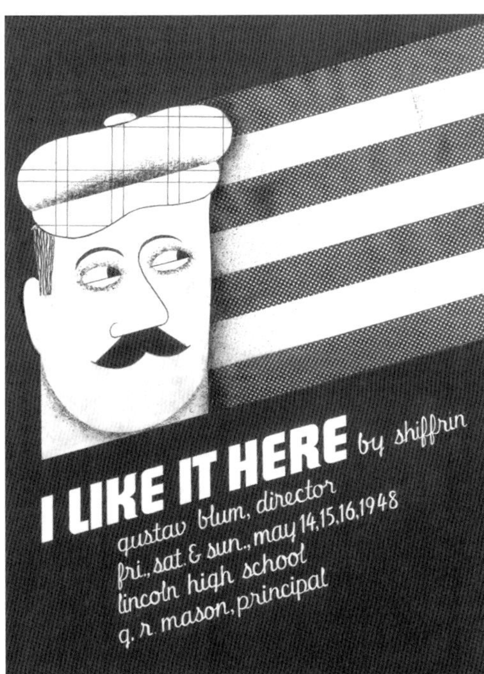

Poster designed at age seventeen, Abraham Lincoln High School, 1948

We were part of a revolution in design and illustration, helped by the fact that we were good at designing with type *and* image. This was unusual because most designers don't draw and most illustrators weren't interested in typography.

Starting with the end of World War II, new production techniques and attitudes opened up creative possibilities. We, and other designers and illustrators, allowed ourselves to look at the past in order to revive styles with new energy. Starting with the charm of Victorianism, we moved on to Art Nouveau, Art Deco, and Streamline of the 1930s and '40s. Realism and sentimentality gave way to graphic and expressive realism. The surrealism of René Magritte flourished, and I still find this style useful. The computer with CGI and animation have made everything possible. We no longer look with amazement at Superman flying.

I still enjoy the use of only two dimensions for my work. Poster design is a sublime medium for me. Its generous size offers unique possibilities, creating work appreciated by collectors and museums. I follow my own design principles: contrast, emphasis, scale, proportion, hierarchy, and dynamic symmetry. Or, I don't.

I would like to thank the many art directors, producers, and entrepreneurs who assigned me posters. The dates for their creation span over fifty years, and unfortunately many of the names of the collaborators are forgotten. If you know who they are, please let me know for inclusion in future editions of this book.

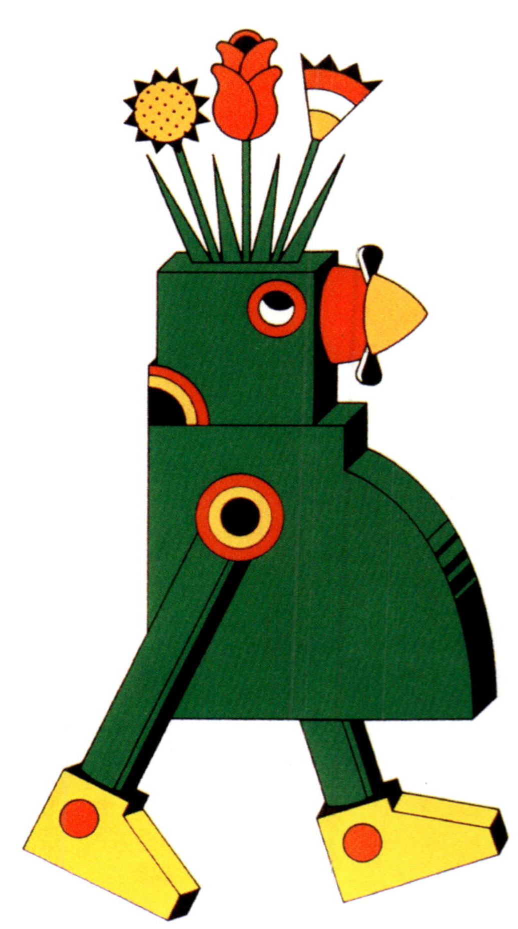